Emergency Psychiatric Care

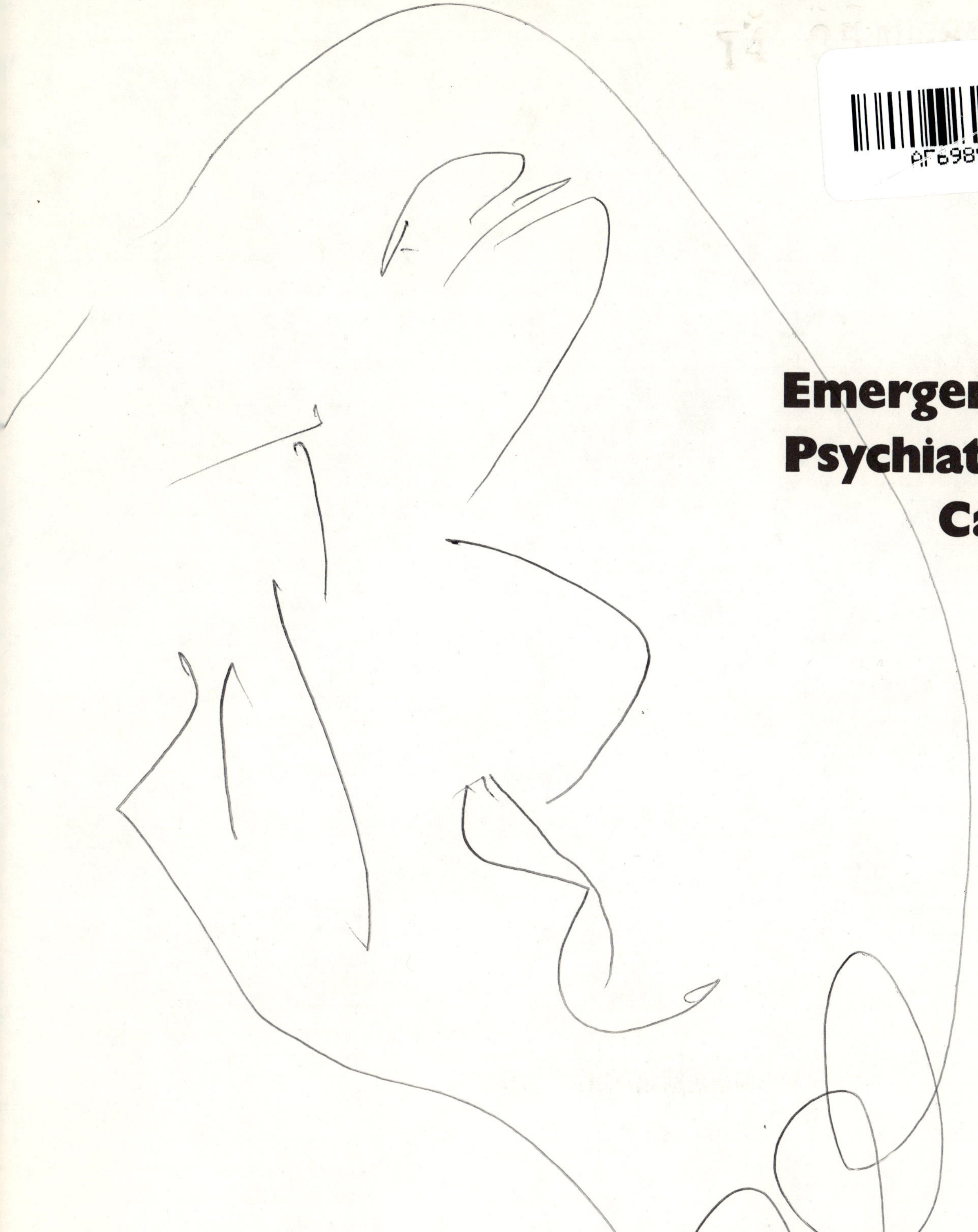

Emergency Psychiatric Care

THE MANAGEMENT OF MENTAL HEALTH CRISES

EDITORS

H. L. P. Resnik, M.D.
Clinical Professor of Psychiatry
School of Medicine, George Washington University

Lecturer in Psychiatry
School of Medicine, Johns Hopkins University

Harvey L. Ruben, M.D., M.P.H.
Assistant Professor of Psychiatry
School of Medicine, Yale University

with

Diane Daskal Ruben, M.A.T., J.D.

SPONSORED BY

The National Institute of Mental Health

THE CHARLES PRESS PUBLISHERS, INC.
Bowie, Maryland 20715

The material in this book, prepared under NIMH contract HSM-42-72-180, does not necessarily reflect the opinion or approval of the National Institute of Mental Health or the U.S. Department of Health, Education and Welfare.

ISBN 0-913486-15-9
Library of Congress Catalog Card No. 74-11791

79 80 81 82 10 9 8 7 6 5 4

Bowie, Maryland 20715

Illustrated by Bruce Bolinger

Contents

Contents

Preface

In July 1972, as part of an overall effort to become involved in upgrading the quality of emergency health care throughout the United States, the National Institute of Mental Health (NIMH) established the Mental Health Emergencies Section. This section evolved from the Center for Studies of Suicide Prevention (CSSP), and the senior editor of this volume, H. L. P. Resnik, chief of the administratively deactivated CSSP program, was appointed chief of the new Mental Health Emergencies Section. The experience of the CSSP in crisis intervention training and the Mental Health Emergencies Section in on-the-scene crisis intervention with both natural and man-made disasters helped the new section evolve rapidly.

As one of its first priorities the staff of the new section attempted to assess the scope of existing emergency care programs to document the varied facilities for providing emergency mental health care to the public and to evaluate the nature and quality of professional and paraprofessional training in emergency mental health care.

Presently in this country the persons involved in the delivery of emergency health care include police, fire fighters, ambulance and rescue squad personnel, and hospital emergency room aides, nurses, and physicians. In addition, there is appearing a new paraprofessional to deal specifically with emergency care—the emergency medical technician.

In traveling around the country, the staff of the Mental Health Emergencies Section became aware that most of the people who render front line, first level emergency health care had neither the background, the training, nor the expertise to deal with the mental health aspects of a medical emergency. Moreover, they were even less equipped to specifically handle a psychiatric emergency or crisis. Even more astounding was that emergency department personnel at all levels—from physicians and nurses to aides—were aware of the frequency with which mental health emergencies were presented to them. However, few had ever received specific training to intervene successfully in such emergencies. To complete the circle, the staff of the Mental Health Emergencies Section discovered that few mental health professionals, including psychiatrists, had received education, training, or clinical experience in crisis intervention and emergency care. If such experience had occurred, it was usually in a community mental health center or an outpatient department; rarely, was this experience gained in the context of a hospital emergency department or an on-the-scene rescue vehicle.

At approximately this time an Emergency Medical Services (EMS) thrust was initiated by the U.S. Department of Health, Education and Welfare, and the representation of NIMH was invited. Dr. Bertram Brown, Director of NIMH, organized the Ad Hoc Committee on Mental Health Emergencies, thus ensuring the coordination of programs such as Alcohol, Drugs, Child and Family, and Suicide and Crisis Intervention. This committee then represented mental health interests in the selection of EMS demonstration sites and in their monitoring. It was shocking to find that less than 10% of the proposals requesting EMS support had even remotely considered psychiatric emergencies as part of their total emergency responsibility to the community.

A systematic approach to the education and training of emergency personnel in the principles and practice of emergency mental health care and crisis intervention was needed. However, no single training reference clearly, concisely, and comprehensively presented the knowledge necessary for emergency medical personnel to deal with mental health emergencies and psychiatric crises. Such a book would need to be written in terms understandable to the broad range of people from various backgrounds who were dealing with these emergencies.

Thus in January 1973 the Ad Hoc Committee sponsored the compilation of this text, *Emergency Psychiatric Care, The Management of Mental Health Crises*, as a training and reference manual for those practicing in the field. The Ad Hoc Committee members who worked on the project were:

H. L. P. Resnik, M.D., *Chairman*
Chief, Mental Health Emergencies Section
Division of Special Mental Health Programs
NIMH

Harvey A. Taschman, Ph.D., *Executive Secretary*
Coordinator, Child Mental Health Services
Center for Studies of Child and Family Mental Health
Division of Special Mental Health Programs
NIMH, ADAMHA

Kathleen A. Bueker, Ph.D.
Chief, Vestermark Center
Division of Manpower and Trainir
NIMH

Gerald H. Dubin, M.D.
Program Development Specialist
Services Research Branch
Division of Resource Development
National Institute on Drug Abuse

Irving D. Goldberg, M.P.H.
Chief, Applied Biometrics Research Branch
Division of Biometry
NIMH

Ford H. Kuramoto, D.S.W.
Executive Assistant to the Acting Director
Division of Mental Health Services
NIMH, ADAMHA

F. Barrie Montague, M.P.H.
Public Health Analyst
Office of Program Planning and Analysis
National Institute on Alcohol Abuse and Alcoholism
ADAMHA

Lucy D. Ozarin, M.D.
Program Development Officer
Division of Mental Health Services
NIMH, ADAMHA

Other contributors to the committee's work included the following:

Abe S. Abraham, M.D.
Special Assistant to the Director
Division of Manpower and Training
NIMH, ADAMHA

John A. Benvenuto, M.D.
Acting Chief, Special Treatment Projects Section
Services Research Branch
Division of Resource Development
National Institute on Drug Abuse
ADAMHA

Gene D. Cohen, M.D.
Staff Psychiatrist
Division of Mental Health Services
NIMH, ADAMHA

Hans M. Schapire, M.D.
Assistant Commissioner
New York State Department of Mental Hygiene
Former Staff Psychiatrist
Community Mental Health Services
Support Branch, Division of Mental Health Services
NIMH, ADAMHA

Each chapter of this book has been written by an expert in a particular area of emergency mental health care. In each chapter the basic clinical picture of each crisis or emergency is described, a method for assessing the severity of the crisis is given, and then practical, step-by-step management instructions are presented. These instructions have been printed in bold italic type that is quickly visible on the page. Thus this book attempts to be a comprehensive "how-to-do-it" description of emergency mental health care prior to the arrival of a psychiatrist or other mental health professional or in situations where such persons or their consultation is unavailable. This task was more easily accomplished for some chapters than for others. The further one moves from the medical model of care (i.e., for drug overdose or alcohol intoxication), the more difficult it becomes to delineate specific care procedures. In that vein, we would very much appreciate any suggestions that our readers may have.

This is not to say that experienced mental health professionals may not find this book useful. We learned many new facts as we were editing it. We believe it is a rare person whose clinical skills with emotional crises are not improved by the suggestions of our colleagues.

The material in this book, prepared under NIMH contract HSM-42-72-180, does not necessarily reflect the opinion or approval of the National Institute of Mental Health or the U.S. Department of Health, Education and Welfare.

H. L. P. Resnik, M.D.

Harvey L. Ruben, M.D., M.P.H.

Diane Daskal Ruben, M.A.T., J.D.

Acknowledgments

The editors would like to express their appreciation to Lansing Crane, Esquire, for his review of the legal aspects discussed in Chapter I, Lenore Weinberg for her editorial assistance, and Candice Farrell, Elizabeth Kyle, and Carol Norman for their typing of the manuscript.

Contributors

John A. Benvenuto, Jr., M.D.

Chief, Special Treatment Projects Section
National Institute on Drug Abuse

Assistant Clinical Professor
George Washington University School of Medicine

Washington, D.C.

John M. Davis, M.D.

Director of Research
Illinois State Psychiatric Institute

Associate Professor of Psychiatry
University of Chicago Pritzker School of Medicine

Chicago, Illinois

Norman Farberow, Ph.D.

VA Wadsworth Hospital Center
Suicide Prevention Center
University of Southern California School of Medicine
Los Angeles, California

Larry Fish

Director, Social Systems Institute
Denver, Colorado

Vernelle Fox, M.D.

Chief, Alcoholism Service
Long Beach General Hospital
Long Beach, California

Edward F. Heffron, M.S.

Deputy Director for Community Services
Hazelton-Nanticoke MH/MR Center
Nanticoke, Pennsylvania

Steven R. Kafrissen, M.D.

Deputy Director for Clinical Services
Hazelton-Nanticoke MH/MR Center
Nanticoke, Pennsylvania

Elisabeth Kubler-Ross, M.D.

Psychiatrist and Author
Chicago, Illinois

Robert E. Litman, M.D.

Department of Psychiatry
University of California School of Medicine
Los Angeles, California

Donald J. Ottenberg, M.D.

Medical Director
Eagleville Hospital and Rehabilitation Center
Eagleville, Pennsylvania

Clinical Associate Professor of Medicine
Temple University School of Medicine
Philadelphia, Pennsylvania

Howard J. Parad, D.S.W.

Professor of Social Work
School of Social Work
University of Southern California
Los Angeles, California

Paul R. Polak, M.D.

Executive Director
Southwest Denver Community Mental Health Services
Denver, Colorado

Mary Reres, Ed.D.

Professor and Chairman
Psychiatric—Mental Health Nursing
School of Nursing

Associate Professor of Psychiatry
School of Medicine

Associate Professor of Education
School of Education

University of Virginia
Charlottesville, Virginia

H. L. P. Resnik, M.D.

Clinical Professor of Psychiatry
George Washington University School of Medicine

Professor of Community Education (Mental Health)
Federal City College

Washington, D.C.

Lecturer in Psychiatry
Johns Hopkins University
Baltimore, Maryland

Former Chief, Mental Health Emergencies Section
National Institute of Mental Health

Alvin Rosen, D.O.

Assistant Medical Director and Clinical Director
Eagleville Hospital and Rehabilitation Center
Eagleville, Pennsylvania

Associate in Medicine
Philadelphia College of Osteopathic Medicine
Philadelphia, Pennsylvania

Diane Daskal Ruben, M.A.T., J.D.

Private Practice of Law
New Haven, Connecticut

Harvey L. Ruben, M.D., M.P.H.

Assistant Professor of Psychiatry
Yale School of Medicine

Chief, Assessment and Acute Treatment Services
Director, Alcoholic Treatment Program
Connecticut Mental Health Center

New Haven, Connecticut

Jack Zusman, M.D., M.P.H.

Professor of Psychiatry
State University of New York
Buffalo, New York

I

Crisis Intervention and Emergency Mental Health Care: Concepts and Principles

Howard J. Parad, D.S.W.
H. L. P. Resnik, M.D.
Harvey L. Ruben, M.D., M.P.H.
Jack Zusman, M.D., M.P.H.
Diane Daskal Ruben, M.A.T., J.D.

A CRISIS INTERVENTION FRAMEWORK[1]

Emotional Crisis and Psychiatric Emergency

Emotional crisis! Psychiatric emergency! What images do these words bring to your mind? Crazy? Urgent? Helpless? Mentally disordered? Dangerous? Hopeless? Upset? Hysterical? Panicky? Off-balance? Anxious? Suicidal? Homicidal? Gravely disabled? Or perhaps a combination of some or all of these conditions?

1. This first section has been written by Howard J. Parad, D.S.W., and H. L. P. Resnik, M.D.

We all hear about, witness, and cope with crises on a daily basis in our health caretaking roles—whether as physicians, nurses, mental health workers, technicians, aides, orderlies, police, or firemen and whether based in an ambulance, helicopter, or emergency room. Each of us must also face emotional crises in our personal lives as mothers, fathers, wives, husbands, children, sisters, brothers, club members, voters, or neighbors.

The word "crisis" is part of our national way of life: the energy crisis, the food crisis, the population crisis, the transportation crisis, the pollution crisis, the political crisis, and crises associated with disasters like tornadoes and floods. Indeed, we are numbed to the point of forgetting the true human significance of individual crisis experiences.

In this source book you will find a great deal of important and useful information about mental health crisis situations commonly encountered by medical, nursing, and paraprofessional personnel in the course of their daily work.

For each type of crisis situation, the chapter author details four basic elements: (1) typical clinical pictures of the crisis and different manifestations of the problem, (2) diagnosis and assessment of the severity of the situation, (3) immediate steps for management at the scene or in the field, and (4) guidelines for emergency room care.

This book is a manual for those rendering front line care. It provides guidelines and practical information for decision-making and for treatment of the crisis by workers who are not psychiatric professionals. It gives advice about whether to take the patient to the hospital, whether to call for psychiatric consultation, and, if so, what to do before the psychiatrist arrives. Because it is designed to be a readable, handy guide for emergency workers, each chapter begins with an extended, paginated outline of its topics for a quick overview and instant reference.

In this introductory chapter, we shall attempt to sensitize you to the general theoretical issues of crisis intervention and of being a crisis intervenor.

The Importance of Emergency Mental Health Services

There is a close interrelationship between a person's mind, body, and social milieu. Hence, every human experience has biological, psychological, and social—or biopsychosocial—aspects. And every health emergency has, in turn, important psychosocial components in addition to the biological and critical life-saving medical aspects. Prompt, effective psychosocial first aid can often facilitate the patient's ability to cooperate with medical personnel, thus: (1) increasing the effectiveness of medical intervention during a physical emergency, and (2) helping to prevent the development of more serious psychosocial problems, perhaps after the physical emergency is under immediate control.

Emergency psychiatric services are now receiving more and more attention from emergency medical service planners throughout the country. These services have been largely underemphasized in the past, especially in training programs. A number of national and state legislative and program developments have stressed the increasing importance of emergency mental health care. These include:

1. The basic provision in the original Federal Community Mental Health Centers Act of 1963 (PL 88-164) requiring 24-hour emergency services as one of the five necessary program features in mental health centers that were to be constructed under the provisions of this landmark legislation.

2. The integration of mental health crisis care capabilities into the total emergency medical services (EMS) planning of the five EMS demonstration sites selected by the Department of Health, Education, and Welfare. This $15-million project, managed by the Emergency Medical Services Branch of the Health Services Administration, has had very close consultation with the Mental Health Emergencies Section of the National Institute of Mental Health and the Ad Hoc Committee on Mental Health Emergencies of the Alcohol, Drug Abuse, and Mental Health Administration (ADAMHA).

3. The policy decision made within many state mental and public health departments to depopulate their state's mental hospitals by providing service to the patient in his own community. This plan will have far-reaching effects as the number of patients discharged steadily increases. It has already challenged the resources of many communities and is also challenging the tolerance threshold of many

families. It will undoubtedly increase the need for local emergency health facilities. The discharged mental patient is all too often sent home from a state hospital without the support of an adequate aftercare plan. Vulnerable to various types of personal, family, and social stress, his coping abilities may be marginal. Under pressure, he may decompensate and require emergency care.

4. Some states, such as California, have passed legislation giving top priority to crisis intervention services, meaning that emergency care has been given preference over hospitalization, residential care, and other forms of outpatient care.

5. The Emergency Medical Services Systems Act of 1973 (PL 93-154), under which emergency medical service programs throughout the country are to be funded, will have a significant impact on increasing the availability of emergency services to all citizens. The operating guidelines for administrating this bill include deliberate reference to emergency medical problems, including *both* physical and psychological emergencies. Specific mental health emergencies, such as suicide, alcohol, drugs, child abuse, rape, and acute psychiatric episodes (e.g., psychosis) have been considered in the operating plan.

6. Under the Crisis Counseling Assistance and Training section (42 USC 5183) of the Disaster Relief Act of 1974, the National Institute of Mental Health is to provide services to victims of disasters and training to disaster workers. This was delineated as a high-priority need during Senator Quentin Burdick's hearings in Rapid City, South Dakota, and Wilkes-Barre, Pennsylvania.

In addition, training and educational programs emphasizing the importance of emotional responses of patients and their families, as well as emotional responses of those who provide emergency medical services, are to be included. Integrating such concepts into all emergency care training programs will help prevent a fragmented and dichotomized approach to the delivery of emergency medical services.

Crisis Intervention or Mental Health Emergency Care: A Question of Semantics?

One common definition of a mental health emergency indicates that "All patients whose condition warrants prompt psychiatric treatment for whatever reason are designated emergencies."[2] Can one go on to differentiate an emergency from a crisis?

Some professionals consider the patient to be in a mental health *emergency* only if he is suicidal, homicidal, or gravely disabled. Others, with a broader view, believe that, if the patient feels he has to be seen right away he's in an emergency. If he can wait up to 24 to 27 hours, he's in a crisis. And, if he can wait even longer, he has an "ordinary" problem.

Clearly, we have semantic problems. Perhaps we can say that *an emergency is a sudden, unforeseen, isolated incident, which, if unresponded to, will result in life-threatening or psychologically damaging consequences.*

On the other hand, a *crisis* often is less impelling, occurring in a psychological setting that has been previously identified and has been gathering momentum over some time. If attended to immediately, it can usually be "dealt with" over the following 12 to 24 hours.

What, then, is crisis intervention? It is the active entering into the life situation of an individual, family, or group to: (1) cushion the impact of a stress that throws the person (or persons) off balance and (2) help mobilize the resources of those affected directly by the stress. In this regard, the crisis worker should try to involve family members and "significant others" in problem-solving and support-giving.

The worker has two basic objectives: first, to reduce the impact of the stressful event and, second, to utilize the crisis situation to help those affected in dealing with present problems

2. J. Thomas Ungerleider, "The Psychiatric Emergency: Analysis of Six Months' Experience of a University Hospital's Consultation Service," *Archives of General Psychiatry* 3(1960): 593-609.

and (to the extent possible) to learn new and more effective ways of coping with subsequent crises. Hence, the familiar observation that a crisis situation brings out, not only danger, but opportunity as well.

The Main Elements of Crisis Intervention

The four stages of a crisis are: (1) a precipitating event, sometimes called stress or "stressor," (2) the perception of the event, (3) the response to the event, and (4) the resolution of the ensuing problem or an impasse.

The precipitating or stressful event

Mental health crises are triggered by a variety of situations, usually involving change-producing events of special significance for the person or persons affected. These stresses may be divided into two categories according to the manner of their occurrence. There are accidental or situational stresses which occur without warning and there are other life stresses which are more or less anticipated. An auto collision or the sudden death of a loved one are examples of unexpected stresses. The upset felt by a recovering psychiatric patient trying to adjust to the community following discharge from a state hospital or the fear of death experienced by a seriously injured victim following an accident are examples of anticipated types of stressful events. Obviously, we are all vulnerable to a variety of both expected and unexpected stresses.

Perception of the stressful event

It is important to understand that almost any kind of event, ranging from those perceived as serious threats from an "objective" medical point of view to those that are of "personal" or "symbolic" importance, can pose a threat to the needs or goals of an individual at a particular time of his life. By a threat to life goals we mean a hazard to such basic security needs as love or affectional ties, a sense of identity, or, most important of all, body integrity, one's very existence.

Thus, for a given person, a change in status or role or a loss of a loved one, a job, or self-esteem may be threatening and may make him vulnerable to breakdown. Of course, every stressful event does *not* lead to a crisis state; only those which are meaningful to the individual and which overtax his current coping capabilities lead to crises.

The response phase

When an event is perceived as threatening, it often shades off into a response characterized by disequilibrium or disorganization. This is called the "crisis state." During this period, the individual feels overwhelmed by the stress confronting him, helpless in coping with it, and unsure of direction. In short, he is upset and finds his inner tension mounting. His "steady" state (equilibrium or balance) has been disrupted, he finds that his customary problem-solving mechanisms do not work, and he needs to find and develop new ways of coping.

Crisis resolution

Crisis resolution refers to the development of effective adaptive and coping devices through the use of the patient's own resources and through the intervention of health care personnel, family members, and significant others who steer him toward a solution to his problem. Thus, tension and anxiety, which have been mounting during the perception and response phases, begin to diminish during this period. Hopefully, the individual will once again be able to rely on his own problem-solving methods, as well as to use the new coping methods he has learned when other problems occur. In this sense, crises afford an opportunity for emotional growth.

We may roughly diagram the crisis sequence as shown in Figure 1-1.

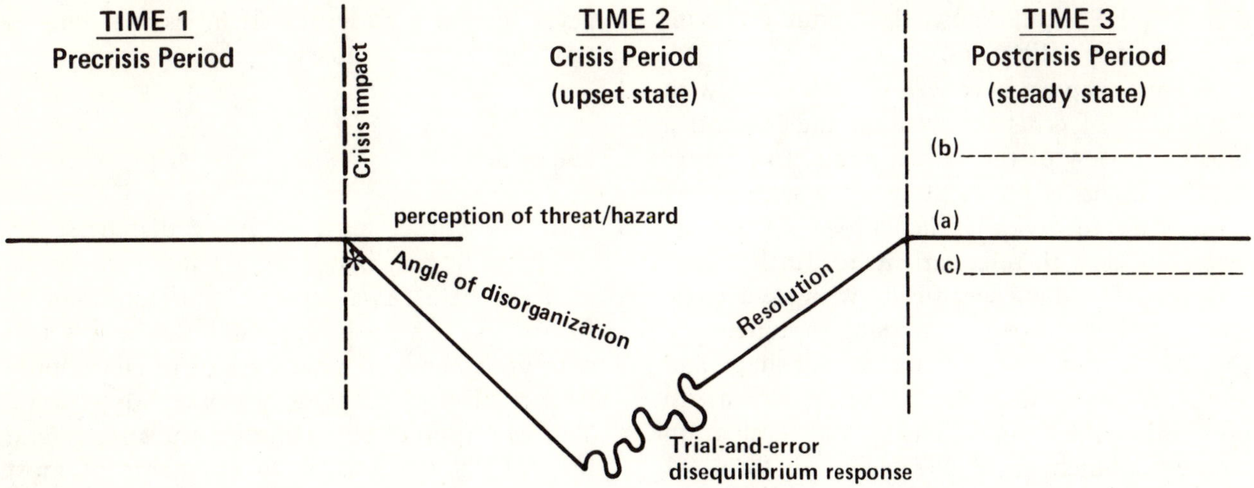

Figure 1-1. Crisis sequence diagram. The asterisk indicates the immediate onset of the crisis period, which occurs directly after the crisis impact. An angle of disorganization develops during the crisis period and may vary from steep to gradual. This variance also occurs during the resolution (recovery or reorganization) phase. During Time 3, the postcrisis period, the level of functioning may be about the same as during Time 1, the precrisis period, or it may be higher or lower, depending on the nature of the stress, available resources, and whether the crisis resolution is adaptive or maladaptive.

In crisis intervention the main point to keep in mind is that, during the disequilibrium phase, when the patient's habitual coping mechanisms are proving inadequate, he is especially receptive to professional intervention. This is the time when a crisis worker can have major impact, insuring that the patient develops new and more effective problem-solving methods and emerges from the crisis with heightened emotional strengths.

THE EMERGENCY TEAM AS THERAPEUTIC INTERVENORS[3]

Having reviewed the theoretical basis for crisis intervention, we are ready to move toward the specific achievement of its goals, which is, of course, the purpose of this book and the rationale of the chapters that follow. However, at this point, it is worthwhile to explore a few characteristics of effective crisis intervenors—no matter what their professional identities—before considering the practical techniques of intervention.

The aim here is not to teach crisis workers to become mental health specialists. Rather, we hope to impart an adequate understanding of various mental health crises which will allow emergency teams to: (1) appropriately assess the situation, (2) arrive at a determination of what needs to be done, and, (3) either respond accordingly or effect an appropriate disposition. It obviously would be very helpful if the emergency team could consult with a mental health specialist—whether in person or by telephone—but we realize that at present this is a luxury. However, we expect this type of resource to become increasingly available as total emergency care systems are developed. Unfortunately, at the present time, mental health care is the most neglected area in emergency medical planning.

To function in this important role, the emergency worker must first understand some fundamental principles of crisis intervention and

3. This section has been written by H. L. P. Resnik, M.D., and Harvey L. Ruben, M.D.

then acquire usable knowledge about the management of specific crises.

This chapter is concerned primarily with the theory of crisis intervention and presents a broad overview of the worker's role. In Chapter II, the focus is on methods of assessing and responding to crises. It includes a section on when and how to refer patients for further care. Chapter III, dealing specifically with psychiatric crises, describes how to conduct an emergency psychiatric interview, obtain an adequate and useful history, and complete the assessment. In presenting these interviewing and evaluation methods, which are applicable in all forms of crises, Dr. Zusman has clearly recognized the worker's limitations in terms of time, setting, and knowledge of specific psychiatric techniques. A careful reading of these first three chapters should provide a sound background for the practical management of the various mental health crises described in this book.

Let us examine the emergency worker's role in more detail. Some of the crises he will encounter as a therapeutic intervenor will have specific psychiatric or mental health content while others, nonpsychiatric crises, involve psychological and/or social ramifications for both victim and family. Frequently, the worker feels more comfortable in dealing with nonpsychiatric crises, and we shall start with this type problem. As an example we can choose a very common situation, an automobile accident in which several people have been injured.

The crisis worker must be attuned to an emergency's psychological components which are all too frequently overshadowed by the more pressing and more obvious physical demands for attention. Numerous patients have recounted that, although in a state of shock, they could recall all the events, both words and actions, surrounding their emergency. Invariably, they stress the usefulness of whatever emotional support they received from members of the crisis team. Remember this need and behave as though the patient is completely in touch with you, regardless of his physical condition. Also, never discuss a patient as if he were a thing—a "psycho" or a "coronary."

Use of Self

The worker must be aware that he, as an emphatic human being, is in himself an instrument of help. Awareness of and responsibility for the use of your body, whether it be to touch with your hands or your eyes or to talk, should be part of every emergency worker's repertoire. You can appreciably minimize the anxiety and fear which are normal concomitants of most accidents by *appropriate talk, touch, and behavior.*

In talking, use a reassuring tone. Resist shouts or increases in your own excitement level; modulate your voice. Establish your introduction by first telling the patient what you are—a physician, a nurse, a policeman. Offer your first name as well as your surname—"I'm Jim Ryan." With the emotional shock of an accident, victims need repetition of all communications to absorb them. It is a good practice to repeat all instructions at least twice. Ask the victim's name and then use it frequently. Notice how he offers his name to you—Thomas Jones, Tommy Jones, or Mr. Jones—and use that form in addressing him. Do not become personal too soon. You do not have the right to call him by his first name unless he allows this. If he does, though, it enhances the intimate relationship between the care giver and the care receiver, facilitating cooperation. Talk to your patient so that he knows you are there. He may be unable to see you or feel you but a steady stream of talk assures him of your presence. For subject matter, tell him without involved detail what you are doing, where you will be taking him, and whether you have notified his family. Let him know you are experienced (if this is so) in a manner that conveys confidence. Inform him about the chain of care he will be receiving —"I'm going to take you right to the hospital" or "We've called a surgeon." In accidents where others have also been injured, do not volunteer such information *unless* the patient asks. Respect his silence or avoidance as an individual of his inability to cope with such information. Everything you say should have a purpose in assisting the patient. If he asks if other people are injured and you know, tell him. Do not give details; let matters stand at "the man has a leg injury" or "the lady has hurt her head." If others have been *killed* at the scene, it is usually preferable not to report this directly to your patient. You might hedge with words like "badly injured," "pretty bad," or "my partner is over there with them now." Obviously, when bodies are covered and apparent, and you are asked, a fact is a fact. (See Chapter VIII.) Be careful to keep your comments to your colleagues brief and professional. Never forget the patient can hear, even if he may have his eyes closed.

Everyone has a need to be touched and to be held. It is a very primitive need, dating back to infancy, and is very normal and quite acceptable under stress. The use of your hands to touch the face, the hand, or the body is a very reassuring gesture to an anxious or frightened person, particularly children to whom specific words may not be helpful. Hold the patient, if the situation presents itself. If in doubt, ask "Would you like to put your head on my shoulder?" or suggest "If I hold you for a minute or two, it might feel better." To be surrounded or held is reassuring and helpful, unless the patient's physical condition indicates otherwise. Certainly, if the victim is of the opposite sex, ask if she wishes to be held. If not, be professional, avoiding any suggestions of being improper. You can touch with your eyes as well as your hands. Look your patients in the eye when you talk. It is a good way to let them know you care.

Your own behavior and actions can help reduce the patient's fears and anxiety. Be calm and create a professional atmosphere. Avoid shouting or running about. Organize your plans and then act deliberately. Also, keep the scene modulated. Bystanders tend to gape and talk and get in the way, to say nothing of frightening the patient. Control the crowd by appointing someone, perhaps an aggressive assistant, to take charge of the situation. He should let the crowd know that they are hampering your efforts.

The Effect of Crises on Workers

It is quite normal for emergency workers to have personal reactions to the plight of others. Although maintaining a professional attitude is important, this does not mean that one must be cold, callous, or dispassionate. You can be an excellent worker and still be responsive as a human being. In some situations you may feel nauseated, upset, scared, frustrated, angry, or impatient. When you begin working in this field, you will probably wonder if your colleagues or supervisors ever felt this way. Ask them and you will find these are common reactions. When you are tired and overworked, you may lose your temper, be belligerent, feel insensitive, and make mistakes. If this occurs, take a break or rest as soon as you can.

When crises affect you adversely, there are natural support systems to which you can turn. The first support is your co-worker. He appreciates what you are going through and can share your feelings. If you've made a mistake, he will understand how and why. The next support is your supervisor. He undoubtedly has considerable experience and can offer you advice, encouragement, and direction. A third level of support is a regular rap session during which the entire emergency team can share experiences, both positive and negative. This group process can serve many purposes, particularly promoting group cohesion and peer support. If a mental health professional is also included, the group process can be greatly facilitated.

Of course, the more a crisis worker can share his burdens with his spouse, the less stressed he is. It is essential that the crisis worker's wife understand the constant, intense strains which lead to weariness, shortness of temper, or unavailability. But what of her needs? Here, too, a group session among crisis workers' wives and a mental health professional would help to get at their feelings and thus allow them to work maximally with their partners, as they would like to do. Wives may feel abandoned, short-changed, deprived, frustrated, and angry. Bringing the two groups together as couples would allow them to share issues and minimize any couple's feeling that their particular stresses are unique.

THE EMERGENCY MENTAL STATUS EXAMINATION[4]

A fundamental part of the emergency worker's role in mental health crises is to assess the severity of the problem. He must make a correct judgment of the degree of mental and emotional impairment suffered by the patient before treatment or referral can be accomplished.

The purpose of the mental status examination is to get a complete picture of the patient's mental state in a systematic way. In this way comparison can be made with other individuals in similar situations and the degree of abnormality of disturbance in the patient can be determined.

In obtaining facts about a crisis, arriving at a diagnosis, and deciding on a course of treatment, a psychiatrist or other mental health professional utilizes a formal interview and evaluation process. The first phase of this process is the mental status examination. This same examination can be adapted by the emergency worker faced with a mental health crisis.

4. This section has been written by Jack Zusman, M.D., M.P.H.

Structure

The examination is structured around a checklist of facts and areas of concern to be covered. Although it is important for the worker to get information about most of the items, rigid adherence to the form of the checklist during an interview is generally neither a good idea nor practical. The order of the items is not particularly meaningful or important, nor is it likely to be the order in which facts will occur to the patient as he relates his story. If you attempt to direct the patient to present information in a prescribed order, the spontaneity of your relationship with him will suffer. The patient may even become angry or upset if you are too aggressive or persistent in structuring his narrative.

Permit the patient to talk freely, at the most offering very occasional direction until the patient "runs down." When the patient has told his story, or the things he feels he must tell immediately, you can begin to fill in the details by asking pointed questions about missing data. Even at this stage, guide the patient only through brief questions and comments; encourage him to respond spontaneously. Finally, when the patient makes it clear that he feels you now have all the information which he considers of greatest significance, consider your checklist, locate the remaining gaps, and ask about them.

Do not hesitate to carry with you a written checklist to which you can refer during the interview. Obvious use of the checklist early in the interview may disturb spontaneity, but once you have developed a relationship with the patient, its presence will not likely bother him.

There are two exceptions to permitting the patient to take the lead at the outset of the examination. First, when there is essential information to be obtained which may be lost subsequently, ask these questions immediately. For example, if the patient has taken an overdose of some toxic substance and may soon become unconscious, you must press right then for answers about the drug, dosage, and time of ingestion. When the management of an emergency hinges on information from the patient, insist upon this data. With patients who are minors, the parents must be located and summoned *before* treatment can be undertaken, unless life-threatening circumstances exist.

Second, in cases where the patient is extremely depressed or minimally responsive for other reasons, you must also take the lead with questions. However, even here in the early stages of the interview, concentrate only on items which you, as an examiner, feel are important to the patient.

If the patient is reluctant to respond to some of your questions, put these aside for later inquiry or for discussion with his friends or relatives. If the patient is pressed too hard about these matters, he may withdraw from the interview completely.

Keep in mind when using the checklist that obtaining a complete, detailed picture of all elements of the patient's current situation and background can be disturbing to the patient and wasteful of precious time. Most likely, a number of items on the checklist will not be relevant to the present problem. Put them aside or make a note to explore them at a later time.

In obtaining facts about events which have led to the emergency situation and in evaluating the state itself, the primary objective is to categorize the patient generally and then decide upon a course of treatment.

Categorization

As the first step in categorization, you must decide whether the patient is in a state normal for him (and therefore not in need of any sort of emergency help) or is in a state of emergency (and therefore requires immediate intervention). Such decisions are not easily made, and the boundaries of the categories are not clear-cut. Each crisis worker must develop his skills for assessing individual patients, learning by experience what the reactions of "normal persons" are to various common stressful situations. Become familiar with the effects which you yourself have upon those whom you interview and take this into account.

Precise categorization of patients is best left to the specialist. However, emergency workers must make a diagnosis in terms of available treatment options. Know what options are open to your patient—hospitalization, referral for outpatient treatment, social welfare agency, or discharge, once emergency treatment is completed. Individual sections of this book discuss how to recognize the varying degrees of seriousness and need for treatment in relation to most of the mental health problems which you will encounter. In every case, however, take into account the treatment options open to you; only in this way are diagnostic categories meaningful to you as an emergency worker.

The Checklist

The following is the mental status checklist of information items which the worker must obtain or evaluate. In most cases the items are self-explanatory. Where they are not, a brief statement of explanation is included. The asterisks indicate those items which are essential or of very high priority with every patient, no matter what the problem.

I. Personal items
   A. Name*
   B. Age*
   C. Residence address and telephone number*
   D. Next of kin, name, address, and telephone number*
   E. Worker's estimate of reliability of the information given by the patient

II. Informant (instead of patient, if patient is unable to provide information, or in addition to patient)
   A. Name
   B. Residence address and telephone number

   C. Relation to patient
   D. Reliability and degree of access to essential information

III. Major problem leading to emergency
   A. Exactly what is the problem*
   B. When did it start*
   C. What makes it better* (e.g., medication, activity, rest)
   D. What makes it worse* (e.g., activity, location, stress)
   E. Has the problem ever occurred before and, if so, under what conditions*
   F. What made the occurrence today an emergency*

IV. Current life situation
   A. Family and living arrangements* (e.g., with whom does he live; to whom does he have responsibilities; which individuals can be called upon to help and take responsibility for him)
   B. Significant others and significant responsibilities* (e.g., who are the individuals important to him and to whom he is important; for what other persons does he have responsibilities; is he a parent of young children who must be cared for immediately)
   C. Employment
   D. Unusual habits/situations* (e.g., how much does he drink; does he use drugs; has he been in trouble with the police)
   E. Is he currently under psychiatric or medical treatment* (with whom and for what)
   F. Socio-cultural background and supporting relationships (e.g., with what group does the patient identify; to what clubs, groups, or social networks does he belong; which groups are important to him or have offered him support and can be called to help in the emergency)
   G. Education

V. Recent history
   A. Changes in life situation* (e.g., loss of job; death in the family; breakup of important relationship; promotion to new job; graduation from school)
   B. Changes in feeling (e.g., increase in sadness or happiness without obvious reason; change in appetite; change in sexual interest; change in sleep patterns; increase in anxiety)
   C. Significant illness (mental or physical)
   D. Ingestion of intoxicants or medication*

VI. Past and family (relatives') history
   A. Illness, suicide, use of alcohol or drugs
   B. Significant events
   C. Relationships

VII. Previous illness
   A. Mental* (where, when, why, how, nature of treatment)
   B. Physical (where, when, why, how, nature of treatment)
   C. Significant symptoms of recent physical illness or injury (e.g., headache; seizures; dizziness; chest pain; vomiting)

VIII. Mental examination
   A. General appearance, manner, and attitude* (particularly as these factors deviate from what is normally to be expected in that particular situation)
   B. Degree of consciousness* (with emphasis on indications of diminished state of consciousness; best rapid indicator of diminution is patient's inability to carry out uncomplicated but repetitive arith-

metic, such as subtracting sevens, in a series, from 100 or counting backwards from 100)

C. Apperception (e.g., ability to grasp new situations, events, and experiences; ability to think in an abstract manner; ability to understand proverbs and analogies)

D. Affectivity and mood (e.g., current emotional state; appropriateness of current emotional state for the present crisis situation; range of emotional expression)

E. Expressive behavior* (e.g., drive and degree of expression in connection with patient's ordinary behavior; disturbances or activity such as overexcitability, apathy, negativism, silliness, or hostility)

F. Associations and thought processes (e.g., degree of logic in the patient's expressions; appropriateness of connection between patient's thought from one moment to the next; ability of patient to express his thoughts in an understandable manner; coherence of his sentences)

G. Thought content and mental trend (e.g., patient's preoccupations; appropriateness of what concerns him; degree of reality in sensations and experiences which he reports)

H. Perception (e.g., patient's ability to correctly interpret his sensations; strength of patient's convictions regarding sensory experiences which he has misinterpreted)

I. Memory (e.g., patient's ability to recall immediate past; distant past; ability to recall specific instructions given five minutes ago)

J. Fund of information (e.g., patient's knowledge of general facts—name of the president of the U.S. or number of states in the U.S.—in relation to his education and apparent intelligence)

K. Judgment (e.g., ability to draw conclusions from a set of facts; ability to predict likely future course of events based on past experience)

L. Insight* (e.g., patient's awareness of nature and seriousness of his problem)

M. Personality type (e.g., patient's general precrisis manner of dealing with problems and way of relating to the world)

IX. Diagnostic impression

A. How serious is the problem now?*

B. How serious is it likely to become in the near future?*

C. Of the options open, which is most likely to benefit the patient; which is the least likely to harm the patient*

1. Should he be treated; is a tranquilizer necessary
2. Should he be taken directly to a psychiatric facility
3. Should his physical condition be checked out first to rule out concomitant illness or injury appearing as an emotional disorder

It should be clear by now that the emergency medical worker is in a critical position. He is the first or only health professional with whom a patient has contact during a crisis. The ultimate successful resolution of the crisis depends largely upon the actions of the worker during this time. Remember:

1. Intervene to the extent you feel capable.

2. Be aware of your own professional limitations.

3. If you feel that you are at the limits of your expertise, seek additional help or consultation.

By following the above three mandates, the

worker, too, will be able to learn and to grow with each new experience.

THE ROLE OF THE EMERGENCY TEAM CHIEF OR SUPERVISOR[5]

Although this manual is directed toward all members of emergency teams, a word should be said about the role of the team chief or supervisor, who must possess certain additional skills and knowledge.

The director of the team will vary according to where the team functions as well as local circumstances. For instance, within a hospital setting, the chief will be a physician, probably the head of the emergency room service, while on-the-scene management may be directed by the supervisor or a police rescue squad. The chief's role is especially important when the emergency involves many people.

Regardless of his position or title, he is the one who must maintain an overall perspective on the task at hand. Whether the crisis is a natural disaster such as a flood or earthquake, a train-wreck or a multiple auto accident, he must operate with an overview of the situation. He must know the total extent of the emergency, the number and types of injured or dead, and the availability of resources. He must establish priorities for treatment which are offered to each individual based on initial triage evaluation. He himself may actually perform the triage function or he may delegate it to a competent senior team member.

Triage refers to the process for deciding who receives what type of treatment in the face of a massive casualty situation. This is equally true for psychiatric and physical casualties. When treatment resources are in short supply, the triage officer must decide who needs help first and who will benefit the most. The victim who is so severely injured that he is not likely to recover regardless of treatment should be given medication to alleviate pain, but probably little else can be done at the moment. The triage officer must decide who is severely injured, but savable. This patient should be treated first. Finally, there are those whose injuries can safely wait to be treated until after the more severely injured have been cared for. With a broad view of the situation, the supervisor is in a position to establish such priorities.

The individual crisis worker cannot afford to develop this macrocosmic perspective. He must concern himself with each individual case, rather than the totality of the problem. Were he to become concerned with the overall picture, he might find himself overwhelmed by the magnitude of the disaster and unable to deal effectively with his assigned patients. He must bring all his skills to focus on particular patients whereas the supervisor must make sure that the individual team members are fulfilling their tasks in a broader sense.

If one team member has more "psychological-mindedness" or specific expertise in this area, the supervisor should designate this person to handle the mental health aspects of the emergency. The team chief can make initial contact with the patient, carry out assessment, and develop the appropriate disposition in co-operation with the team member.

The supervisor is responsible for developing the team's overall approach to the catastrophe. He must help the members decide whether or under what circumstances they will touch or hold victims (for psychological rather than medical reasons). Also, he establishes priorities to determine the extent of the involvement of team members in the mental health aspects of the emergency. He bears the responsibility for notifying the family and checking back later on referrals that he has made. If the chief does not assign himself or a particular person to fulfill these functions, it is easy for each team member to assume another is performing them. Thus,

5. This section and the following section (Why Emergency Teams Sometimes Fail) have been written by Harvey L. Ruben, M.D., M.P.H., and H. L. P. Resnik, M.D.

ultimate responsibility for success or failure of the crisis team rests with the supervisor.

The director must also be prepared to offer psychological support and understanding to his team. As mentioned previously, the supervisor should actively strive to create a feeling of easy accessibility, strength, compassion, and understanding so that when members of his team are troubled they will seek him out individually. When possible, the supervisor should identify an outside mental health consultant experienced in crisis intervention who can regularly meet with the entire group to discuss emotional crises confronting them. Such a program is preventive mental health care for the staff. Many a good emergency worker is lost to his program because his own mental health has not been considered.

WHY EMERGENCY TEAMS SOMETIMES FAIL

There are a number of practical rules and techniques for intervention which are spelled out throughout this manual. If followed, they can ensure success in most emergency situations. Yet, unfortunately, failure, both partial and complete, does occur, and frequently for very familiar reasons. The following list, while not inclusive, summarizes some of the difficulties which most frequently prevent the crisis team from successfully resolving the situation:

1. Priorities for handling a massive disaster are inadequately established. Triage function is not properly carried out. The team members end up dissipating their energies in many different directions, and few people, if any, are adequately handled.
2. Team members are so overwhelmed by the physical aspects of an emergency that they fail to deal with the psychological aspects, either for the patient or the family.
3. Workers assess the psychological aspects of the crisis, but fail to adequately deal with them. Staff members attempt to function beyond the limits of their own expertise, failing to seek consultation and making inappropriate dispositions for care on follow-up.
4. The team assesses the situation correctly but fails to follow through to make sure that the patient reaches the resource to which he is referred.
5. The worker allows his own personal feelings about certain types of patients or problems to interfere with his adequate handling of the case. He becomes blinded by his emotions so that it is impossible to make an appropriate assessment or develop the disposition. A most frequent illustration of this situation is dealing with the alcoholic patient.

LEGAL ASPECTS OF MENTAL HEALTH EMERGENCIES[6]

Emergency team members, both professional and paraprofessional, and the hospital must be aware of the legal implications of their assessment and treatment of individuals. Issues of responsibility, consent, confidentiality, and civil liberties should affect the point of view and the activities of the informed emergency worker. On the one hand there is the interest of the state in conforming certain types of behavior to its statutes, for example, laws governing reporting of crimes, civil commitment, drug addiction, and alcoholism. The state may also protect the individual in certain ways, possibly guarding the patient's communications to his doctor or providing for Good Samaritan care by the professional. On the civil side, the law may allow monetary recovery from the treater to a wronged patient, for example, medical malpractice, improper commitment, or insufficient protection of a suicidal patient. But here, too, experience shows that there is considerable latitude in emergency diagnosis and treatment.

It is essential that every worker is aware of

6. This section has been written by Diane Daskal Ruben, M.A.T., J.D.

the state laws that govern his responsibilities and actions. In all of the areas discussed below, there are variations in local standards. You should know, before your inquiry is an emergency, such information as: What are the commitment procedures and standards? Is there extensive statutory protection of confidences? What patient conditions and activities must be reported? Need every automobile driver consent to an alcohol-level test? How does your jurisdiction handle avowed drug addicts? Familiarity with these laws is as important as your familiarity with various local resources.

Accepting, Referring, and Releasing the Patient

According to early common law, there is no legal duty for a layman or a medical professional to come to the aid of a person in trouble. Moral imperatives aside, today there is no positive legal responsibility to rescue or treat. Of course, professional canons of ethics for medical personnel emphasize the *ethical duty* of the doctor or nurse to aid the injured victim. When a special relationship between individuals exists, such as between parent and child, there is a legal duty to help. Similarly, firemen and policemen do have a clear duty to help a victim within their jurisdiction.

The law does recognize that, once aid is offered, it must be done properly; nor can the assumed responsibility be abandoned. Thus, a good swimmer is legally permitted to stand on the shore and watch another person drown. But once he dives in and pulls the victim out, he cannot abandon him, without opening himself to financial liability.

Analogously, a hospital has traditionally had the right to turn away unwanted patients at the emergency room door. This is no longer true. If a hospital holds itself out as offering emergency facilities, it owes an institutional duty of treatment to patients who seek its services. Moreover, it warrants the availability of competent staff, decent equipment, and reasonably attainable physician back-up. The hospital may transfer or refer a patient when appropriate, but only after the immediate danger to the patient is past and when he has been *stabilized before transfer.* Thus, if you see an alcoholic in the emergency room and determine that he should be referred to a detoxification center, his physical and mental condition must be sufficiently stable before he is safe to transfer—there must be no immediate danger of concussions, asphyxiation, or suicide. Therefore, he may very well need some treatment in a holding bed in the emergency room prior to transfer.

A patient who is released prematurely can later sue the staff and the facility which allowed him to leave. For example, in one case an unconscious patient was brought to the emergency room. He had been found in his underwear on the lawn of a hotel and could not give his name or any history. His vital signs and chest sounds were normal. No x-rays were taken. The staff released him to the police as a drunk. He died in jail that night from a puncture of the thoracic cavity by undiagnosed broken ribs. The hospital was found liable for his death.

If the patient is unwilling to remain under your care, you have three alternatives. If he is a suicide risk or so emotionally disturbed that he is incapable of protecting himself, he may be suitable for involuntary commitment (see below). Likewise, if he is in life-threatening danger, but unwilling or unable to consent to treatment, you are able to proceed, based on the emergency nature of the situation (see below). Otherwise you will have to permit him to sign himself out of your care "against medical advice." If he refuses to do so, carefully note on his record that you warned him of the serious potential danger to himself and that he refused to submit to your care.

Liability for Negligence

In general, the emergency team is granted broad discretion in its handling of a victim, from the initial contact through the referral or hospitalization which terminates the contract. The need for the patient's consent is waived in an emergency; the law encourages the treatment team to freely and quickly take whatever assessment and management steps it judges appropriate. Past cases recognize that the worker does not guarantee the success of his technique and that the nature of the emergency can demand bold, resourceful, and rapid decision-making.

While it is a rare exception to the norm, an emergency worker—physician, nurse, and possibly physician's assistant—can be sued by a patient for money damages when a court determines that the professional or paraprofessional deviated from the proper standard of care. It must be established that misdiagnosis or mistreatment by the worker breached his duty to the patient and was the legal cause for injury or damage to the patient. This cause of legal action is called *malpractice.* A doctor may be liable, as well, for the errors of the employees and staff working under his actual or imputed supervision and control.

Nurses are specifically responsible to wronged patients for improperly following orders or for following orders where they should have used independent judgment to the contrary. For instance, where a physician orders a certain dosage of medication intramuscularly and the nurse administers it without objecting that the usual method is intravenous, that lack of discretion might make the nurse liable. Nurses' liability may arise when bedrails are not provided and a patient is subsequently injured in a fall. Nurses should be careful never to rely solely on a monitoring machine to the exclusion of their own observation and care.

The physician's liability for negligence may exist, as we have said, when improper management of the patient causes harm. He may also be responsible to the patient on various other grounds for wrongs he or his assistants have done—failure to advise the patient of potential dangers of treatment, failure to consult with a psychiatric specialist where such consultation is required, failure to protect a patient against his own suicidal actions, improper commitment, or even failure to warn third parties of realistic potential dangers to themselves from patients. Successful recovery on these grounds is not common, but the team member is wise to understand these possibilities.

The Good Samaritan law is a statute adopted in various forms by almost all states. It provides that a professional who renders good faith emergency care at the scene of the accident will be protected from future liability, barring gross negligence. The different forms of the law vary as to who is covered (nurses are included in about half the states), whether the qualifying treatment must be free of charge, what exactly is the definition of emergency, and the degree of misconduct which will be tolerated. These laws have generally not been updated or interpreted to include paramedics and physicians' assistants. This statute does not apply to situations in which you are called to an emergency in an official capacity or in response to a telephone call. It applies to the situation in which you come upon an accident as a private citizen who also happens to be a crisis worker.

The law was adopted because of a hesitancy on the part of professionals to render accident care on the scene for fear of possible suit. The origin of this fear is not evident; there are no reported cases of malpractice suits in such a situation. Even if your state has no such statute, you would be unrealistically conservative to withhold your competent and much needed help at the scene of an emergency.

Beside professional malpractice, the other potentially liable party is the hospital, which is financially responsible for negligent injuries it causes or fails to prevent. A hospital corporation can be found liable for injury or death to patients who have entered into its sphere of control, where an error or omission legally caused such injury. This applies not only to admitted patients, but to emergency patients seen by its staff. The hospital's duty of care includes providing safe premises, hiring competent staff, and taking reasonable precautions to protect the patient, *even from self-inflicted injury*, where this possibility is foreseeable.

For instance, if sodium amytal is given intravenously to a patient without the immediate availability of oxygen and injury occurs, the hospital might pay a penalty. In cases of physical diagnosis, the hospital has been found wanting for not having a specialist consultant available. The same doctrine might well be applied by the courts where the extent of a mental health disorder is too grave to be handled by the nonspecialist.

A common ground for suits against team leaders and hospitals is *wrongful death*, an action brought by the state or next of kin if a patient allegedly dies from an error of diagnosis, treatment, or management. For example, if a patient arrives in the emergency room distraught and anxious but the staff fails to determine his suicidal potential, leaving him unprotected, his subsequent suicide may be a basis for recovery. The courts often rule that the hospital and its employees should foresee when a patient will attempt a self-injurious act and should protect him from these impulses.

In one case, the psychiatrist superintendent of a general hospital was liable for $10,000 after a patient deemed already suicidal was left alone in a locked room. The nurse who was to observe him through a peephole in the door had at least 12 other patients. While she was busy, the patient strangled himself with some tubing in his room.

To guard against such situations, do not fail to make an assessment of suicidal lethality of a disturbed patient. Put this assessment and its basis in the record. If suicide precautions are deemed necessary, specify what degree of care should be followed. If you, as staff, have any doubts about what specific measures are ordered, ask the person who wrote the order. The law is replete with cases of patients who leap out of windows, escape from wards, dive through hedges, bolt from technicians, and "creatively" destroy or injure themselves.

Consent to Treatment

Under nonemergency circumstances, the competent, conscious, adult patient should be informed of the needed medical treatment and asked to give his permission—if feasible, written consent. Under such circumstances, your unauthorized treatment, even in good faith, could be held a recoverable technical battery upon the patient. However, the law recognizes several broad exceptions to the need for obtaining consent: the incompetent adult, the unconscious patient, the victim in crisis, and the individual openly assenting to treatment.

A child or minor is unable to give consent for himself, and so, barring emergency or immediate danger, his parent or guardian must give permission for him to be treated. The exception here is the emancipated child, a minor who does not live with or depend upon his parents for anything. This individual has either actually or constructively severed his ties with home and is capable of consenting to his own treatment.

A patient may be so disturbed, bizarre, or ill that he is considered by the court unable (incompetent) *legally* to give informed consent. In this case, a guardian or responsible family member must give permission for him (unless another exception applies). Where the patient is competent to consent, he must grant permission with some informed knowledge of what he is agreeing to. Failure to disclose the dangers in a course of treatment may open a health worker to suit for battery (the consent is invalid because he does not understand its nature) or for negligence (where failure to disclose the inherent risks is a breach of duty owed to the patient). This is so, regardless of the skill used in treatment or the success of the care.

When the conscious patient willingly submits to treatment, consent is implied by his nonprotestation. Consent may also be implied by the law in *situations of emergency*. If there is immediate urgency to treatment or immediate danger to the life or health of the patient, you may proceed freely without obtaining permission. A drug overdose, an hallucinating schizophrenic, a badly battered infant—these are examples of emergency situations in which you may proceed without hesitation with involuntary treatment.

Occasionally, a seemingly competent individual will refuse to consent even to treatment which the staff deems life-saving. What is the law's reaction to such a self-destructive gesture? There are times when the state steps in and, without consent, requires compulsory treatment, for example, where contagious diseases are concerned. However, the courts are divided on whether they will order a transfusion to save the life of a patient who refuses to grant this permission on religious grounds. Usually, the court will order the transfusion where there are children or family who will suffer the loss; other times a principled individual may be allowed the civil liberty of saying "no."

This is different from the case of a disturbed, unstable, or severely depressed individual who expresses a fervent desire to be allowed to kill himself. Suicide attempts are often cries for help. It is your responsibility to protect the patient from these impulses until he can reconstitute himself.

The Involuntary Patient

The principles of civil rights urge that an individual should not be robbed of his freedom without good reason and without due process of law. A severely disturbed patient may be hospitalized against his will where the diagnosis, need and method of commitment correspond to the standards established by the local law. Every crisis worker should be familiar with the substantive and procedural requirements of his own state statute. There are basically three definitions of severity which the various states adopt in their commitment laws: "dangerous to self or others" (probably the most stringent standard), "in the need of treatment and care," or "in the best interest of the patient and society" (a rather malleable guide).

There is a fine line between incarceration for treatment and for punishment. Society often punishes deviant behavior by removing the individual, whether to jail or to a mental hospital. The patient who is hospitalized against his will should ideally be equally afforded procedural safeguards equal to those available to criminals—notice of the action, judicial hearing of his care, and adversary proceeding with an attorney for him with the possibility of jury review of an adverse decision.

The officers or physicians who certify a patient for commitment (see below for procedure) must find by personal examination that the patient meets the standard of illness prescribed in the state law. Failure to do so may open them to suit for improper commitment or malicious prosecution. For example, in one case, two mental health officers committed a patient, relying entirely on the husband's description of his wife's illness. The court awarded her a verdict of $20,000 because she was committed without probable cause.

On the other hand, if you commit a patient, whom you have actually examined, for a temporary observational commitment, the risk of recovery on such a suit is minimal. There is no reported case of a physician sued successfully for a wrongful observational commitment, and you may be averting a potential tragedy by such an incarceration.

These civil liberties considerations do not mean that you should feel helpless to hospitalize a protesting patient who is seriously threatening the life of a relative or who recently made a suicide attempt. In fact, when you owe a special duty to the individual (i.e., patient), you could be held responsible for injuries from your failure to commit a dangerous person. Such considerations mean that you should not commit a patient who is disturbed and would benefit from treatment, but does not meet the legal standard imposed by your state law. A number of witnesses may tell you that the patient was hallucinating wildly an hour ago, but it must be on the basis of your judgment of current mental health that a patient is committed.

There are two processes to achieve commitment. The first is by judicial commitment, a hearing, then confinement. The second is by medical certification in which one or two medical opinions (it varies according to the state) establish that the patient is legally disabled, followed by brief observational hospitalization and a hearing. Be familiar with your own statute to know its requirements and methods.

Civil commitment of drug addicts is now an available alternative to penal incarceration. Since 1962 it has been unconstitutional to jail an addict for his habit since addiction is judged an illness, not a crime. However, an addict may be jailed for drug offenses, drug-related offenses, and nondrug offenses. Most addicts, outside of New York and California, still receive criminal, as opposed to civil, disposition, which may include treatment.

Many jurisdictions have shifted to civil disposition for the disease of alcoholism. The Supreme Court has ruled that it is cruel and unusual punishment to consider alcoholism as a criminal condition per se. In some places an alcoholic may still be incarcerated for public drunkenness, though it is a product of his disease; in more enlightened communities, the chronic alcoholic will be treated instead of jailed.

Confidentiality

A patient has the right to expect that his private communications to you will remain private. Confidentiality, essential for honest treatment, is a tenet of medical ethics. Many states have codified the protection of these confidences by enacting a privilege statute, which allows the patient to keep you from revealing such matters in court. Mental health information is used by the courts in criminal proceedings, custody decisions, divorce decrees, and other situations; but you should see yourself as an extension of the patient, not as a functionary of the courts.

As a worker doing emergency treatment, you should not reveal private information in a court unless it is subpoenaed. You should not discuss your clients and their cases with third persons—including friends of yours, seemingly amicable relatives of the patient, law enforcement personnel, or even doctors unaffiliated with you or the case—without obtaining the patient's permission for such disclosures. Legal sanctions for violation of such confidences are weak, but a suit for libel or slander could conceivably ensue.

Keep an accurate record, noting objective findings and information rather than speculation, which may later be injurious if revealed. The personal history which you note should not be based solely on information given you by someone other than the patient. You should not release hospital records nor show them to anyone who asks unless they have a subpeona or court order.

Some states have a privilege law which protects (in court) the revelation by a doctor or a psychotherapist of information told him by his patient. You should be aware that the wording of some such statutes extends its protection to cover confidences to people who are not physicians, but you can assume that personnel—like technicians, nurses, or medical students are generally not covered. Moreover, as an emergency worker, your contact with the patient may be brief enough so that a true physician/therapist/patient relationship is not even formed.

The moral and legal exceptions to the protection of patient confidences are situations in which the patient reveals his serious intent to immediately commit a crime or when the information runs counter to a strong public policy, as expressed in the laws. For example, many states require you to report any suspected cases of child abuse either to the welfare department or sometimes to the police. On the other hand, some states may strengthen privilege to permit a patient to seek treatment. A few states have a statute protecting the name of an addict and his request for treatment and rehabilitation of drug dependency. Without such a law you could legally make a voluntary report to public authorities concerning such a drug abuser. Even a general privilege statute would not be violated, since that law protects in-court statements only. But you should be aware of the negative, chilling effect which cumulative reports like this may have upon the addict population's seeking medical assistance.

Relationships with the Police

As an emergency worker you will have to square the ethical and legal requirements of confidentiality with the citizen's duty to report offensive behavior. As we have said, there are some areas in which the law puts a special premium on disclosure—child abuse, gunshot wounds, and sometimes addiction.

If a patient confesses a past crime to you, such a confession is not privileged information, but mere knowledge of the crime does not make you an accessory. It is criminal for you to help the criminal or to hinder the prosecution of him, but generally there is no legal obligation to come forward. Here again, one's moral obligation is a different question depending, as it does, upon the nature of the crime, the type of patient relationship, and the current status of the patient. The confidence of an intent to commit a future crime is similarly ambiguous. How well-formed and imminent is the intent? How severe is the crime? Is the patient's ability to verbalize his feelings—not act on them—in itself therapeutic? Are you being manipulated by this threat? Is the patient a long-time acquaintance or a one-time encounter? Will your intervention serve a good purpose to protect either a third person or the patient himself?

Your main function as a crisis intervenor is to promote the physical and emotional health of your patients. You should not rely exclusively upon the reports of a police officer to obtain the immediate history of your patient. You should not consider your function to be one of investigating or deciding if your patient has committed a crime. Whether it be rape or spouse abuse, you should aim to provide treatment and arrange future help where necessary, not to determine the victim's past sexual conduct nor to pin blame on the assaulting family member.

One special area you may be called upon to act as an adjunct to law enforcement agencies is a blood test for alcohol level. Many states have laws which say that, by driving on their highways, a citizen automatically consents to a blood test when this is desirable. Such a law surmounts the constitutional objections that an involuntary blood test is an unreasonable, warrantless search and seizure (Fourth Amendment) or a forced self-incrimination (Fifth Amendment). Police find the results of such a test useful as evidence for proving that a driver was driving under the influence or to prove intoxication or impaired driving capability. Even where consent is not obtained, the Supreme Court held, in 1966, that the blood test is physical evidence, like photographs or fingerprints, and, as such, is not forced self-incrimination.

How far should you go in overruling the individual's vociferous objections to the blood test? The individual does have a right to refuse the test, and his refusal cannot be the basis for revocation of his license, nor can it be used against him in court.

As an emergency worker, you are not obliged to perform a blood test for the police. You need not insist on seeing a magistrate's order before performing an involuntary blood test, but you should hold out for a written request by the police for such a sample. The request should show a reasonable cause. You should have the approval of the physician who will be ultimately liable, since you are acting as his agent. If the patient is actively protesting, you might ask that a police doctor perform the test. If the patient is unconscious, you should have the certification of a doctor that an intoxicated condition is suspected, since consent is not possible. Should the patient absolutely refuse to cooperate in being tested, do not attempt to physically force the test; the likelihood of injury to him is too great, and you could conceivably be sued for battery.

II

The Practice of Crisis Intervention in Emergency Care

Howard J. Parad, D.S.W.
H. L. P. Resnik, M.D.

INTRODUCTION

The theoretical bases for crisis intervention were reviewed to emphasize that any stress can be perceived by an individual in such a way that his equilibrium is disrupted. The inability to deal with stress through habitual coping patterns creates a turmoil or crisis state in which the person attempts to find new ways to cope with or solve the problem. This state leads to an interim or long-term resolution of the crisis, or if unsuccessful, a nervous breakdown. You will learn about specific types of emotional disorders in the following chapters.

In simpler language, when a person is confronted with a new and overwhelming problem, he may respond with a temporary state of emotional disruption. Since his usual way of dealing with such difficulties proves inadequate, he must find a new solution, perhaps using some new or different resources. If he is able to do this, he successfully resolves the problem and thus acquires for himself a new problem-solving method for use in his future life. The situation may be equated with emotional growth or maturation. If, however, he is unable to solve the problem successfully, despite his attempts to find a solution, this may lead to a state of continued and increased inner turmoil and ultimately to diagnosable mental illness.

The period of emotional imbalance or disequilibrium, when an individual has found established coping methods inadequate and is searching for a new way to solvc thc problem, is the time the person is most receptive to the brief intervention of the helping professional. This places the emergency worker at a unique advantage. He has access to the person at the exact time when minimum intervention can have maximum effect on the person's life. This is the very essence of crisis intervention. By being attuned to this fact and being knowledgeable in crisis-intervention techniques, the worker can have major impact in helping the individual to resolve the crisis. With this in mind, you need to consider the necessary steps in the practice of crisis intervention.

IDENTIFYING THE CRISIS-PRONE PERSON

Profile

Typically, the crisis-prone person lacks or is unable to utilize the personal, family, and social supports that help everyone to cope with stress while functioning in everyday roles. Often alienated from meaningful and lasting interpersonal relations, he may exhibit some or perhaps all of the following interrelated problems:

1. Difficulty in learning from experience
2. A history of frequent crises, ineffectively resolved because of poor coping ability
3. A history of mental disorder or other serious emotional disturbance
4. Low self-esteem, which may be masked by provocative behavior
5. A tendency toward impulsive "acting-out" behavior (doing without thinking)
6. Marginal income
7. Lack of regular, fulfilling work
8. Unsatisfying marriage and family relations
9. Heavy drinking or other substance abuse
10. History of numerous accidents
11. Frequent encounters with law-enforcement agencies
12. Frequent changes in address

Precipitating Events

Emergency mental health workers typically deal with the following commonly encountered individual, family, and social occurrences that often have crisis-inducing effects, especially for vulnerable or crisis-prone individuals:

1. An accident, with or without physical injury
2. An arrest or court appearance
3. Birth of a baby
4. Change in housing situation
5. Change in income
6. Change in job (including demotion or promotion)
7. Change in school status
8. Death of a significant person
9. A delinquency episode
10. Divorce, desertion, or separation—actual or impending
11. Entry into school
12. Out-of-wedlock or unexpected pregnancy or abortion
13. Physical illness
14. Acute episode of mental disorder
15. Retirement

In addition, there are many other catastrophic environmental events, such as tornadoes, hurricanes, floods, fires, and earthquakes, that have significant mental health implications for individuals and populations as well. Of course, there are many variations to the stress/crisis/response model outlined in the introduction to this chapter.

Individuals vary greatly in the way they view and react to stress situations. What overwhelms one person with great anxiety and tension because of personal sensitivities or psychosocial deficiencies can challenge another person, stimulating his feelings of satisfaction and mastery. The crisis-prone individual is very sensitive to relatively minor stresses. Moreover, as behavioral science has demonstrated, all persons have a breaking point. Even the strongest individual will be vulnerable to certain types or accumulations of stress.

It is not unusual for a person or family to experience many stress situations at the same time. For example, perhaps mother suddenly has to go to the hospital for gynecological care on the same day or soon after father has found out that he might be laid off from his job. Suppose that at the same time one of the children has the flu and the other has just had a minor auto accident. Although any one of these stress situations might produce anxiety but not induce a crisis, the combination of stresses may throw the person or family off balance. Individuals or families can usually mobilize untapped psychological resources. But when mobilization is impeded because of simultaneous stresses or diminished individual or joint resources, crises materialize.

You will often provide emergency health care to persons who have recently been exposed to a life-crisis situation, whether precipitated by a physical cause, such as the death or accidental injury of a loved one, or a psychosocial one, such as marital separation or loss of job. Understanding the meaning and impact of these personal or family events will often assist you in helping the patient. Some individuals and families emerge from crisis encounters feeling stronger and more effective, others become weaker, and still others may be overwhelmed.

TYPES OF EMERGENCY MENTAL HEALTH SERVICES

Contexts of Crisis Intervention

Crisis intervention is a form of active, focused emotional-environmental first aid. It may be carried out in any health setting within the context of any health emergency by any trained medical and paramedical personnel. The preconditions for effective crisis intervention are that the patient is in an upset state and in need of immediate attention. The health worker must be able and willing to listen empathically and attentively, understand the patient's predicament, offer the patient the needed reassurance, emotional support, and clarification, and aid in finding an appropriate health and/or social service.

Settings for Crisis Intervention

In various settings, the crisis worker provides instant first aid, comfort, support, and information to the victim and others involved. Given your knowledge of the diverse resources in your community, you must decide where the patient should be transported: an emergency room, a crisis clinic, a nursing home, or the nearest physician's office. Settings for crisis intervention include the following:

1. The field site, while giving emergency medical care.
2. The ambulance, rescue squad, or police car en route to the hospital.
3. The emergency room, while the patient waits or receives the needed medical care.
4. The walk-in psychiatric clinic offering crisis counseling to ambulatory patients.
5. Hotlines (or rap lines), offering suicide prevention and other crisis-intervention telephone services to troubled individuals. (These services may be independent of, or part of, emergency medical and mental health services. They rely mainly on telephone counseling by trained volunteers—ideally, with professional mental health consultation available on a backup basis.)
6. Emergency departments, where health care personnel offer aid to persons suffering from injuries and other medical and/or mental health problems.
7. Waiting rooms adjacent to treatment areas, where the worker may offer assistance and support to the families. (This is essential and should not be forgotten.)
8. Mobile psychiatric services (often called home treatment teams or psychiatric emergency teams), usually staffed by two or more team members—ideally, one female and one male. (These consist of psychiatric social workers, clinical psychologists, mental health nurses, psychiatric technicians, and other mental health workers, with a psychiatrist available on call. Sometimes the psychiatrist is a

member of the team, which visits and provides consultation to persons who call (or on whose behalf other people may call.)

IDENTIFYING A MENTAL HEALTH EMERGENCY

Identifying a mental health emergency may seem like a simple task, but in practice it is a very complicated one. The answer often depends on the nature of the health service you are providing, your own background and values, and the training and experience you have had in working with emotionally upset and mentally disordered persons.

The person experiencing the painful upset of a severe emotional crisis may shout, cry, gesticulate, or otherwise behave in a highly emotional and dramatic manner. In a "steady," noncrisis state, he may behave calmly and unemotionally. Another individual may signal a severe crisis by showing apathetic and depressed behavior contrasting markedly with his previous pattern of activity and lively interest in his family, friends, and work.

In order to be a helping agent in a crisis, you will often find it useful, although not always possible, to obtain information from the patient's family, friends, neighbors, or bystanders about the patient's precrisis behavior. The important aspects to note are disruptions in previous behaviors and modes of functioning that signal a person's inability to cope in his customary way. The following nine "senses" have been found most useful by crisis workers at the Benjamin Rush Center for Problems of Living (Los Angeles Psychiatric Service).[1] A practical profile of the person in crisis includes a sense of:

1. *Bewilderment:* "I never felt this way before."
2. *Danger:* "I feel so nervous and scared—something terrible is going to happen."
3. *Confusion:* "I can't think clearly, my mind isn't working right."
4. *Impasse:* "I feel stuck, nothing I do seems to help."
5. *Desperation:* "I've got to do something—don't seem to know what, though."
6. *Apathy:* "Nothing can help me, I'm in a zero situation."
7. *Helplessness:* "I can't manage this myself, I need help."
8. *Urgency:* "I need help now."
9. *Discomfort:* "I feel miserable, so restless and unsettled."

DEALING WITH A MENTAL HEALTH EMERGENCY

The crisis-oriented health worker should be attuned to three general questions:

1. What is troubling the individual?
2. Why does he come for help *now*? If the person is an ambulatory patient, why has he gained access to the system as an emergency? If he is an involuntary patient or the victim of an accident, how did he get into this predicament?
3. What can I do to help him/her *now*?

The first two questions tell us about the individual's "presenting problem" and his view of the crisis-producing stress; the third deals with implementing the actual method of crisis work.

A Practical Approach to Crisis Counseling

Among the many concepts relating to crisis-intervention counseling as a part of emergency care, the four most important ones are (1) immediacy, (2) assessment, (3) focused activity, and (4) problem-solving or adaptive coping.

1. Appreciation is expressed to Martin Strickler, M.S.W., Deputy Director, Los Angeles Psychiatric Service, for this profile material, which has been adapted for use in this chapter.

Immediacy

By its very nature, the crisis requires instant intervention or emotional first aid appropriate to the patient's situation. We know from experience that now is the important word for crisis intervention. Why? Because the anxiety, tension, and out-of-control feelings associated with the crisis state make the patient cry out directly or indirectly for immediate attention, response, and relief from distress.

The health worker must try at this point to accomplish several things: (1) relieve anxiety and guilt, (2) prevent further disorganization or decompensation, and (3) see that the patient is protected from injuring himself or others. To delay in responding to the patient's immediate need is to risk his becoming increasingly upset, even to the point of disability. Intervention, then, begins the moment you see the patient.

Assessment

Assessment refers to your on-the-spot evaluation of the patient's situation. You must quickly, but accurately evaluate his biopsychosocial condition—his needs, his resources, his weaknesses. Circumstances will dictate which questions are appropriate to ask. It makes a big difference whether you have been called to the scene of a highway accident, an urban street, a nursing home, or a private residence. In each of these situations, you have varying degrees of time and privacy to explore the situation. When circumstances are appropriate, you may want to ask the following questions: How are you feeling? What is upsetting you? Why do you need help now? What has happened in the last hour, day, or week?

If the patient is in an emotional crisis, attempt to identify the nature of the precipitating or stressful event and its meaning. You may go on to ask the following questions:

1. Have you recently lost someone? (Even the loss of pets has precipitated crises in people who have limited interpersonal contacts.)
2. Is there an impending loss or separation of a boyfriend, girl friend, husband, wife?
3. What changes have recently taken place in your life? (Check off:)
   (a) Illness
   (b) Accidents
   (c) Change of job, loss of an old job, or stress from a new job
   (d) Other changes
4. How do you feel about these things? (When there are positive responses to the above questions, ask the following: Do you feel scared inside? Depressed? Anxious? Overwhelmed? Fearful you might hurt yourself or someone else?)

The attempt here is to assess the actual (objective) as well as the symbolic (subjective) meaning of whatever change of events of "loss" experiences may have occurred. Are the experiences perceived as threatening or hazardous to the individual's security needs or ties with loved ones? (Remember, the patient's perception of threat or hazard triggers a crisis response.)

You should pay as much attention to what the patient does as to what he says. Note the patient's body language and nonverbal behavior (posture, body movements, eye glances, mannerisms) as well as his verbal behavior. The patient's feelings may be communicated to the worker through nonverbal means.

Focused activity

The interviewer's approach and direction at this initial state of the interview, in contrast to the patient's upset and panic, must be characterized by a reassuring calm, steady warmth. The worker must be attentive and empathic ("even though I am not you, I try to feel your feelings"). He must be outreaching so that the patient can talk, offer practical help and support whenever possible, and generally convey the attitude of a concerned, caring person.

You can help the patient through your attitude and demeanor by remaining calm, not overreacting, being willing to listen, inquiring about the precipitating stress, and asking about similar situations from the recent or remote past. The worker should approach mentally disturbed people as patients who have injured minds and feelings.

As we have said, it will make an enormous difference whether you are administering first aid at the scene of an accident, counseling in an emergency department enclosure, or making an emergency visit to a home during a family crisis.

Up to this point, the determination of the nature of the precipitating event and how it is perceived—that is, the actual and symbolic meaning to the patient—has been your primary concern. Now, the patient's response to that event must be assessed. How has the patient tried to cope with his crisis dilemma? You may not find this out by direct questions.

Although there are times when your most helpful role is simply listening, more typically you will be an active, outreaching person. Two factors become important at this point. One of these is your attitude of openness, warmth, and support. This will do much to reassure the patient and establish good feelings between you and the patient. It will encourage the patient to unburden himself. Getting him to see you as a helping, facilitating person is often, in itself, a way of relieving tension ("I want to help you" or "What can I do to help you?"). The other factor is your skill in actively asking questions such as the following: What is the trouble? How are you feeling? What have you done about this? Is there anyone around we can talk to about this?

Problem solving

Of course, the purpose of the actively focused crisis intervention is to steer the individual (and his family, if possible) toward adaptive coping and away from maladaptive coping. This means recognizing and facing up to problems, using trial-and-error methods to experiment with new, hopefully better ways of coping, sharing information, and expressing or controlling feelings more effectively than previously. The crisis worker energetically encourages the patient to mobilize his own resources and those of his family and friends on his own behalf.

Although certain aspects of this approach should always be tried at the scene—whether on the street or in the emergency department—often it is not possible to offer reasonable and viable solutions on the spot. When that is the case, say so, but do it in a way that holds out hope. Then act to bring the patient to the appropriate resource. You might say, "I can see you really have a tough and complicated problem. I think the crisis counseling center is better set up for helping with this than we are. I am going to help you make contact with the crisis center." (See the section, Referral to Mental Health or Human Service Programs, below.)

The activity of the health worker must be directed toward limited and specific goals that are meaningful to the patient or his family. In crisis intervention, the worker does not try to unravel chronic character problems or attempt an involved psychotherapeutic overhaul. Instead, the worker must relate to the patient, assess the disability, act to minimize distress, and facilitate a proper disposition by transport, telephone, or referral.

Emergency department and rescue personnel often ask if they can comfort and reassure by touching, as when they have to tell the family that the patient is dead on arrival. Here, the worker should be guided by his own good judgment and, of course, by the response of the person he's trying to help. Obviously, we're talking here about the judicious communication of concern and caring, not about heavy, inappropriate grabbing, clutching, or massaging. Watch for the person's body English. Is he responding to or recoiling from your sensitive touching? Is he responding to your move toward him or the actual touching experience?

Time Factors

In emergency crisis intervention you will usually have only one interview with the patient, lasting from a few minutes to an hour (rarely more). The length of the interview will depend on numerous variable circumstances, among them, where the encounter takes place, the patient's mental condition and cooperation, the presence of others, the worker's training and skill, and the function of the health program.

This leads us to another important point about crisis intervention. *A crisis is more or less time limited or "self-liquidating."* It has been said that emotional crises can last a few weeks, depending on the severity of the precipitating event, the way it is perceived and responded to by health care workers, and the coping abilities and resources of the person, his family, and the community. Thus, the emergency episode may last a few minutes to a few hours. Any longer requires specialized techniques that are available from specialized mental health personnel, psychiatrists, psychiatric technicians, nurse clinicians, social workers, and psychologists. In many communities, psychiatric emergency teams have been constituted to back up emergency medical services personnel. Such teams are prepared to work with a given problem in time-limited, problem-oriented psychotherapy of up to about six visits. Whatever the time involved, experienced psychiatric and paraprofessional personnel engage in meaningful crisis intervention from the first moment they deal with the patient.

How the attending health care worker responds to the patient's plight sets the tone for the interview. During a serious accident when the emphasis is on life-and-death type of intervention, you should give comfort to the patient as realistically as possible within the constraints of the emergency situation. Talking with the patient is as important as asking him how he feels. Simple, brief interventions, perhaps lasting only a few moments, may long be remembered by the patient.

Giving specific information to the victim of an accident, insofar as this is possible, can bolster him. "Yes, your head is bleeding, but the wound doesn't seem to be too serious," or "We're carrying you into the ambulance and then to the hospital where you will get medical attention, and the doctors will take care of you" are a few examples.

Sometimes ambulance attendants, knowing that they will probably never see the patient again, sit in stony silence on the way to the hospital. Terrified, the patient listens to the shrill shrieking of the ambulance siren and observes the frightening play of lights as the ambulance speeds toward the hospital. It is at this time that asking the patient how he feels (if he is able to talk) and giving whatever realistic reassurance is possible prepares him for what will happen next. In a real sense, you make a kind of alliance with the patient, however brief, to help him deal with his human plight.

REFERRAL TO MENTAL HEALTH OR HUMAN SERVICE PROGRAMS

When to Refer

No mental health emergency takes place in a social vacuum. Perhaps an emergency patient's bruises have resulted from a quarrel, which in turn was triggered by a family crisis. What happens if the doctor and nurse in the emergency room attend only to the patient's skin wounds and ignore the psychic wounds the patient and his family have inflicted on each other? Most likely, without crisis intervention, the patient and his family will continue their marital battles, perhaps to the point of increasingly violent encounters. The final result could be a family breakdown, with great pain and anxiety for the parents and the children.

After a brief but helpful crisis-counseling session, the emergency room nurse can often refer a patient to a crisis intervention clinic within the same hospital. Here, the patient and his family can receive further help with the personal and family stresses which precipitated the crisis situation.

These guidelines can help you decide when to refer a patient:

1. *When the patient or his family exhibit*

emotional problems that require crisis counseling (brief or extended service) beyond the scope of the emergency room, referral is a necessity. To facilitate the process, the worker must convince the person that he needs specialized care rather than return to the same upsetting circumstances.

For example, if you have just pumped the stomach of a patient who has taken an overdose or sutured the wounds resulting from an alcoholic person's fight with his wife or neighbor, you should make a strong attempt to refer the patient to a crisis counseling or mental health service, either within your own facility or in the community. During a crisis, the patient is more amenable to such help than he will be when the crisis is over. Now is the prime time to convince the patient he needs further care.

2. ***When the patient and his family need help in obtaining social resources beyond the scope of your emergency health program (such as dental care, job placement or training, housing, public assistance, homemaking care, transportation, help with recreation plans), referral to an agency that can meet these needs is required.*** Indeed, the patient may well be in an emergency because of the lack of resources and supports within the existing system of care in his community. Many mental health emergencies represent casualties of the family and social systems.

Unless some needed resources can be marshaled for the patient and his family, it is usually predictable that the patient will again come to the emergency room door—perhaps even further disorganized or decompensated in his psychosocial functioning.

In other words, we must start to help the person build a new "support system" for himself when we note important psychosocial deficiencies contributing to his health emergency. A support system is a social network that will sustain and strengthen him in coping with everyday stresses and in gaining sources of supply (security, recognition, and practical help from others). For the emergency room patient who is often without meaningful family attachments, such a support system includes these basic building blocks: a decent place in which to live, a job (or other source of income such as public assistance if the patient is unable to work, and a social club, community center, or other place where the patient can find friends and develop satisfying social relationships.

How to Refer

An effective referral insures that the patient will receive promptly the health and social services he needs to cushion the impact of stress and to strengthen his coping capabilities. The following guidelines for successful referral are suggested.

1. ***Refer a patient to the health or social welfare resource most likely to offer the help he needs.*** In most communities, the United Fund, or similar agencies (Red Feather Agency, United Crusade, or Community Chest), publishes a directory of health and welfare resources and also offers an information and referral service. Emergency room personnel should know the service's telephone number. You can also get further information from the nearest family service agency. Throughout the United States there are over 325 accredited family counseling agencies affiliated with the Family Service Association of America. Additionally, local mental health clinics or the local health department should have information about crisis-oriented mental health programs.

One simple call to the agency to which you are referring the patient can establish whether the needed help is available and is likely to be given. Sometimes a patient, already confused and distressed, is referred to inappropriate resources. If he feels that he is being put on a referral merry-go-round, he may shun further help.

2. ***Arrange a definite appointment for the patient with a specific helping person in the***

designated agency or program. Perhaps a note or card for the patient with the name of the new worker will further ease the referral process.

*3. **If the patient is being referred to a service in the same hospital or health facility, invite the mental health worker to meet with the patient in the emergency room.*** This eases the transfer and increases the likelihood that the patient will continue crisis counseling. Recent studies show that the patient who has received emergency room care for a suicidal, alcoholic, or family-crisis episode is unlikely to follow through when referred to the hospital's psychiatric or mental health clinic. But, this technique of the overlapping interview—that is, inviting the mental health worker or psychiatric clinic staff member fo join you—has been effective in reducing the frequency of "no-show" cases or treatment dropouts. Valuable medical time can also be used more economically.

*4. **Provide for some feedback on how effective your referrals have been.*** Check back with the agency or service to which you have referred the patient to make sure that the service was delivered or at least offered. Feedback can help you to make future referrals increasingly effective.

*5. **Do not condone the establishment of an emergency room or ambulance "black list" of troublesome callers.*** Making an effective referral with persistence, patience, and skill is more important than deciding whether to reject.

If the Patient Refuses a Referral

The preceding two sections on referral have assumed that the patient accepts the referral willingly. Sometimes, however, a patient refuses to agree to follow-up treatment. Several suggestions to help you deal with such a situation follow:

*1. **Insure that the patient understands your reasons for making the referral.*** Explain fully to him your assessment of his situation and how follow-up treatment can help.

*2. **Do not argue with the patient about the diagnosis.*** Patients, particularly those with certain types of emotional problems or afflicted with alcoholism, may refuse to accept the diagnosis. Agree with the patient that you can see how he might believe that, for instance, he is not an alcoholic. Discuss with him, then, how his behavior has been affected by alcohol and how alcohol has played a role in his current crisis. Suggest to him that, even though he does not consider himself an alcoholic, it would be useful for him to explore further how alcohol is causing him problems in a follow-up interview at an appropriate agency.

*3. **If the patient still refuses referral and yet is willing to see you again, arrange an appointment in the near future.*** Hopefully, when the patient has had some time, he will be more receptive and in a better position to understand the reason for the referral.

*4. **If the patient rejects all of the above, let him know that you have not rejected him.*** You probably are his only contact with a helping resource. Let him know that you are disappointed that he will not accept the referral, but allow him to return to you again in the future if he should wish to talk about this problem further. Perhaps at that time he will be ready to accept further treatment.

CONCLUSION

Crisis intervention is an important component of emergency medical care programs. The key concepts in crisis counseling include (1) immediate availability to the patient, (2) quick assessment of his emergency situation, (3) purposeful, focused activity that guides him toward adaptive coping, and (4) problem solving. The crisis worker who works with these concepts must give special attention to the stressful event that has thrown the patient into crisis, the meaning of that event to the patient, and what psychosocial methods can help him resolve the crisis.

Crisis intervention can help make emergency medical programs, rescue squad work, and other emergency activities all the more effective as vital human services.

SUGGESTED READINGS

Barten, Harvey H. *Brief Therapies.* New York: Behavioral Publications, Inc., 1971.

Bellak, Leopold, and Small, Leonard. *Emergency Psychotherapy and Brief Psychotherapy.* New York: Grune & Stratton, Inc., 1965.

Caplan, Gerald. *Principles of Preventive Psychiatry.* New York: Basic Books, Inc., 1964.

Glasser, Paul H., and Glasser, Lois N., eds. *Families in Crisis.* New York: Harper & Row, 1969.

Jacobson, Gerald F. "Emergency Services in Community Mental Health: Problems and Promise." *American Journal of Public Health* 64(1974): 124-28.

Langsley, Donald G., and Kaplan, David M. *The Treatment of Families in Crisis.* New York: Grune & Stratton, 1968.

Lieb, Julian et al. *The Crisis Team.* New York: Harper & Row, 1973.

Parad, Howard J., ed. *Crisis Intervention: Selected Readings.* New York: Family Service Association of America, 1965.

Parad, Howard J. "Brief Ego-Oriented Casework with Families in Crisis." In *Ego-Oriented Casework,* edited by Howard J. Parad and Roger R. Miller. New York: Family Service Association of America, 1963.

Strickler, Martin, and Allgeyer, Jean. "The Crisis Group: A New Application of Crisis Theory." *Social Work* 12(1967):28-32.

Ungerleider, J. Thomas. "The Psychiatric Emergency: Analysis of Six Months' Experience of a University Hospital's Consultation Service." *Archives of General Psychiatry* 3(1960):593-609.

Wolberg, Lewis R., ed. *Short-Term Psychotherapy.* New York. Grune & Stratton, 1965.

III

Recognition and Management of Psychiatric Emergencies

Jack Zusman, M.D., M.P.H.

DEFINITION OF AN EMERGENCY

A psychiatric emergency, for the purposes of discussion here, is the sudden appearance of unusual, disordered, or socially inappropriate behavior. Since the term covers a wide range of problems, it is impossible to provide a simple definition identifying every problem and excluding instances which appear to be psychiatric emergencies, but actually are not. The definition inevitably overlaps other problem categories like family problems or individuals who have made deliberate decisions to lead life styles quite different from the life style of the majority. But, whatever the problem is called, the measures which must be taken to deal with the problem often are clear.

Let us examine the key words in the definition. Sudden appearance means that the problem develops over a period of days or weeks rather than years. Long-standing psychiatric problems are best left to the mental health professional. In addition, a situation which has been present for years usually can wait a few days or weeks more rather than require the prompt but brief service of the emergency worker.

Unusual indicates a different behavior for that person or persons like him. It does not mean unusual for you, the emergency worker, or most of the people you know. In our country, acceptable styles of behavior and of life differ widely. You must not impose your own ethical or health standards in evaluating a person. Make an effort, instead, to consider what you know about individuals who have grown up with the same background or are living under the same circumstances as the person in question. The individual who seems very strange, but behaves similarly to his friends and acquaintances probably is not suffering from a psychiatric emergency.

Disordered behavior lacks pattern or purpose. What the person is doing one moment seems to have absolutely no relationship to what he does next. Such movements provide no clue to help the emergency worker understand what the person is attempting to accomplish. Even if he is able to describe what he intends, his behavior will not help him to accomplish the intention; most likely his actions have no direct connection.

The presence of inappropriate behavior, however, can help identify most psychiatric emergencies. The behavior is inappropriate because it does not—in nature or degree of intensity—fit the circumstances in which the person finds himself. Keep in mind that there is a time and place for everything, and consider whether the behavior in question corresponds to that time and place. For example, it is appropriate to take off one's clothes before taking a bath or to wield a knife when cutting food. Clearly these same actions become inappropriate in other circumstances. The expression of emotions must be carefully observed since this is a very common area where the mentally ill show inappropriateness. The individual who is not struggling with tears after having witnessed the death of a loved one or registers no emotion while awaiting news about an injured relative should alert you to a potential psychiatric problem. In evaluating inappropriateness, make certain that an individual's inappropriateness does not result from a difference in his cultural background or from his misjudgment in a strange situation about which he was insufficiently informed.

Behavior is used here in a broad context: observed and reported verbal behavior like speech and writing as well as emotional. While obvious signs of physical illness are excluded in this context, it is important to remember that, at times, a psychiatric emergency appears in the form of acute physical symptoms.

Recognition of psychiatric emergency depends upon the opinion of the examiner. Unlike many physical illnesses, there are no definite physical or laboratory measures which can be used to establish the presence of a mental illness. Few general, objective standards are available to the worker. Proficiency in recognizing a psychiatric emergency is best developed under the tutelage of experienced mental health workers. By examining large numbers of people under different circumstances, you can develop reliable standards of normality and appropriateness. You must be aware of the typical and expected behaviors of cultural groups, age groups, occupational groups, and other major categories in the vast human population.

Psychiatric emergency is often inseparable from social problems and physical illness. Sometimes all three—psychiatric emergency, social problem, and physical illness—are present in one individual crisis so that it is impossible to determine which came first or which is the most important. Usually the physical illness requires most immediate treatment. The psychiatric problem then is evaluated by exclusion—that is, symptoms not attributable to the physical illness are assumed to have resulted from the psychiatric problem. The social problem generally receives lowest priority.

One major hallmark of psychiatric emergency is emotional distress. The problem usually produces emotional distress in the person and often in those who are closely associated with him. The presence of great distress without reasonable explanation is a sure signal to search for an emergency.

SYMPTOMS OF THE EMERGENCY

Most individuals suffering from psychiatric emergency show one or more of a number of easily recognized patterns of behavior. Sometimes these patterns can also be found in normal persons not suffering from a psychiatric problem, but who may be in realistic distress from some unfortunate circumstance. Psychiatric emergency is distinguished by the inappropriateness or extreme degree of the person's behavior in comparison with the event which seems to have set it off or the circumstances in which it is taking place.

Fear

The common symptom of fear can revolve around particular persons, activities, or places. An individual may become fearful at the sight of certain friends or relatives, whole categories of individuals such as policemen or teachers, or a person who attempts to come close or show friendliness. He may fear an activity such as driving or riding in a car, speaking before a group, or riding a bicycle. He might fear places such as small, enclosed rooms, heights, or open spaces.

He may express a fear directly by simply saying he is afraid, or he may hide it, making complicated excuses to avoid whatever he fears. When he cannot avoid the feared object, his behavior then suggests fear—for example, perspiration, trembling, or faintness—or he may attempt to calm himself by using alcohol or tranquilizing drugs. The psychiatric problem of fear often appears first as a physical problem. Physical signs accompanying fear such as shallow, rapid breathing, or sharp chest pain are sometimes mistaken for symptoms of a cardiovascular problem. Fear can also cause attacks of abdominal cramps and diarrhea or can bring on nausea and vomiting.

Anxiety

While closely related to fear, the symptom of anxiety differs in that it is not associated with any person, activity, or place. It is a fearful feeling which comes on without any obvious reason or in relation to anything which has occurred. Anxiety can be even more disabling than fear because there is usually no way a person can avoid setting it off. Mild anxiety appears as a sinking feeling in the "pit of the stomach." It may be accompanied by dryness of the mouth, rapid beating of the heart, perspiration, and dizziness. Anxiety in its strongest form produces a feeling of immediate, impending doom or death. The individual may react by screaming, cowering in distress, or becoming unconscious.

Depression

Another major frequent hallmark of psychiatric emergency is sadness or depression. In its mildest forms, depression can be a persistent pessimism and a tendency to cry easily at emotion-provoking events. It is more severe if the person expresses strong feelings of hopelessness and isolation. He may cry frequently and be unable to function at work or at home. He may even withdraw from all social relationships and feel extremely tense and irritable. Some depressed persons become agitated. Unable to remain still for a moment, they pace, wring their hands, rock in their chairs, and may out of desperation bang themselves against hard objects. Severe depression is frequently accompanied by sleeplessness, loss of appetite, loss of interest in sex, and constipation. Some severely depressed persons have deep feelings of worthlessness or guilt. They believe they are being or should be punished for some very bad act or desire. Because suicide is more frequent in cases of severe depression than in other psychiatric emergencies, you must be constantly alert for possible signs of self-destructive impulses. (See Chapter VI on suicidal depression.)

Mania

The opposite of depression is mania or a manic state. Individuals suffering from mania are unrealistically optimistic, freely communicating the optimism to others. Mild mania may not ever become a problem. After all, painting a brighter picture than really exists is a common human inclination. But a more severe form of mania can be very serious. Its victim might take many unwarranted risks, show poor business and personal judgment, agree to pay for purchases or carry out projects beyond his needs and capacity, or experience no sadness at serious defeat or loss. Someone in a severe manic state may move around continually and incessantly, and never pause to eat, drink, or sleep—even to the point of physical prostration or death. Individuals who suffer from mania often alternate between the two extremes of mania and depression.

Anger

Inappropriate anger can indicate psychiatric crisis. In its mild form an individual may be easily hurt and insulted by minor slights which in normal circumstances would pass without notice. He may be argumentative and determined to stand up for his rights, even when argument is not in his best interest. The crisis reaches a more severe stage when an individual interprets all sorts of actions by others as intended insults and assumes that persons who may not even be aware of his presence are deliberately acting provocatively or challenging him to do battle. He may frequently get into self-defeating conflicts with authority figures and behave overcautiously in protecting himself from expected, though often unreal, physical attacks. He may even go to the extreme of arming himself for protection when clearly no need exists, provoke gun battles with police after minor altercations, or "cut off his nose to spite his face" rather than give in to another person.

Anger can be brief but destructive. A person may explode wildly in violent temper outbursts after some actual or imagined provocation. The intensity of his outburst is out of proportion to the situation. Then the anger quickly passes. The individual becomes ashamed and apologetic or tries to justify his behavior.

Confusion

A person who is confused experiences a reduced state of alertness or awareness of his surroundings. He may not know where he is, what day it is; he might not recall his name and address. Perhaps he is unable to dress himself properly or attend to personal hygiene. His confusion may become apparent when he is unable to answer simple questions or when he behaves inappropriately.

Confusion, like most psychiatric problems, exists in degrees, beginning with the normal forgetfulness we all experience under stress. Most persons occasionally forget, and as they grow older, their memories are not as sharp as in their youth. But the "absent-minded professor" who comes to class dressed in pajamas or who forgets where he parked the car may have gone past the point of normal confusion. If he reaches its most extreme phase he will be completely disabled and dependent upon others.

Confusion can result from physical damage to brain tissue (as in a stroke), disruption of the body's "internal environment" (as in alcohol intoxication), or intense preoccupation with matters other than the present situation. The absent-minded professor presumably is preoccupied with complicated research. The seriously ill psychiatric patient is concerned with his fears and possibly hallucinations.

Reality Contact

Serious psychiatric illnesses cause problems in "reality contact." Every normal individual is in good contact with reality: he knows what is happening around him; he can reasonably predict the outcome of his actions; he is able to distinguish clearly between what is going on inside his own body (e.g., the pain he feels when he has a headache) and what is going on outside (e.g., the pain he feels when someone sticks a needle in him). He can distinguish between what he wishes would happen and what is really happening. He knows that whether his feelings toward another individual (e.g., affection, fear, or anger) are or are not reciprocated depends on more than his own perceptions. Furthermore, he knows that no one can be aware of his feelings until he has expressed them.

When reality contact is lost, one or more of these normal barriers between an individual and the world around him breaks down. He may come to feel that others can read his mind or that the simple act of wishing for something brings it about. He may have trouble distinguishing voices, noises, sights, smells, and other perceptions which exist in his imagination from perceptions formed about the external world. He cannot predict how others will react to his behavior. The ability to distinguish between close friends and strangers eludes him. He may express his thoughts in language incomprehensible to other people—without recognizing its incomprehensibility. The effect of all of his experience with the physical state of the world may be lost so that he comes to believe, for example, that he is able, by wish or will, to control the actions of those around him.

An individual who has poor reality contact may report hallucinations (false perceptions) or delusions (false beliefs). If the problem is moderately severe, the individual will recognize that something is wrong and will feel uncertain about his perceptions. Where the problem is more serious, uncertainty will disappear so that he will lose any ability to distinguish between the world he carries inside and the world outside. He may express himself in language which makes no sense or, in milder forms, only partial sense, requiring the listener to guess at the meaning.

Loss of reality contact often appears with other symptoms. For example, someone who is depressed, fearful, and estranged may believe that he has committed some serious crime and that the police are searching for him. He may then barricade himself in his home and be prepared to shoot it out with the police because he feels in any case he is a subject for execution.

Withdrawal

Sometimes an individual loses interest in or withdraws from persons, events, and objects which were previously important to him. He may give up activities, no longer care for personal belongings, neglect personal hygiene, express little emotion about events which normally would be important to him. Habits may change: he may sleep all day, stay up all night, and discard possessions for which he has worked very hard. Withdrawal, while often part of depression or loss of reality contact, can appear by itself.

Behavioral Deviance

Although rarely occurring alone, behavioral deviance can give an indication of psychiatric emergency. The person who abruptly changes his life style, relationships, philosophy (either expressed or implied), and close associates may be acting from a carefully considered decision during which he weighed all the benefits and disadvantages. In this case it is *not* an indication of psychiatric crisis—no matter how much the worker may disagree with the individual's decision. On the other hand, an unconsidered radical change may be the first sign of serious illness. You can determine which is the case only by questioning the individual, particularly about his deliberation before the decision and his awareness of the consequences.

Physical Symptoms

It is not unusual for physical symptoms to occur during a psychiatric emergency, and their presence requires close scrutiny. There are few physical illnesses which cannot be mimicked by a psychological problem, but the fine points of diagnosis are best left to experts. Since the physical illness in question is usually more of an immediate danger to life and first-aid treatment is readily available, you should generally assume that physical symptoms indicate physical disease. Bear in mind, though, that occasions can arise where previous diagnosis and a person's repeated pattern of development of physical symptoms clearly indicate that he is suffering from a psychiatric problem.

There can be other reasons why you must assume that the problem is psychiatric rather than physical—until proven otherwise. The most common physical symptom accompanying psychiatric problems is anxiety. The three systems of the body apparently most susceptible to psychiatric symptoms are the cardiovascular system (heart and blood vessels), the gastrointestinal system (stomach and intestines), and the central nervous system (the brain and spinal cord). Some physical signs of emotions like blushing or crying are common and people are barely conscious of them. But intense chest pain, diarrhea, or fainting can be abnormal, but not uncommon responses to psychological stress.

ASSESSMENT OF PSYCHIATRIC EMERGENCIES

Determining what is wrong with a person depends upon collecting a series of important facts, putting them together in a logical and balanced pattern, and then measuring the picture which develops against the standards of normality for the person and for the community from which he comes.

First, ascertain exactly what has happened: which behavior suggests a psychiatric crisis and which is causing the distress? You can determine these facts by interviewing the person and those close to him. Although the person lacks objectivity, he still has seen and can describe more of the situation than anyone else involved.

Next, the person's present state is examined to determine his condition and to provide a basis for estimating the reliability of the information he has provided. The examination is also the first step in management; how it is conducted can do much to improve the person's condition or to worsen it. To a lesser extent, you need to sift through information from other individuals to determine how valid and biased their information actually is.

Third, the worker must seek information

about the community from which the person comes and about its standards. Hopefully, you will already be familiar with the person's background. However, information you do not know should be obtained. Without it, you can be seriously misled in estimating the person's condition.

Finally, you assemble all the facts to determine the following:

- Is something wrong?
- Must I take action?
- What available action will be most effective and least harmful?
- How urgent is the situation for the person and in comparison with the needs of others you are also serving right now?

History-Taking

Collecting details of the person's recent past, particularly those directly related to his problem, requires a determined effort. Without being inflexible, you must be fairly clear about what facts are needed and how to ask clear questions if these facts are not volunteered by the person and others. Your objective is two-fold: obtain a detailed, complete history of events which led up to the present crisis and of events which have happened since the onset of the crisis. As individuals are telling you their stories, make an effort to pin down specific details: dates, times, places, and names. By the end of your investigation, you should be able to construct the whole story of the person's problem, using the many pieces of reliable information as building blocks.

Valuable facts can come from talking with those who knew the individual before his crisis. No matter how rushed you may be, appear relaxed and patient when you are interviewing so that those with whom you are talking can offer a full account. You might begin by asking what the problem is and then permit the individual to respond without interruption until he runs down. Once you have his full account, ask particular questions. For example, you might want to ask the person:

- When did the problem start?
- How did you know something was wrong?
- Has this ever happened before, and if so, what usually brings it on?
- When it has happened before, what measures have helped and what measures have made it worse?
- Who usually cares for the patient when he is upset; is there a doctor involved; is there some member of the family who has a special relationship?

Having a complete picture of the person's problem is important. Avoid a situation where you discover that there is additional information that is urgently needed but which is now difficult to get.

In some instances you will be unable to obtain necessary information from the person himself, and other pertinent individuals will not be available. Other means can be used. A telephone call to the person's family physician or to a relative can be far simpler than attempting to drag information out of the confused person or having to make a guess to fill in the gaps.

In contrast to emergency management of many physical problems, handling a psychiatric emergency is a time-consuming operation which requires considerable involvement and concentration by the worker.

The Interview

The principal tool for examining a person in a psychiatric emergency is the interview, a structured conversation carried out between you and the person or you and someone who knows the patient. You must provide the structure for the interview without making your subject aware that the conversation has in fact been carefully structured. Your ability to appear unhurried will also encourage a person to open up.

The interview is both a means for collecting information and a critical step in your own management of the problem. For these reasons, interpersonal elements, developed relationships, and the physical setting become significant.

Rapport

You need to develop feelings of trust, dependence, and mutual respect with the person you are interviewing. The technical term for this relationship is rapport. A careful mixture of relaxation, confidence, and empathy on your part can encourage the person to the point of sharing his innermost thoughts and feelings without embarrassment or fear. By sharing, he obtains some relief from the unpleasant disturbing feelings which have caused or are part of the crisis.

Physical setting

Rapport between worker and patient is encouraged by an appropriate physical setting for the interview, preferably some quiet, private area devoid of exciting or disturbing elements and conducive to concentration. The room should be comfortable, possibly suggesting the professional, special, helping kinds of activities which go on there.

If you are out in the field when the emergency arises, choose a room in a home where you can talk undisturbed. At the scene of an accident or a disaster where rooms are not available, use an outdoor area away from noise and activity or select a car or truck located in a quiet place. If you are in a hospital, avoid using the emergency room with its sounds and tools of crisis, but instead find an isolated office. Some hospitals have specially designed and prepared psychiatric interviewing rooms.

Consider the comfort of the person you are interviewing. If he has not eaten or had anything to drink for any length of time, try to provide these needs. Encourage him to smoke if he wishes and to act informally.

Safety

Another major consideration in the setting is safety. Occasionally, a disturbed person jeopardizes his own safety or that of others. In a fit of temper or out of fear or confusion, he may attack the worker with furniture or fists; in one unguarded moment he might attempt suicide. Regular interviewing offices should not have objects which can easily be used as weapons.

Interviewers should never work in situations where they cannot call for help or where suspicious activities remain unnoticed. If a disturbed person must be left alone the setting should be designed so that someone is always around to keep an eye on the scene and to summon quick assistance. Some unobtrusive signal system located in the interview room can help the worker when occasionally he is trapped with an individual who refuses to let him leave the room. In providing food and drink for the patient, remember that plates and glasses can become weapons and that hot coffee is a particularly dangerous item.

By no means should you view every person as potentially dangerous or see that strenuous precautions are taken in every case. However, when the setting is prepared in advance for the worst possible eventualities, you need not resort to last-minute measures which might increase anxiety.

Structure

The interview should always begin by permitting the person to talk freely at length about whatever most concerns him. Usually, this will be some aspect of the crisis, but it may not be directly related. Nevertheless, if the person does not have this opportunity for self-expression, he is likely to return again and again to the subject of his greatest concern, disrupting later portions of the interview.

Just asking a vague question at the outset will provide an opportunity for talking. For example, ask why he is here or what the problem is. Usually after he has talked five to ten minutes the person will pause. At this point you can go back to clarify issues which the patient has raised or to fill in missing details.

In some cases, the person is not willing or able to talk freely so that details are not provided. In that case, you must lead the conversation into areas which are important or ask specific questions. The person cannot be allowed in this special situation to set his own pace. Valuable time would be lost. If the person is unaware of what his problem is, describe to him how you see the problem and work from that point to obtain his reactions and further details. It is possible that the person and you might disagree about what the problem is. Rather than seek any agreement, explore the details from each point of view.

There are some persons who are compulsive talkers. After providing far more detail than you need, their interest in the present emergency lags and they switch to something else completely unrelated. As soon as you recognize this, attempt, without being rude, to steer the person back to the matter of concern. Often verbal effusiveness can be stopped by asking a question which requires a simple yes-or-no answer. Once the person pauses, you can then ask a question which is more relevant.

History

In addition to the details about the psychiatric emergency, you must get some basic information about the person's life and background. Find out immediate facts like name, address, age, nearest relative, previous psychiatric treatment, current medications. Gather enough information about the person's sociocultural background to be able to place him in a group in order to draw meaningful comparisons.

Note-taking

Do not hesitate to make notes during the interview. Few workers can wait until an interview is over to write a detailed report of what transpired without losing some of the essentials. Although persons being interviewed are occasionally disturbed by the note-taking and workers themselves may find that the writing conflicts with concentration, it is better to write than to lose the information. Instead, try to develop a skill of writing automatically as the person speaks, without having to take your attention from him. Train yourself to write the material only once, completing the case record as you listen. Whichever technique you adopt—writing the detailed case record, taking abbreviated notes, or using a personal code to record the facts—some system for note-taking is necessary during the interview in order to provide an accurate reconstruction.

SPECIAL PROBLEMS

Among the most common special emergency problems are children; persons who are fearful, paranoid, or uncooperative; victims of violent attacks; individuals who are confused, amnesic, or mute; and those who are suicidal.

Children

Because they are less able to express themselves verbally than adults and have less self-control in stressful situations, children have more difficulty in cooperating with the worker. Once children are frightened, the extent of their fears can be much greater than in adults. Conversely, though, children may be less frightened, even untouched by something which an adult would find severely distressing. Less subject to the effects of social pressure, children may be harder to convince to do something they do not wish to do, and they may not even experience emotions such as shame or guilt.

Attempting to help a child involves a legal issue: a child cannot be treated without consent of a parent or other responsible adult, except where the child's life is endangered. Except for a child or adolescent who is suicidal and therefore must be hospitalized, this danger point occurs rarely in psychiatric emergencies. Children's reactions are harder to judge than those of adults. It is even more difficult in the case of adolescents, who have an even wider range of normal behaviors.

Follow these guidelines in dealing with children:

1. *In interviewing a child, deal with issues indirectly* since the child may not feel comfortable talking about them and, in any case, may not recognize their relevance. A game may help you establish rapport; through story telling or picture drawing, the child may provide information he was unable to give when questioned directly. You can ascertain the condition of a child by watching him at play and by his interactions with others rather than by direct questioning.

2. *Provide food.* This action is even more important than for adults.

3. *Make the interview short* since a child's concentration span is much less than an adult's.

4. *Despite your wish to please the child or shield him from unpleasant information, do not lie to the child.* Reveal unpleasant facts to him gradually and carefully, but never tell him falsehoods which later will become obvious and which will erode his trust in medical workers and adults in general.

5. *Enlist the cooperation of his parents or other responsible adults.*

Paranoid Persons

Fearful, angry, uncooperative persons are generally suspicious and easily misunderstand attempts to help as threats against them or efforts to injure them. These individuals may be prone to violence against others or even against themselves. Despite every effort you make to reach and help them, these individuals may still see themselves as prisoners of war, with you as the symbol standing for the enemy.

Follow these guidelines in dealing with paranoid persons:

1. *When attempting to interview a paranoid person, explain all your actions fully and carefully.* Offer opportunities for questions and answer his questions fully. Never lie, no matter how unpleasant the facts. Make your role and responsibilities clear, particularly separating yourself from law enforcement personnel or other authorities.

2. *Before an interview, be certain that the individual is not armed and that help is available if he should become physically violent.*

3. *Do not be friendly or informal.* Such persons easily mistake attempts at friendliness or helpfulness for efforts to overcome or injure them through subterfuge. Therefore, maintain some distance and act businesslike without being abrupt. Unusual privileges or helpfulness may be misinterpreted. Offer no special services unless the person clearly requests them and explains why he feels they are necessary.

When the person's offensiveness or hostility becomes annoying, threatening, or physically dangerous to you, back off and limit the conflict. Strong countermeasures—either through use of force or increased friendliness—may well provoke stronger attacks. Clearly state your feelings of annoyance or hurt at what the person has done, your belief that his fears are groundless, and the limits beyond which you will not permit him to go. Then attempt to continue with the task at hand.

4. *In cases where it is absolutely necessary to overpower the person, overwhelming*

force must be used. It is extremely dangerous for the person to feel attacked and equally dangerous for him to have the slightest suspicion that he can overcome the force which is to be used against him. When force is threatened or used, the struggle must be as brief and painless as possible. If it is clear to a paranoid person that he cannot win, he will usually give in without a struggle.

5. ***When the patient is armed and barricaded, negotiate continually to convince him that no harm is intended and listen to his conditions for giving up the battle.*** Rather than engaging in a gun battle, police should surround and isolate the person, then allow him time to think and to become hungry and thirsty. During negotiation the hopelessness of his winning the battle should be stressed and, in contrast, the help which is available if only he will permit it.

Victims of Violence

Those suffering from violence, including rape victims, require special treatment because of the major psychological effects. Normally, a person views the world as a relatively safe and pleasant place in which people have control of their lives. When a violent episode occurs—particularly at the hands of another person—the victim's view of self and of those around him is radically changed. Rape, for example, stirs up sexual anxieties as well as effects from violence for the victim.

Immediately after the violent episode, the victim is likely to be in a state of emotional withdrawal, numbness, or apparent apathy. Most likely, he feels that the event will recur and that he is helpless to prevent future attacks. In a rage reaction he may strike out at anyone who seems to resemble the attacker. Robbery or burglary victims, even when not physically assaulted, may feel that their possessions have somehow been dirtied. Most victims of violence do not require long-term treatment, particularly if help is given immediately.

Follow these guidelines in dealing with victims of violence:

1. ***Encourage the individual to wash or change clothes.***

2. ***Note the need to consult with the police so that no evidence is destroyed.*** But you must encourage the police to act rapidly for the sake of the victim's mental health—your area of concern.

3. ***Focus your interview on encouraging the victim to ventilate, to relieve the anxiety of the episode, to regain emotional control, and to consider the impact on his life.*** The worker serves primarily as a sympathetic audience, offering occasional comments and directive statements.

4. ***For the first few days and nights after the assault, the victim may benefit from mild tranquilization and sedation.***

5. ***Arrange a follow-up appointment for several days later.*** By this time most victims are on the way to psychological recovery.

Persons with Amnesia

The confused, mute person who has lost his memory requires special treatment because of the difficulty in communicating with him and obtaining necessary information. Where the symptoms come from loss of reality contact, the person feels little distress because of the protective aspects of the illness. Otherwise, he is likely to be extremely anxious over his inability to communicate. The pressure upon him is worsened by an anxious group hovering around attempting to help him clarify his thoughts or recover his memory.

Follow these guidelines in dealing with those with amnesia:

1. ***Remove the person as quickly as possible from any anxiety-provoking elements.*** If necessary, leave him alone for a short time so that he can calm down and gather his thoughts.

2. ***Proceed slowly and indirectly.*** To ensure the comfort and relaxation of the person, give him something to drink or eat, and encourage him to smoke if he wishes.

3. ***If the problem is memory loss, make a few attempts to jog his memory by offering hypotheses suggested by indirect evidence.*** For example, where an elderly individual has lost his way and cannot remember his name and address, it may be obvious that he comes from some nearby home. Mention names of nearby streets to him in the hope that he will respond to one of them.

4. ***Recovery from an episode of confusion, amnesia, or muteness may take many hours or even longer; be prepared for possible long-term treatment.***

Suicidal Persons

There are many kinds of suicidal persons (see Chapter VI). Since deliberate suicide almost always involves a depressed state of mind, any interview with a depressed person should explore this possibility. However, not all suicidal patients display depression. Some spend a long period of time during a depressive episode considering the issue of suicide and then, deciding to end their lives, feel relatively relaxed. These individuals may not appear seriously depressed in an interview and only reveal their intentions through direct questioning. Other individuals, losing their hold on reality, will deliberately injure or kill themselves without recognizing exactly what they are doing. Still other individuals choose self-injury as a means for calling attention to their need for help and have no actual intention to commit suicide. But each case poses real danger, whether injury is deliberate or accidental. Also, once injury has occurred, the danger of another attempt is real.

Since most persons have difficulty in talking about suicide or self-injury, it is not uncommon for a worker to neglect raising this issue with those he is helping. Even when the question is brought up, if careful groundwork has not been laid, the person may respond to the shock of the issue by denial or evasion.

Follow these guidelines in dealing with a suicidal person (see Chapter VI for more discussion):

1. ***Even when suicide is a remote possibility, discuss the person's current emotional state as well as periods in the past when he was seriously depressed.*** Ask him if he has ever felt so bad that he thought he could not go on. If the person answers yes, ask if he has ever thought seriously about hurting or killing himself. If so, ask if he has ever done anything like that. If he answers no, ask how close he may have come. Did he actually make a plan or did he just get ready to do it? Each question leads naturally to another one more personal and emotion-laden. By answering the first question positively, the patient has given the worker permission to ask the next.

2. ***Assess suicide risk.*** Remember that children and adolescents can commit suicide, and even nine- or ten-year-olds sometimes should be questioned about this issue.

3. ***Make an appropriate disposition and referral.*** Suicidal persons should be put under the care of a professional. Until that care is arranged for, they should not be left alone.

DIAGNOSIS OF PSYCHIATRIC EMERGENCIES

Categories for Treatment

Cases can be grouped to help you plan their management. Medical diagnosis is not central to this kind of assessment. The most useful categories center around treatment: what kind, how soon, and how extensive. The following paragraphs describe each category, beginning with the most serious.

Life-threatening emergencies are those in which the person has access to or is carrying a deadly weapon, is frightened to the point of actual or probable violence, has barricaded himself so that he cannot be easily contacted, feels invincible because of losing contact with reality, or seems determined to kill or injure himself in the near future.

Serious emergencies are those in which the person is confused to the point of being unable to care for himself, is unwilling or unable to protect himself from dangerous situations, seems likely to behave in a violent or suicidal way in the near future, or has a history of sudden violence or suicidal attempts.

Potentially serious emergencies are all other cases in which psychiatric crisis is clearly established, but without any of the mitigating circumstances described below. When in doubt, a case should be classified as potentially serious.

"No immediate danger" is a category for cases in which a long-standing problem is currently stable, having been previously diagnosed and adequately managed by a mental health specialist. Such cases generally come to the worker's attention because of some unrelated problem (e.g., the same individual's involvement in an automobile accident), but these past problems indicate psychiatric difficulties. Such persons may be referred for evaluation or sent back to their own therapist for follow-up.

"Another problem" refers to individuals who come to the worker's attention for what first appears to be a psychiatric emergency but which, upon careful examination, turns out to be another type of problem, e.g., physical illness. These individuals should immediately be referred for appropriate treatment.

"No problems" includes those who have no psychiatric emergency or problem of any other nature. Bear in mind that most everyone, when subjected to searching scrutiny, would be found to have some mental health discomfort or difficulty. But only some actually need intervention or referral for specialized treatment.

Exclusion of Other Diagnoses

One common source for symptoms resembling those of psychiatric crisis is a disease of the central nervous system. Stroke, bleeding inside the skull, and brain tumor commonly cause confusion, amnesia, loss of reality contact, and allied symptoms. Frequently, symptoms suggesting psychiatric problems are accompanied by other symptoms which show clearly that there is a central nervous system disorder. When the patient exhibits paralysis, severe headaches, unequal and/or unresponsive pupils, or obviously increasing confusion, a life-threatening emergency is present and immediate neurological consultation must be obtained. None of these symptoms may be clearly present, and yet, if a central nervous system disorder is suspected, a neurological examination should be arranged as soon as possible.

Myocardial infarction, or a heart attack, produces symptoms similar to those of anxiety. Often, even medical specialists cannot be certain about the cause of symptoms without taking an electrocardiogram and other laboratory tests. When the patient complains of chest, shoulder, or arm pain; seems to be in shock without any bleeding; has persistent and unexplainable vomiting; and is of an age when heart attacks are common, he should be treated for heart attack rather than for anxiety until a medical specialist directs otherwise.

Past or recent drug ingestion can cause symptoms of psychiatric emergency (see Chapter V). The so-called "psychotomimetic drugs" like LSD, STP, or amphetamines can produce loss of reality contact, anxiety, depression, mania, and most any other significant symptom. Sometimes the person or his friends can provide information about the drug. At other times no information is available. An individual who has used drugs repeatedly may suffer "flashbacks" when some minor stress produces recurrence of the symptoms, even though the last use was months ago.

A final major cause of symptoms is alcohol intoxication. Almost any symptom can be produced by alcohol, but usually the history, appearance, and odor of the individual make it clear that alcohol is the cause (see Chapter IV). It must be kept in mind, however, that an individual may suffer a psychiatric disorder after having taken just enough alcohol to put the odor on his breath, and thus mislead the worker. Occasionally, individuals use sedatives instead of alcohol to produce intoxication so that there is no odor. Diagnosis in these cases is best left to a medical specialist.

MANAGEMENT OF PSYCHIATRIC EMERGENCIES

General Principles

The basic approach to persons suffering from all types of psychiatric emergencies is the same, with few exceptions. Persons in a psychiatric emergency are usually anxious, stressed, and in pain. Their behavior is frequently disorganized, they are in an unstable state, and they can quickly move toward becoming better or worse.

Follow these guidelines in managing psychiatric emergencies:

1. *Calm the person, relieve the anxiety and stress, and limit the extent of the disorganization.*

2. *Remove the person from the crisis situation and exclude all disturbing persons and objects.* Give him the opportunity to relax in a comfortable setting.

3. *Right from the beginning make every effort to explain to the person what his problem is, what is being done about it, and what the likely positive outcome will be.* In attempting to reassure, do not go beyond what you actually know.

4. *Communicate confidence in yourself, firmness, and reasonableness on important issues.* Your attitude is very important. Show an interest in the person and a concern with what has happened to him. Listen willingly if he disagrees with the treatment offered and consider whether he may be right.

5. *Rather than agree or disagree with a person's distortions of reality, realize that these distortions are real for him.* For example, he might ask if you hear voices. You would be fair in saying, "I don't hear any voices except yours and mine, but you may certainly be hearing other people speaking."

6. *When the person is not relating or is unable to sit and relax, encourage him to do so.* Offer him some food and drink and find a pleasant place to sit. Get him talking about what interests him.

7. *Contact members of his family or close friends not involved in the emergency to stay with the person.* He will feel reassured. It is best to obtain the permission of adults before contacting anyone about them. However, the request should be handled in a specific rather than a vague way. You might say, "I would like to notify your family on where you are and how you are." The person then has the opportunity to object, but if he does not, you are free to proceed. Where a child or a younger adolescent is involved, notify the family—regardless of objections. In cases where the person is already in treatment for his condition, notify his physician and ask the physician either to take over management or to offer advice regarding the emergency treatment.

8. *Remember that when the emergency is viewed as a temporary difficulty likely to resolve quickly and without aftereffects, recov-*

ery is quicker and more complete than when the person is treated as seriously ill and likely to have a prolonged, incomplete recovery. According to "the expectancy principle," patients tend to behave in the way which those around them expect and directly or indirectly communicate to them. The expectancy principle does not mean that all persons will recover easily; it simply means that more will do so when it is clearly expected. You must be prepared, however, to deal with individuals who do not recover as you had hoped. Basically, expect the best, but be prepared for the worst.

9. Encourage the person to speak freely about whatever is on his mind, allowing him to ventilate his feelings. This is one of the most effective ways of producing relaxation and a return to the person's pre-crisis stability. Often, in reliving his experience and sharing it, the person comes to see it in a better perspective. His feelings—whether loneliness, helplessness, hurt, or anger—can be relieved.

10. When the person begins talking, interrupt as little as possible. Do not guide the patient's story or ask details which the patient omits. Details can come later. Do not make effusive expressions of sympathy which require the person to stop; if he finds them inappropriate or offensive, the period of ventilation may end. Be brief and controlled in your expressions of sympathy. Questions which the person asks during this initial period should be looked upon as only rhetorical, unless it is clear that he definitely wants a specific answer. Even then, give brief answers and toss the ball back to the person as an encouragement to continue. When the person seems to be having difficulty in talking about his feelings or incidents, ask gentle questions. Generally, persons who have gone through a crisis and are unable to express their feelings directly are more likely to have disruptive symptoms than those who can talk it out.

11. After the person has told his full story, you can ask for details. Go back over the story to establish facts and sequence. For example, "You have told me about how this began and how it made you feel, but I am not sure exactly when it started."

12. Try to build a sense of structure as you talk with the person. He may view the situation as absolutely chaotic, unexplainable, and insoluble. To cope with the effects of the emergency, he must feel that you understand what has happened, that you know what to do, and that you can communicate some of this understanding to him. Begin to build in your own mind and in discussion with the person a logical connection among the events. Show him how to look at them and how to deal with the problem. For example: "You see, you are the kind of person who needs to be busy and feel productive. When you lost your job, you really went into a tailspin. You became very depressed, gave up friends and interests, and saw life more and more as hopeless. Then you were feeling so bad you could not go out to find another job."

13. Do not argue with the person if he disagrees with you. Simply point out that there are many different ways of looking at a situation. In providing your view, you realize that it could be wrong and that he is free to agree or disagree. If you are in doubt about how he might react to any statement, it is best to say nothing. In fact, this is a cardinal principle in working with troubled persons. Rather than speak up and risk offending or hurting the patient, remain silent and participate in the interpersonal relationship through nonverbal communications such as listening, nodding, or smiling.

14. As soon as possible, contact and gain information from those interested in the patient. A less involved observer can provide missing facts or a broader view of the crisis. Often the person is unaware of details or unable to provide an objective view. In other cases, the person will seem to provide a very complete picture of the events, his feelings, and the feelings of those around him. However, after contacting others, you learn with some surprise that the person's view differs from that of a less involved observer. Those close to the situation can help in other ways. Most persons involved in an emergency will not require hospitalization or major psychiatric treatment, but they do need help from friends and neighbors or a local social service agency. The person may need to move in with a friend for a day or two, someone to take him to social activities or a loan of a few dollars. Solve the problem as simply and quickly as you can without unnecessarily involving the cumbersome, expensive, time-consuming major psychiatric agencies and treatment modalities. Once you determine that the emergency is likely to subside with minor help, use a common sense approach to meeting the person's needs.

15. If the person was in treatment prior to the emergency, contact his therapist. You can update the person's situation for the therapist and he can give a good deal of background about how to help the patient. If the situation permits at this point, you can simply terminate your service and refer the person back to his therapist. If you discover that the person has been taking a prescribed medication and you are unable to reach the therapist who prescribed it, give the appropriate dose of the medication. Medications such as a major tranquilizer can often have a very useful effect within 30 to 60 minutes. Remember, though, medication should be given only after you are certain that the person has not recently taken an intoxicant, some incompatible medication or enough of his own medication to pose an overdose problem if he takes any more.

Use of Force With the Uncooperative Person

When you are convinced by the evidence that the uncooperative person poses a serious potential danger to himself or others and he refuses evaluation by a specialist or he will not cooperate with the necessary treatment, force may have to be used. This is a dangerous and complicated issue for several reasons. The threat or use of force by one person against another is a crime unless there are extenuating circumstances. Thus, the worker risks both criminal charges and a civil suit. If the person resists physically, he or the worker might be injured. If the person comes to the worker for help and suddenly finds himself a captive, the loss of trust may make it more difficult for the worker to help him. Therefore do not resort to force until you have reviewed the particular circumstances carefully and know which state laws apply here.

On the other hand, failure to use force or detain an obviously dangerous patient may leave you open to criticism or legal liability if the person then injures himself or another person. If possible, consult with a more experienced colleague before making your decision. Persuade the person to wait briefly until the consultation is completed.

The legal position of the nonmedical person who is contemplating using force is weaker than that of the medical person. Although state laws and traditions differ, the English common law on which most state laws are based suggests that one person may restrain another to protect life or prevent injury. When the worker is not a medical person, strong evidence must show that, without use of force, there would have been injury or loss of life. The worker, for example, actually must see the individual engage in a dangerous activity or hear the individual make serious threats. It is not enough to suspect or even know that the individual may be dangerous.

Medical persons generally can act more freely on suspicion and without such clear-cut proof. As experts, their responsibilities to the welfare of their patients and to society are clearly established. State laws often provide them with specific powers to restrain the mentally ill. Law enforcement personnel have similar powers in some states. For the emergency worker, familiarity with the laws of his state on using force is absolutely essential.

If there is a case in which force is justified as a means to restrain a patient, before any action is begun be certain that enough people are available to overpower the person without any difficulty. Moreover, it must be clear to the person that there is no point in struggling because he cannot win. Four persons can usually handle the resisting adult. During or immediately after the use of force you should firmly explain to the patient: "We feel you are very upset and will need to go to the hospital for at least a few days. I know you don't want to go, but we are worried that if you don't go to the hospital you may hurt yourself or someone else. We have decided, therefore, that you will go to the hospital even if you don't want to, and the law gives us the right to decide that." If the patient then struggles or attempts to escape, assistance is near.

Tranquilizing medications can also be useful in case of struggle. This, of course, requires a physician to prescribe and a trained person to administer. But if tranquilizers cannot be used when a struggle appears certain, use physical restraints rather than attempting to wrestle with the person. It may even be best to place the person on a stretcher in a comfortable position, with limbs tied down by cloth straps and a strap across the chest. Check that the ties do not restrict circulation. The person should never be out of sight of the worker. However, often a restrained person quiets down much more quickly if he believes he is alone. You can be outside of the room and still be able to observe unobtrusively. Once the patient is under restraint, transport him quickly to a hospital where medication is available.

Personnel called to restrain a patient should first remove articles like eyeglasses, ties, or rings to prevent injury to or by the person. Law enforcement personnel should unload their guns, preferably removing them and storing them safely.

Specific Management for Treatment Categories

Life-threatening

When the person is armed and barricaded or threatens suicide (e.g., standing on a window ledge), all measures must be slow and deliberate. Never push, crowd, or rush the person. Usually there is nothing to lose and everything to gain by delay. Attempt to engage the person in conversation. This will distract his attention, help him to relax, and possibly begin a dialogue which might eventually convince the person to accept help. Do not meet threats of force with counter threats, and avoid using force to meet force. Instead, the person should be surrounded at a distance. If force is necessary to overcome the individual, do not act until there is sufficient manpower to accomplish the job quickly and with minimum risk of injury. Also, prevent the person from retreating into another situation where he again is in control.

When overpowering the person, make every effort to avoid injuring him. His behavior may be extremely anger-provoking, but he cannot be held accountable for it.

Great care must be exercised in transporting the restrained person. If a car is used, lock all doors and have a worker sit next to him. There should be no opportunity for him to disturb the driver. If transported by ambulance, the person should be permitted to lie or sit, whichever he wishes. Sufficient personnel should be in the ambulance to control him if he becomes excited.

If no psychiatric facility is available, take the person to a general hospital where tranquilizing drugs and special-duty nurses are available. If hospital facilities are unavailable, keep the person under control at home, using medication and special-duty nurses or trained workers, until he can be admitted to a hospital. In dealing with a potentially violent individual, avoid situations in which you may be overpowered.

If the person's problem is mania or confusion, make certain that he is receiving adequate food, water, and sleep. If necessary, employ medical intervention to provide nourishment and fluids, either by nasal-gastric tube or by intravenous administration. Tranquilizers or other physical measures may be necessary to prevent the person from exhausting himself to the point of serious illness or even death.

Serious

Persons in the serious category must be taken fairly soon to a hospital or a mental health specialist. First, though, take time to interview the patient and those who know him. Information obtained at the scene will be extremely helpful later. Many times, in fact, only the worker in the field can get this information.

When a family member or friend is available, ask him to accompany the person to the hospital. His presence will help to calm the person and provide a source of information for later examiners. He can be the link with the other members of the family, informing them of developments and helping to coordinate the treatment plan.

Potentially serious

You should interview a person in the potentially serious category exhaustively at the scene and seek out other available individuals who know him well. Frequently, immediate hospitalization is not necessary if someone will accept the responsibility for watching him and arranging later professional help. Find out who will assume responsibility for the person, what the living conditions are, what kind of back-up is available if his condition worsens, and whether needed professional follow-up is accessible. Potentially serious individuals should not be released unless it is clear to responsible parties that, should the situation become worse, assistance will be sought.

No immediate danger

Persons in no immediate danger generally require minimal follow-up investigation by the worker and a less than thorough investigation of home conditions. Some of these cases, already in treatment, can simply be told to return to their physician or therapist. Others can be told that, while professional evaluation and treatment may be helpful to them in the future, there is no urgency. Inform them, however, how they can obtain help if they decide to seek it.

No psychiatric problem

Persons who are temporarily upset but turn out not to have any sort of mental health problem should be told frankly of their situations. Without such a clear statement, many persons assume that their mental health has been jeopardized and they must seek treatment. They may also limit their activities. Let them know that their problem is only temporary.

Physical illness

When you feel that a person's problem is not a psychiatric emergency, but perhaps physical, arrange for the appropriate examination and treatment. Provide for some follow-up if the illness is severe enough.

Studies have shown that most persons directed to visit clinics, to see their private physicians, or to obtain further service do not follow through. Once a crisis passes, the pressure eases so that a person will tend to procrastinate and neglect. If you are seriously concerned about a person's need for follow-up, schedule an appointment for him yourself and give pertinent information to the person himself or a family member, arrange to have someone take the person to the appointment, write a referral letter which the person can take to the appointment, and indicate your strong interest in the follow-up. Beyond that, you can call the person to find out if he did keep the appointment.

Emergency Room Care

In general, measures which have been described here for the emergency worker apply also to medical personnel working in the hospital emergency room. Of course, a physician—though not a psychiatric specialist—is expected to take medical responsibility, including concern with mental health issues. The general physician should not forego a physical examination when a patient's problem is clearly psychiatric since a physical problem can exist in addition to the psychiatric one.

Follow these guidelines in emergency room care:

1. ***When hospitalization is necessary, attempt to admit the patient without formal psychiatric diagnosis until specialist consultation can be obtained.*** In many states, admission of a psychiatric patient to a hospital requires a special legal procedure, and most general hospitals may not be authorized to accept such patients.

2. ***When the involuntary patient must be hospitalized, obtain specialist consultation before restraining the patient.*** Most general hospitals are not equipped to deal with involuntary patients beyond a short period of time. The legal and practical issues of restraining the patient and preventing escape of the patient make specialist consultation very important.

3. ***For legal as well as medical reasons, keep complete records of the patient's case.*** The sketchy notes used by some hospitals to record emergency room visits will be inadequate in many psychiatric cases.

4. ***Make a determined effort to obtain a complete medical and psychiatric history.*** If a patient has been previously treated, the emergency room physician should consider prescribing any previously effective medication. He may also help assess whether the patient is likely to be dangerous on the basis of past experience. The decision to use medication will depend largely upon knowing the patient's previous reactions to medication as well as any recent ingestion of other medication or intoxicating substances and any known allergies.

5. ***If the patient is brought to the hospital in restraints, do not release him immediately.*** The restraints may be disturbing the patient or make him uncooperative, but premature release could be a mistake. Instead, learn about the patient's state, relate to him, and obtain some idea of how he will react when the restraints are gone. Occasionally, a patient has been released from restraints and the attendants dismissed, only to have him go on a rampage. When restraints are going to be removed, the patient should be placed in a relatively safe room. A number of personnel should be standing by for possible help. Talk to the patient about his agreement to cooperate once the restraints are removed.

6. ***Consider all psychiatric patients to be escape risks, at least until you have the full information about the problem.*** Take unobtrusive measures to prevent escape. This may involve no more than seating the patient in an inner room where he cannot leave without going past the hospital staff. If a patient does attempt to leave, unless it is clear that the hospital can properly detain him, do not resort to forceful restraint because he is clearly dangerous to himself or others. Instead, try persuasion and find out where he is going and who can be notified of his departure and the recommended treatment. Often under such conditions, patients will stay willingly for a period of time until the matter is settled.

7. ***Provide ordinary comforts: enough to eat and drink, a bathroom, dry clothing.*** Too often in the emergency room rush of business this basic side of patient care is forgotten. This action is particularly valuable in establishing rapport with a psychiatric patient.

Medications

The most frequently used classes of medication for psychiatric patients are the major and minor tranquilizers. As with all types of medications, the physician is best advised to become familiar with a few members of each medication class, learning how to use these properly, rather than attempting familiarity across the board.

Minor tranquilizers are used to relieve mild to moderate anxiety, to encourage sleep, and sometimes for a placebo effect. Major tranquilizers are used for severe anxiety and agitation as well as for anti-psychotic properties. Occasionally hypnotics are used to induce sleep. Antidepressants and stimulants are also available, but these classes of drugs are best reserved for the specialist.

Medications are given only after it is known that the patient has not recently ingested any substance which, combined with the medication, could lead to an overdose. Also, the possibility of drug allergies should be checked. If the patient or anyone else knows of medications which have been effective for him in the past, these should be tried first.

For detailed information about available medications, consult sources like *AMA Drug Evaluations*,[1] by the American Medical Association. However, some of the salient points are discussed below.

Minor tranquilizers

Chlordiazepoxide (Librium), when given orally, is an effective drug for allaying mild to moderate anxiety, agitation, and depression. It is available in 5-mg, 10-mg, and 25-mg capsules and tablets. An average-sized adult who has never taken the drug before will feel some effects from a 10-mg capsule (oral medication usually takes from 45 to 90 minutes before the drug is fully effective). For larger than average adults having more severe symptoms, up to 100 mg orally may be given, continuing with maintenance of 25 mg, three or four times a day. Where more rapid action is necessary Librium can be injected intramuscularly or intravenously. Usually a dose of 50 mg is sufficient for the average adult, although in severe agitation 100 mg can be used. Where very quick action is necessary the intravenous injection is preferred. However, generally the candidates for intravenous injection are those patients who are most agitated and difficult to handle. It is, therefore, quite a problem to hold them down and keep them still enough to accomplish venipuncture and slow injection of the medication. Since there is always more danger in using intravenous medication, intramuscular injection is preferred.

Diazepam (Valium), when used for psychiatric problems, is similar in indications and effect to Librium. The major difference is the magnitude of the dose; Valium is several times as potent by weight as Librium.

Meprobamate (Miltown or Equanil) has somewhat milder effects than Librium and Valium. When given orally, an adequate dose for an average-sized adult is 400 mg and maintenance dose is 400 mg three to four times a day. It is available in 200-mg and 400-mg tablets or in liquid form.

It should be noted that most minor tranquilizers are known to be at least psychologically habituating, if not physically addicting.

Major tranquilizers

Chlorpromazine (Thorazine), the most commonly used major tranquilizer, can be taken orally or by injection. An adequate oral dose for an average-sized, moderately agitated adult is 50 mg. However, there is a relatively high margin of safety with Thorazine; if necessary, up to 200 mg can be given in a single dose. The maintenance dose varies widely (it can be up to 2,000 mg per day), but the nonspecialist had best restrict treatment to 100 mg four times a day. Thorazine is given only intramuscularly when injected, with an injected dose having approximately twice the potency of an oral one. The maximum injected dose is 100 mg, and an average-sized adult will respond to 50 mg. A large dose of Thorazine by injection normally puts the patient to sleep within two hours.

Thorazine has significant immediate side

1. AMA Department of Drugs, *AMA Drug Evaluations*, 2nd ed. (Acton, Mass.: Publishing Sciences Group, Inc., 1973).

effects, particularly, hypotension. When injected with Thorazine, the patient must be cautioned about this problem and observed carefully because he may faint after rising from a prone or sitting position. In the elderly, hypotension may lead to more serious cardiovascular effects.

Hypnotics

Commonly used hypnotics are sodium ammobarbital (Amytal) and pentobarbital (Nembutal), given in doses of 100 to 200 mg for insomnia. In patients who cannot tolerate barbiturates, chloral hydrate is a useful substitute when given in a dose of 500 or 1,000 mg. Sodium ammobarbital (Amytal) may be used intravenously or intramuscularly to control excited or uncooperative patients when it is necessary to put them to sleep rapidly. The maximum intramuscular dose is 500 mg. The intravenous dose is administered slowly to allow time for observing the patient's reaction. A single dose should not exceed 1,000 mg.

One of the more difficult situations facing the emergency room physician and crew is the attempt to control a dangerously overexcited patient through use of medication. Injection of medication in itself requires a group of persons to hold the patient and involves some risk of injury to both patients and staff. The physician, therefore, is reluctant to use repeated small doses of medication since they increase the risk of injury. He wishes to inject in one dose the appropriate amount which will calm the patient or put him to sleep without leading to a dangerous respiratory depression or hypotensive crisis.

You should attempt to enlist the patient's cooperation, asking him either to take the medication orally or to submit to an injection. If he refuses, then gather the necessary staff. Depending upon the size of the patient, prepare an intramuscular injection of 50 or 100 mg of Thorazine or 50 or 100 mg of Librium (intravenous administration is generally not recommended). Working rapidly and smoothly, the staff should pin down the patient and remove the necessary clothing for the injection. After the injection, transport the patient to a room where he may be left alone, but observed closely. Within 30 to 45 minutes he should calm down and then fall asleep. Once a patient has received parenteral medication, he cannot be released on his own until he has recovered from the effects of the medication.

After the patient has received the necessary emergency service, he will then be either admitted to the hospital, referred to another facility for inpatient or outpatient care, or discharged. Issues of referrals have already been discussed. Bear in mind, though, unless special measures are taken, many patients will not follow through on referrals nor will they continue to take prescribed medication. Each patient must be seen with the view that this occasion could be his first and last contact regarding the problem. You must accomplish as much as possible, then, during the visit without counting on follow-up.

PSYCHOLOGICAL EPIDEMICS

The Problem

Emergency workers are often involved in the treatment of seriously disturbed behavior among groups of people. The term we have chosen for this type of problem is psychological epidemic. The definition of a psychological epidemic is the outbreak of behavior in a group which, if it were seen in an individual, would be considered psychologically abnormal.

A case example will give you a good idea of a typical epidemic.[2]

> Suddenly one morning, thirty of thirty-nine women workers in a data-processing center became ill. Symptoms were dizziness, vomiting, nausea, and faint-

2. Sidney M. Stahl and Morty Lebedun, "Mystery Gas: An Analysis of Mass Hysteria," *Journal of Health and Social Behavior*, 15(1974):44-50.

> ing. Ten of the women were so sick they had to be taken to a hospital. The center had to be evacuated and closed. A gas or impurity in the air was suspected as the cause of the problem. Despite careful studies of the air in the center and of the blood and urine of affected workers, no abnormalities were found. The next day the center reopened and several workers again became sick, requiring another evacuation and closing of the center. Only after steps were taken to deal with the psychological situation among the workers was the center able to reopen.

This episode is typical in several ways of what the emergency worker may find in a psychological epidemic. The group involved is usually well defined and long existing, e.g., a school class or a work group in a factory. The outbreaks of psychological epidemics seem to be more common among groups of women. The symptoms often suggest physical illness and poisoning by gas, food, or water (usually gas is suspected). Careful investigation does not turn up any evidence of genuine illness or poisoning.

Epidemics have involved the spread of false belief in an entire community: that an attack was being made on a community by creatures from Mars; that persons were damaging car windshields in a neighborhood; that an outbreak of bites was from a mysterious insect.

Epidemics also extend into widespread acceptance of false rumors, often involving political or other public figures. These situations do not concern us here. The emergency worker most often is called in where the episode resembles physical illness.

Typical Patterns

Most psychological epidemics occur in closed groups of individuals who are in frequent communication. Exposed to the same circumstances, they also frequently have been developing some unrecognized psychological stress. Perhaps a factory or classroom may be the site of the epidemic. Typically, a gradually increasing number of individuals suffer over a period of several days from symptoms of unknown cause. At first the cause is suspected to be a widespread, physically noxious element, such as leaking gas. But lack of any physical explanation plus the previous absence of any such symptoms in that particular setting offer the first signs that the epidemic is psychological. First-aid workers, summoned to the scene of such outbreaks, usually administer oxygen or rush the victims to a hospital. Measures may even be taken at the scene to establish the presence of a noxious agent, but any results—often delayed for several days—cannot help in making an immediate diagnosis.

Psychological epidemics, of course, must be distinguished from physical illness; otherwise, something which is treatable and potentially serious will be neglected. It is damaging to treat a psychological problem as a physical illness. The emergency worker who arrives on the scene must guess as to the problem's cause and risk treating it without definitive information.

Follow these guidelines in managing a psychological epidemic:

1. As soon as you determine that a psychological epidemic is present rather than a physical illness, emphasize to the victims that there is a psychological cause. Do not belittle the victims' plight with a derogatory manner, such as, "It's all in your mind; just forget about it." Instead, reassure them—"Right now there is no gas in the air which could make you sick. Perhaps there was in the past; we're really not sure. However, worrying about the possibility has made you oversensitive to the situation and nervous. The most important thing now is to calm down and you will find that you feel much better. There is nothing here now to make you feel sick."

2. Demonstrate to the victims that the situation is actually harmless. Enter the supposedly affected area or engage in the activities which the victims assume are making them ill.

3. Disrupt the group interaction among the victims which has contributed to the development of the situation. Separate the most affected victims from each other, leaving them to communicate mainly with unaffected individuals.

4. Give all others a chance to discuss how they feel as a group and as individuals about the symptoms and other common problems. Balance the discussion with reassurance from experts on the scene.

5. In cases where the epidemic seems to be a reaction to human exhaustion, unreasonable work demands, or an unsatisfactory setting, consider a change in the situation. Give victims other tasks. Work hours might temporarily be decreased. Any measures likely to enhance the psychological atmosphere should be taken.

6. Avoid unnecessary treatment for physical illnesses. If it is clear that the group is experiencing a psychological epidemic, discontinue measures like inhalation of oxygen, increased ventilation of work areas, or repeated testing of air content. Under the circumstances, these measures only serve to strengthen the feeling among many of the victims that they are physically ill. Treat as many individuals as possible at the scene without removing them to hospitals. Only those so psychologically upset that they are disturbing everyone else should be removed.

7. Do not give placebo medication. Although this action might be immediately useful, it will add support to the belief that physical illness is present.

8. Early intervention is preferable to allowing the situation to continue or intending to intervene later. The earlier you recognize the epidemic, the less difficulty you will have in stopping it.

SUGGESTED READINGS

Aguilera, Donna C.; Messick, Janice M.; and Farrell, Marlene S. *Crisis Intervention: Theory and Methodology.* St. Louis: C. V. Mosby Company, 1970.

Bloch, S. H. "Army Clinical Psychiatry in the Combat Zone." *American Journal of Psychiatry* 126(1969): 37-46.

Bridges, P. K. *Psychiatric Emergencies: Diagnosis and Management.* Springfield, Ill.: Charles C. Thomas, Publisher, 1971.

Bushard, Bruce L. "The U.S. Army's Mental Hygiene Consultation Service." In *Symposium on Preventive and Social Psychiatry*, Walter Reed Army Institute of Research. Washington, D.C.: U.S. Government Printing Office, 1957.

Hankoff, L. D. *Emergency Psychiatric Treatment: A Handbook of Secondary Prevention.* Springfield, Ill.: Charles C. Thomas, Publisher, 1969.

Hansell, N., et al. "Decision Counseling Method." *Archives of General Psychiatry* 22(1970):462-67.

Kerckhoff, Alan C., and Back, Kurt W. *June Bug: A Study of Hysterical Contagion.* New York: Appleton-Century-Crofts, 1968.

McGee, Richard K. *Crisis Intervention in the Community.* Baltimore: University Park Press, 1974.

Quarantelli, E. "Images of Withdrawal Behavior in Disaster: Some Basic Misconceptions." *Social Problems* 8(1960): 68-79.

Stahl, Sidney M., and Lebedun, Morty. "Mystery Gas: An Analysis of Mass Hysteria." *Journal of Health and Social Behavior* 15(1974):44-50.

Tyhurst, James S. "Problems of Leadership: In the Disaster Situation and in the Clinical Team." In *Symposium on Preventive and Social Psychiatry,* Walter Reed Army Institute of Research. Washington, D.C.: U.S. Government Printing Office, 1957.

Zusman, J. "Secondary Prevention." In *Comprehensive Textbook of Psychiatry*, by Alfred M. Freedman, Harold I. Kaplan, and Benjamin Sadock. 2d ed. New York: Williams & Wilkins, forthcoming.

IV

Acute Alcoholic Emergencies

Donald J. Ottenberg, M.D.
Alvin Rosen, D.O.
Vernelle Fox, M.D.

THE PROBLEM

Acute alcoholic intoxication and the alcohol withdrawal state constitute two of this country's most frequent mental health crisis situations. In this chapter, acute intoxication means significant alteration of behavior and/or of the state of consciousness as a result of drinking alcohol.

How much alcohol is ingested is the prime concern, not which beverage. A person drinking beer, wine, or shaving lotion may become more intoxicated than one who has been drinking whiskey. Nor is the image of the skid row bum as the typical alcoholic correct because persons of all types become acutely intoxicated. A well-dressed, neatly groomed person may be hiding or minimizing an acute alcohol problem, whereas a poorly dressed or disheveled individual can appear superficially, but not actually, intoxicated.

Negative attitudes by people in general toward intoxication and intoxicated persons must not be allowed to interfere with proper care. Intoxicated persons are individuals needing help. The tendency to see the intoxicated person and his behavior as funny obscures the serious nature of the crisis situation.

While not everyone who is drunk requires emergency care, those who do should be viewed as a potential health crisis. In assessing the situation, consider hazards to other persons as well as to the intoxicated individual.

Acute intoxication may present itself as a life-threatening emergency where seconds count

—as in the case of internal bleeding due to a ruptured blood vessel in the esophagus. It may be a minor annoyance, for example, when a patient with a bit too much to drink exhibits minimal hand tremor, slurred speech, and slight lack of coordination. The emergency team must rapidly assess the patient's degree of alcohol-induced impairment, and then treat or refer him to the appropriate treatment agency.

Decide whether alcohol is the prime cause of the emergency situation or whether other factors are the true precipitators of the crisis. In dealing with either the acutely intoxicated person or one in a state of withdrawal, be alert for other disease processes and/or traumatic injuries masked by the alcoholic state. For example, an unconscious person with the odor of alcohol on his breath may, in fact, have had a cocktail with dinner, but then suffered a stroke or head injury.

Drugs other than alcohol may be the primary or significant contributing cause of the immediate problem. For example, an unconscious person smelling of alcohol may be suffering from a barbiturate overdose or the combination of barbiturates with alcohol. A history is obviously helpful here. Quite frequently, alcoholics are clear enough in the beginning of the emergency to give an adequate history, but then develop acute brain syndromes in the next 12 to 24 hours.

Withdrawal from intoxication may comprise a series of increasingly serious stages. In making on-the-spot judgments be aware that the patient may progress to a more critical stage a few hours later. The chronic drinker or alcoholic who stops drinking may precipitate a withdrawal crisis. Those symptoms may well be more serious than those of intoxication itself.

How severe withdrawal is depends on these factors: duration of intake, amount ingested, abruptness of the cessation, ingestion of other drugs (sedatives or tranquilizers), type of alcohol, person's age, general physical health, and individual susceptibility to alcohol.

Once the crisis associated with acute alcoholism has been stabilized, attempt to refer the person for continuing help with the drinking problem to a local alcoholism treatment facility, the community mental health center, and/or Alcoholics Anonymous.

Punishing the acute alcoholic in no way deters his future involvement with alcohol. The understanding but firm crisis worker during an alcoholic crisis can lay the foundation for a patient's serious attempt at rehabilitation.

CRISIS RECOGNITION AND MANAGEMENT

Acute Alcohol Intoxication

Symptoms of acute alcohol intoxication are precipitated by short-term consumption of the sedative agent alcohol. This consumption may or may not be accompanied by the ingestion of other drugs; if so, the picture is complicated and the crisis usually has longer effects. Keep this possibility in mind, particularly with the younger patient. Attempt to get a valid history or what facts you can from the patient or others in the early minutes of the crisis. Also determine the amount, time interval, and nature of the alcohol consumed.

An acutely intoxicated person without complications probably will smell and behave like someone "under the influence." More serious degrees of intoxication usually are indicated by: (1) nervous system disturbances such as loss of physical coordination and equilibrium or impaired consciousness varying from drowsiness to coma; (2) emotional and psychic symptoms such as inappropriate laughing and crying or extreme belligerence; or (3) organic manifestations such as broken limbs or bleeding from an obvious or hidden injury.

In every case, the crisis staff should find answers to these questions:

1. Is alcohol the cause of the crisis?

2. How long has this drinking episode lasted?

3. When did the person have his last drink?

4. Has the person a long history of drinking excessively?

5. What has the person been drinking? (e.g., whiskey, beer, wine, sterno, shaving lotion, other substances)

6. Have convulsive seizures occurred previously?

7. Have hallucinations occurred previously?

8. Has delirium tremens (D.T.'s) occurred previously?

9. Has the person taken Antabuse within the past 5 days?

10. Has the person taken other drugs in the past 5 days?

11. Are there other diseases known to be present? (e.g., diabetes, peptic ulcer, heart disease)

12. Is there any previous history of internal bleeding?

13. Have any severe injuries occurred during this drinking bout? (e.g., falling down, being struck by an object or another person)

If the answer to any of questions 6 through 13 is affirmative, the patient will require further professional help.

You should know the following basic management procedures that apply to all types of acute alcohol intoxication:

- Keep breathing passage open and remove any object from mouth or throat, including mucous, blood, and false teeth.
- Turn head to the side in case of vomiting to prevent flow of liquid into airway and hold tongue forward and down.
- Maintain continuous observation and check vital signs frequently.
- Speak firmly with understanding and assurance; never laugh, ridicule, or verbally challenge.
- Obtain a history of the nature and quantity of alcohol, and perform a physical examination to exclude diseases, including diabetes, pneumonia, other infections, head injuries and other traumas, and ingestion of other drugs (such as barbiturates).
- Offer fluids by mouth in small amounts, including fruit juice.
- Refer for continuing care of the drinking problem, using resources such as psychiatric clinics, alcohol counseling services, pastoral counseling centers, and Alcoholics Anonymous.

There are several distinguishable types of intoxication with which the emergency team may deal: intoxication without complications and intoxication with complications of disorientation, assaultive behavior, depression, alcoholic stupor, convulsive seizures, and unconsciousness. Methods of recognition and management of these crisis situations follows.

Uncomplicated intoxication

If the patient's only symptoms are alcohol odor, unsteady gait, slurred speech, and nausea or vomiting, both problem and treatment are relatively simple. He might also exhibit mild lack of coordination and may be giddy or uninhibited. Assist the person home or to some facility providing a bed and arrange for observation by other persons.

Intoxication with disorientation

Varying quantities of alcohol in the inexperienced drinker can produce acute disorientation. The very young, the elderly, and people with organic brain damage are unusually susceptible to the effects of alcohol. Normal adults usually have to drink enough to manifest gross sedation before becoming disoriented. The crisis may be simply that an intoxicated person does not know who and where he is. This occurs when alcohol is taken with other drugs. Complications can occur with fear or panic or in the case of an already disturbed personality, the mere presence of a calm, firm person working to reorient the patient solves much of the difficulty. The disorientation should disappear spontaneously within 3 to 6 hours.

Follow these guidelines in dealing with the disorientation factor:

1. *Try to obtain an accurate history of alcohol and drug intake.*

2. *Induce vomiting or gastric lavage if the person seems very sedated, particularly if he seems to become more sedated as time passes.*

3. *Collect a sample of gastric contents.* Analysis of the sample is more important for differentiating simultaneous drug toxicities than for the alcohol problem alone.

4. *Do not collect a sample for blood alcohol level.* This information will not help you assess the situation.

5. *Check vital signs.* They should be within normal limits, except for some elevation of pulse and blood pressure.

6. *Support and observe the patient for the first few hours.* If possible, do not leave the intoxicated, disoriented individual alone because his behavior is unpredictable. He may even harm himself.

7. *Avoid sedation.* The action frequently compounds the problem and risks over-sedation. If the individual is so difficult that drugs must be used, choose non-potentiating, non-hypnotic ones such as diazepam (Valium) or hydroxyzine (Vistaril); administer an intramuscular dose of 10 mg of one of these drugs.

Intoxication with assaultive behavior

A more common crisis call is for the intoxicated individual who is psychotic, aggressive, destructive, belligerent, or paranoid. Just the smell of alcohol and some degree of slurred speech, confusion, and ataxia frequently mislead people to blame the entire situation on alcohol. While most people tend to become louder and more aggressive when intoxicated, they are also able to be managed by family, friends, or authorities. People who respond to alcohol with gross disturbance, confusion, and belligerence usually have some underlying or concomitant problem.

The simultaneous ingestion of drugs and alcohol is a very common problem, particularly hallucinogens and stimulants. Because bizzare drug reactions complicated by alcohol are on the rise, assume that the individual's disturbed behavior could be drug-related.

Relatively small amounts of alcohol can surface such psychiatric problems as rage, hysterical reactions, homosexual panic, and suicidal depression. People frequently use drink as a response to acute schizophrenic reactions, toxic and other organic psychosis, or manic states. When the alcohol effects wear off in a few hours, a clearer picture of possible psychosis emerges. If the problem is only alcohol intoxication, the individual will have recovered from the crisis. But, if more persistent symptoms are present at this point, you need to look to other factors such as longer acting drugs or underlying psychiatric problems.

Follow these guidelines in dealing with the disturbed alcoholic:

1. Do not attempt to handle the patient alone.

2. Approach the patient slowly and carefully. Do not touch him before you have explained his situation. Attempt in a firm, reassuring manner to "talk him down" by persuasion and cajolery.

3. Transfer the patient to the emergency room if you feel that further treatment is necessary. Use physical restraint only as a last resort, and leave the desirability of medication to the emergency room staff.

4. Once in the emergency room, establish initial control of the situation. Protect persons in the environment, calling in extra staff if necessary. Question the patient firmly about the cause of his anger, and avoid threats or challenges.

5. Obtain an adequate history of the substances he has ingested. If this is impossible, analyze gastric contents or blood samples.

6. Defer medication about one hour in order to establish if the patient is developing evidence of progressive over-sedation.

7. If medication is necessary, use mild tranquilizers. Hydroxyzines and diazepams are recommended, keeping the initial dose relatively small (Vistaril 100 mg, Librium 25 mg, Valium 5 mg) and repeating hourly. Initially avoid sedatives like barbiturates or phenothiazines, which risk potentiation of previously ingested sedatives.

8. If the patient is still out of control, administer sodium amytal of 0.25 to 0.5 grams intravenously. Be very careful to give it slowly and only in the presence of equipment for maintaining cardiopulmonary function, e.g., airway, suction pump, respirator and an intravenous setup through which other medications can be administered rapidly.

9. Refer for further evaluation and follow-up care.

Intoxication with depression

People with acute and chronic depressions often feel freer to act out their feelings while intoxicated. The suicidal person may get drunk in order to overcome his fear of pain associated with self-destruction. (See Chapter VI for suicide prevention techniques.) However, do not discount the individual's words and actions just because he is intoxicated. Whenever a person in this condition speaks about suicide, treat his words seriously.

Proceed with the basic suicide prevention techniques, including restraint if he may harm himself or others. The intoxicated person who is also emotionally disturbed will act aggressive, verbally abusive, and agitated. He may shift quickly from laughing to crying.

In the case of physiological depression or over-sedation, massive doses of alcohol can produce stupor, nystagmus, ataxia, disorientation, and coma. If these symptoms are severe, you should immediately suspect other hypnotic sedative drugs. Check also if the individual has widely dilated pupils and if he is sweating. If alcohol is the cause, he is not subject to respiratory depression as much as the person with an overdose of barbiturates.

The remarks at the beginning of this chapter on the general alcohol intoxication problem apply to the patient in physiologic alcohol depression. Except when the patient's case history is full and reliable, it is difficult to distinguish alcohol overdose in the one-time abuser from the chronic abuser. In the latter situation, stimulants are not advised.

Follow these guidelines in dealing with the depressed alcoholic:

1. Attempt to convince the person of the need for further help.

2. *Keep the patient in sight and be able to control him physically if that becomes necessary.*

3. *Talk directly to the patient about his self-destructive thoughts in light of his life stresses, conflicts, and feelings.*

4. *Take all anti-suicide precautions (see Chapter VI).*

5. *Administer a tranquilizer such as chlordiazepoxide (25-50 mg three times a day) for 24 hours.*

6. *Refer the patient for continuing psychiatric care.*

Intoxication with alcoholic stupor

The typical patient in this category sits or lies listlessly or even slumps over. His face is flushed, he breathes deeply and loudly, and the odor of alcohol is evident. He will respond to painful stimulation—pinching, poking, sticking with a pin—or to very loud questioning. Though his vital signs are within the normal range, he must be checked carefully because there is a history of prolonged, excessive alcohol ingestion.

Follow these guidelines in dealing with persons in an alcoholic stupor:

1. *Follow the first five steps of the basic management procedures for acute alcohol intoxication given above.* Observe the patient for several hours or until he is more responsive.

2. *Should pulse become weak, transfer the patient immediately to the hospital.*

3. *Avoid sedation because it may worsen the condition and produce coma.*

4. *Monitor vital signs continuously to assure that the patient's condition does not worsen.*

5. *When the patient is responsive and alert, treatment for withdrawal from alcohol is usually indicated.*

Intoxication with convulsive seizures

This type of patient will have involuntary twitching and jerking of muscles in the arms, legs, hands, feet or entire body. He may drool, perhaps bite his tongue; his eyes stare and his pupils are rolled up. During the seizure—rarely lasting longer than 30 or 60 seconds—he will be unconscious. This frequently indicates the beginning of delirium tremens (see the following section on delirium tremens), but it also can indicate an existing seizure disorder in the intoxicated person. Immediately after the seizure, the patient goes into a deep sleep for a period of time. Upon awakening, he usually does not recall anything that has occurred. At this point, though no direct assistance is needed, transfer the patient as quickly as possible to the emergency room for further evaluation.

Follow these guidelines in dealing with an intoxicated person having a convulsive seizure:

1. *Protect the patient from harm, using the first three steps of the basic management procedures.* The actual seizure is brief, so there is time for little else.

2. *Prevent tongue biting by forcing open his jaws and inserting a tongue blade, comb, wallet, or other firm object.*

3. *Hold the head firmly to prevent it from striking the ground.*

4. *Stabilize the patient.* Use diazepam (Valium), 5 to 10 mg given intravenously and slowly (more effective in status epilepticus); diphenylhydantoin (Dilantin), 100 to 200 mg given intravenously and slowly; or sodium phenobarbital, 100 to 200 mg given intravenously or intramuscularly.

5. *Take a skull x-ray.*

6. Obtain neurologic evaluation and consultation to check out other causes of seizure besides alcohol withdrawal.

Intoxication with unconsciousness

Such a patient is also listless or slumped over, but he does not respond to loud questioning or painful stimulation such as pinching, poking, or sticking with a pin. There may be irregular breathing and a purplish cast to the skin and lips.

Use these guidelines in dealing with the complication of unconsciousness:

1. Follow the first four steps of the basic management procedures.

2. Administer artificial respiration if the patient is not breathing.

3. Administer oxygen, if available.

4. Once in the emergency room, insert nasal or oral pharyngal airway.

5. Apply mouth-to-mouth resuscitation or employ available mechanical ventilation methods. Use the stethoscope to confirm that air is entering the lungs.

6. If no pulse is present, give the patient a sharp slap on the chest.

7. Take supportive measures to correct shock. These measures include intravenous fluids and the administration of whole blood, oxygen, or oxygen/carbon dioxide mixtures.

8. Do a complete history and physical exam, once life support mechanisms have been assured. Exclude conditions other than alcohol intoxication such as: concussion, fractured skull, subdural or subarachnoid hemorrhage, cerebral embolism, subdural hematoma, uremic or diabetic coma, other drug intoxications (particularly barbiturates), internal bleeding, or infections.

9. Perform necessary studies for differential diagnosis. Include a complete blood count, urinalysis, blood sugar, blood alcohol and barbiturate levels, blood urea nitrogen, spinal tap, chest x-ray, skull x-ray, and studies to identify infection.

Alcohol Withdrawal States

The major emergencies created by alcohol dependency are the acute withdrawal syndromes. They range from mild, miserable shakes and nausea and vomiting, through hallucinations, to severe delirium tremens where the death rate has been reported from 5 to 30 percent. Withdrawal symptoms begin 12 to 24 hours after the blood alcohol begins to fall. The individual may still be drinking at the time. The person with conditions such as superimposed infection, trauma, surgery, or pancreatitis has an increased chance for developing severe withdrawal symptoms.

Wernicke's syndrome, though uncommon, can be a substantial medical emergency. Early treatment is essential to prevent permanent damage. In this nutritional complication of chronic alcoholism the patient—usually a daily drinker—manifests extra-ocular muscle palsies, confusion, and ataxia. In its early phases the syndrome may involve only impaired recent memory. If you are in doubt, treat the patient anyway. Substantial doses of thiamine given intramuscularly in three or four doses (100 mg every 3 or 4 hours combined with oral administration for at least several days) provide prompt and dramatic relief. Many authorities, feeling that lesser symptoms of Wernicke's syndrome are fairly common, recommend the routine prophylactic use of parenteral Vitamin B complex in a minimal amount of 100 mg of B_1, 5 mg of B_6, and 50 mg of niacinimide daily for at least the first 3 days of abstinence for the known alcoholic. The treatment is believed to be contributing to less permanent organic brain damage for these patients.

Thiamine deficiency may be the cause of

the alcoholic patient's congestive heart failure. He will show signs of a high output failure with anasarca (massive edema) and a short circulation time. Unlike the patient with alcoholic myocardiopathy, though, he will respond well to parenteral thiamine replacement therapy.

Susceptible patients may experience one or several withdrawal seizures during the first 3 days of declining blood alcohol level. The peak incidence of seizures occurs on the fourth to sixth day for mixed alcohol-barbiturate or other sedative withdrawal patients and between the seventh and fourteenth day for alcohol-chlordiazepoxide (Librium) or alcohol-diazepam (Valium) withdrawal patients. The seizures, self-limited, are accompanied by hyperventilation, respiratory alkalosis, and extreme sensitivity to light. The most dangerous aspect of these seizures is the possibility of fractures or other major injuries from falling, maceration of tongue, and aspiration of vomitus. Withdrawal seizures differ from intoxication with convulsive seizures because the patient is not currently intoxicated. Rather, they occur as part of severe withdrawal or delirium tremens. The following remarks on management of these seizures apply to all alcohol withdrawal states in which they are found.

When they occur, alcohol withdrawal seizures are indistinguishable from any other seizures. Although the seizures are usually grand-mal, some patients—especially those who were taking Dilantin or sedative drugs the past few days—may experience a range of abortive attacks which are confusing. Very rarely, an alcoholic will develop prolonged recurrent seizures (status epilepticus). During such a neurological emergency, it is mandatory that you hospitalize the patient, paying careful attention to the maintenance of an adequate airway, high parenteral doses of anti-convulsant drugs, and protection from self injury. Alcoholic patients frequently have no prior warning about the seizure; in fact, they frequently "feel fine" up to the moment it begins—whether or not they have a history of previous seizures. The commonest cause of first seizure in individuals over 40 years old is withdrawal from alcohol or other sedative drugs.

Follow these guidelines in dealing with withdrawal seizures:

1. ***Protect the patient from injury.*** (See steps 1 to 3 on managing intoxication with convulsive seizures.)

2. ***Control the patient with medication.*** Diazepam (Valium) 10 mg or sodium luminal (phenobarbital) 120 mg intramuscularly or intravenously will suffice in most cases. Dilantin and other anti-convulsants, even if given parenterally, are of doubtful value.

3. ***Hospitalize the patient immediately.*** Commonly, a seizure is the first sign of progressively severe withdrawal symptoms. It is frequently followed (in anywhere from a few hours to 2 days) by acute hallucinosis, with or without a paranoid component, or delirium tremens. Both incidence and severity of these serious disabilities can be reduced by starting treatment early. Withdrawal seizures, for example, can be drastically reduced by prompt preventive measures like daily declining doses of diazepam (Valium), chlordiazepoxide (Librium), or short-acting barbiturates for the first 3 or 4 days after drinking has stopped.

4. ***Consider causes other than withdrawal from alcohol.*** If an individual has more than two or three seizures during a withdrawal episode, if the seizure occurs more than 72 hours after the cessation of drinking, or if the individual does not recover from the post-seizure confusion and lethargy in less than an hour, you need to investigate the strong possibility that he has other problems in addition to the alcoholism. Mixed alcohol and drug abuse and old or new head injury are common occurrences, but all other etiologies must be weighed.

5. ***Postpone diagnostic procedures, until the withdrawal syndrome has abated.*** When the person with known alcohol and/or drug prob-

lems has a seizure, but does not manifest any other neurological sign, also hold off performing a spinal tap, brain scan, or similar tests.

Uncomplicated acute withdrawal

Mild to moderate withdrawal. The diagnosis of this state is based on alcohol odor, mild agitation, slight tremor or lack of coordination, heavy perspiration, slurred speech, and increased pulse and blood pressure. You have found no evidence or history pointing to other diseases or injuries aside from alcohol ingestion.

Follow these guidelines in dealing with the mild to moderate withdrawal state:

1. *Reassure the patient that he will be helped.*

2. *Provide for bed rest.*

3. *Give him fluids by mouth—e.g., water and fruit juice—taken in small sips.*

4. *Do not resort to alcohol to quiet the symptoms.* It simply prolongs the withdrawal.

5. *Refer the patient to a physician or clinic the next day.*

Severe withdrawal. Perhaps the patient shows the same signs of moderate withdrawal, but in a more dramatic way. Add to the picture that he has a history of other diseases and that you know his drinking has stopped or diminished within the last few hours.

Follow these guidelines in dealing with moderate withdrawal with some complications:

1. *Younger persons and adults in apparent good health usually do not require hospitalization.*

2. *Patients with other diseases like diabetes, heart conditions, and peptic ulcer and those beyond the age of 50 may require immediate hospitalization.*

3. *If the patient has a history of convulsive seizures, give him diazepam (Valium), 10 mg 4 times a day for 24 hours, then a reduced quantity of 5 mg 4 times a day.*

4. *If he has no history of convulsive seizures, give chlordiazepoxide (Librium), 25 to 50 mg 4 times a day for 24 hours, then reduce as symptoms subside.*

5. *Follow the general procedures listed earlier for moderate withdrawal.*

6. *Give intravenous fluids when indicated and when the patient cannot tolerate them by mouth.* Once his condition stabilizes, gather a thorough history and examine him physically to check out possible traumatic injuries, diabetes, pneumonia, and other infections and possible ingestion of another drug like a barbiturate.

Alcoholic hallucinosis

The acutely agitated, hallucinating alcoholic encountered for the first time in the emergency situation can be a very difficult patient. The syndrome, usually appearing 24 to 72 hours after the patient has stopped drinking, may be accompanied by a seizure. By this time he rarely shows any signs of drinking or sedation, and he is likely to deny having any history of alcohol abuse, maybe even claiming to be an abstainer. But the picture belies the words: agitation, panic, visual and aural hallucinations and delusions, frequently with a good deal of paranoid ideation. While overt physical signs like an alcohol odor, slurred speech, or ataxia are absent, some less obvious physical signs can help distinguish acute alcoholic hallucinosis from other acute psychotic episodes. The patient frequently still has a small, rapid, lateral nystagmus that gives him a bird-like appearance. His pulse is frequently elevated, between 100 and 120. There may be a fine tremor and sweating may still be present, but the patient is fairly well oriented as to time and place. He might not even look particularly toxic or sick.

Chances are he is a male, between the ages of 30 and 50. Typically, he may agitate to leave to go somewhere, having "just heard his baby had been run over" or saying his "wife just called to say she has been threatened." The stereotyped hallucinations about insects or talking animals seldom apply here. He is usually more distractable than the acute schizophrenic patient. Complete accuracy in diagnosis is not essential for handling his crisis situation. Take the patient into protective custody, preferably hospitalizing or otherwise restraining or incarcerating him.

Once he has slept under sedation, the patient will be reasonably clear when he awakens. Although he will still be intermittently confused, his hallucinations will be less severe in recurrence for the next 24 to 72 hours. Often, differences between these hallucinations and various acute psychotic episodes are not apparent until the patient fails to clear his mind. In any case, if any doubt about diagnosis remains, it is safer to overprotect the patient and keep him under lengthy surveillance than to risk his harming himself. Generally the hallucinating alcoholic is seldom violent or assaultive, but he can become so in response to arguments, confusion, or aggressive interference with his hallucinations. While he is less a risk to others, he is a definite risk to himself. Further, the superimposing of acute agitation and hyperactivity upon an already strained and possibly damaged cardiovascular system can lead to other acute medical complications. Gradual sedation is particularly essential.

Three syndromes commonly confused with acute alcoholic hallucinosis are paranoid schizophrenic reactions, hyperthyroidism, and acute toxic drug reactions.

Follow these guidelines in dealing with hallucinating alcoholics:

1. *Try to keep the patient in touch with reality.*

2. *Obtain a history.* Check out any previous psychotic episodes.

3. *Attempt to distract him from his delusions.* If the patient is agitated about a horrible hallucination he has just experienced, distract him with questions (what did he last eat?) or procedures (taking his blood pressure); then attempt to talk him out of his hallucination. If he readily responds to such distractions, it is safe to suspect acute organic hallucinosis.

4. *Avoid having a crowd around the patient.*

5. *Keep the patient in a well-lighted room to avoid shadows.*

6. *Once in the emergency room, sedate the patient as soon as possible.* Give somewhat smaller doses than you would to severely disturbed psychotic patients and repeat the doses at hourly intervals until the patient is able to rest. Recommended are chlorpromazine (Thorazine), 25 mg; promazine hydrochloride (Sparine), 75 mg; mesoridazine (Serentil), 25 mg; chlordiazepoxide (Librium), 100 mg; diazepam (Valium), 20 mg; sodium amytal, 250 mg; and sodium phenobarbital (Luminal), 200 mg. Although the first dose seldom sedates the patient sufficiently, it is better to start low and then repeat with the same or another drug than to risk over-sedation or a hypotensive crisis. In older patients or individuals with marked tachycardia or borderline hypotension, give drugs other than the phenothiazines initially.

7. *Maintain a constant, supportive, and tranquil environment.* When the patient begins to quiet down, he will feel more secure if loosely restrained. The presence of a calm, reassuring person whom he knows is as beneficial as most medications. This other person—family or friend—should quietly shift the patient back to the immediate when his conversation wanders.

Delirium tremens

A clear-cut case of delirium tremens or DT's is more easily diagnosed than managed.

Add to that the danger of frequent fatality. DT's has become a loose term referring to shakes and vague confusion. It is actually a clear-cut syndrome characterized by increasing agitation, tremor, pallor, greasy sweating, confusion, terror, profound disorientation, and predominantly visual hallucinations. Seizures may or may not have preceded it. The patient with delirium tremens is not easily distracted. Left alone, he converses indefinitely with his hallucinations. He cries out or responds physically or he answers questions like, "where are we?" with "on the dock at the lake." He may pick at the bedsheets, walk continuously, flail his arms and legs, or act combatively.

Delirium tremens is a life-threatening syndrome that may last for several days and for which hospitalization is mandatory. It appears most commonly in patients having other significant medical problems like pancreatitis, post-op status pneumonia, cirrhosis, uncontrolled diabetes, sepsis, or trauma. When fully developed the syndrome and the concomitant illnesses are rarely subtle or difficult to diagnose. Even landladies or neighbors usually recognize that these patients are physically ill as well as mentally disturbed.

The greatest asset in the treatment of delirium tremens is to be anticipatory. When an individual with a known history of alcoholism—especially a patient over 40—develops an infection, suffers trauma, undergoes surgery, or is treated for another significant illness, he should be watched most carefully for the early signs of DT's. If he is confused, tremulous, or agitated, control these symptoms by progressively sedating him—giving large doses of parenteral vitamins. He should avoid overhydration and external stresses.

Follow these guidelines in dealing with delirium tremens:

1. *Reassure and, if necessary, restrain the patient.*

2. *Transfer him quickly to the hospital.* The delirium tremens emergency often develops after the patient has been hospitalized for another reason. If delirium tremens develops at home, the other illness may have progressed untreated so that the patient is in some state like impending vascular collapse. Take him to the hospital for a complete, prompt diagnosis.

3. *Once in the emergency room, ignore the patient's objections to admission.* Someone other than the patient must assume responsibility for admission and information-giving. At this stage, the patient is incompetent and he is headed for a more severe state if untreated. Fortunately, despite strong verbal objections, he usually responds voluntarily to quiet, authoritative direction.

4. *Sedate the patient.* Recommended is chlordiazepoxide (Librium), 100 mg intramuscularly every 2 to 4 hours, with dosage from 50 to 200 mg.

5. *Determine fluid and electrolyte loss and replace as indicated.*

6. *If the delirium continues after 4 to 6 hours out of control, administer sodium amytal 0.25 to 0.5 gm intravenously.* Be careful to give it slowly and only in the presence of equipment for maintaining cardiopulmonary function such as airway, suction pump, respirator, and an intravenous setup through which other medications can be administered rapidly.

7. *Administer magnesium sulfate in 50 percent solution, 2cc intravenously every 6 hours for 24 hours.*

8. *Physical restraints like leather wrist and ankle straps should be used only as last resorts.*

9. *After stabilization, do a thorough history and physical exam.* Be on guard for any infections, including pneumonia. A number of examinations will help: a complete blood count, urinalysis, blood sugar, blood urea nitrogen,

blood alcohol and barbiturate levels, chest x-ray, and skull x-ray.

Alcoholic Dependence

Chronic alcohol dependency—in the form of either plateau or spree drinking—can lead to medical problems of varying seriousness and urgency. These complications or damages fall into five major categories: accidents, bleeding, infections, specific tissue damages, and psychosis.

Managing these complications does not differ substantially from managing the non-alcoholic patient, except for the danger of severe withdrawal syndromes which threaten a patient's chances of survival. Against such odds, it becomes vital to obtain an adequate history and to institute adequate medical management of the acute withdrawal syndromes while treating the complications.

The list of common complications is long, among them: automobile, pedestrian, and household accidents; seizures with fractures; burns; massive gastro-intestinal hemorrhage; respiratory and genito-urinary infections; acute liver insufficiency coma; hypoglycemia; drug overdose; acute cardiac arrhythmias; acute congestive heart failure; and protracted vomiting and/or diarrhea with electrolyte imbalance. Any one of these complications requires hospitalization.

The greatest emergency that occurs in chronic alcoholism is acute cardiac arrythmias and cardiac arrest. This poorly understood phenomenon occurs fast and is usually fatal. All the procedures of acute cardiac rescussitation should be applied, even though they are not usually successful. The individual—especially a male over 45 with or without a history of prior cardiac disease—who experiences persistent pounding tachycardia (120 to 160 beats per minute), with or without premature beats, during the first few days of abstinence is particularly susceptible. He should be given an increased amount of sedation and 200 mg of Dilantin stat, followed by 100 mg four times a day for five days. Only arrythmias of alcohol withdrawal consistently respond to parenteral Vistaril.

Over half of the deaths due to alcoholism occur within the first 36 hours of hospitalization. Emergency workers have two extra responsibilities in dealing with acutely ill alcoholics: they must not overlook major disabilities just because the individual is intoxicated and they must try to obtain and record a detailed, accurate account of the individual's alcohol and drug intake. An admission record merely stating "patient drunk" or "known alcoholic" is not enough. Pertinent details can be invaluable. For example, the record might read: patient consuming X amount of liquor for X days, weeks, months; eating or not eating; taking medications or not; has or has not a history of previous severe withdrawal syndromes.

Associated Problems

Alcohol-Antabuse reactions

Some of the more confusing alcohol-related crisis situations result from the patient's response to a mixture of alcohol and other drugs. Alcohol plus Antabuse (disulfiram) reactions can be fairly critical as well as frightening to the patient. Alcohol consumed by a person taking Temposil (calcium carbamide), Flagyl (metronidazole), or some oral hypoglycemics produces a similar, though less severe reaction.

The presence of these drugs interferes with the complete metabolism of alcohol and leads to large, rapid increases in acetaldehyde, producing dramatic symptoms. The larger the amount of alcohol, the more severe the reaction. Usually, the reaction starts within five to 15 minutes of the first drink. The patient will show most, though not necessarily all, of these symptoms: flushing a slight bluish or dusty red color, mostly on his face, neck, and upper trunk; marked conjunctival injection; distinct smell of acetaldehyde; nausea and vomiting; hypotension; headache; hyperventilation; and chest discomfort and palpitations which are accompanied by feelings of panic and of not being able to breathe, followed by drowsiness.

Patients taking Antabuse may or may not be carrying an Antabuse card. Most are so frightened that they give a reliable history. Occasionally—especially with low dosage of Antabuse, small amounts of alcohol, or the other drugs plus alcohol—the reaction may be milder and the patient does not know what is happening. The milder reaction is easily confused with drug or other allergies.

Follow these guidelines if you suspect drug complications:

1. *Explain to the patient what is happening.* Reassure him there is no cause for alarm if a small amount—a few ounces or less—of alcohol has been taken.

2. *Keep him supine, with legs elevated, and warm.*

3. *Once in the emergency room, give medication based on the severity of the symptoms.* Recommended are 500 cc of normal saline with 500 mg ascorbic acid given intravenously plus intramuscular antihistamine, such as 12 mg of Chlortrimeton, 50 mg of Benadryl or 25 mg of Pyrebencamine to control most of the reaction in an hour or so.

4. *Take necessary anti-shock measures.* Place the patient in a supine position with legs elevated, oxygen, and norepinephrine.

5. *Position the vomiting patient to minimize aspiration.*

6. *If the patient is in respiratory distress, try oxygen by nasal catheter.*

7. *Keep the patient in bed.* Check for hypotension for several hours. If systolic blood pressure drops below 100, additional intravenous fluids may be needed. Severe or protracted reactions may require repeating the intravenous, vitamin C, and antihistamine.

8. *Contact the physician or facility which dispensed the Antabuse.*

Internal bleeding

Alcoholism has a high incidence of cirrhosis of the liver, which can present a common complication of esophagial varices due to portal hypertension. Consequently, alcoholic patients frequently have symptoms of internal bleeding if the varices rupture. Furthermore, since the intoxicated individual is also prone to trauma, you must check out the possibility of other types of internal bleeding, such as genitourinary. Look for these telltale signs of internal bleeding: generalized weakness or prostration, extreme pallor, weak or rapid pulse, hypotension, abdominal pain or tenderness, vomiting of older blood, black and tarry stools, or bright red or dark bloody urine.

Follow these guidelines in dealing with cases of internal bleeding:

1. *Keep the patient quiet, inactive, and warm.*

2. *Start intravenous fluids.*

3. *Type and cross-match for blood transfusions.*

4. *Treat for shock as indicated.*

5. *Determine site and cause of bleeding.*

Traumatic injuries

The alcoholic greatly risks traumatic injury if he becomes intoxicated, unsure on his feet, and disoriented. Since he may be unable to feel or express the site of pain, he must be carefully examined for evidence of any injuries relating to intoxication or withdrawal. Examine him for evidence of skin discoloration, bruises, cuts, and lacerations, with particular attention to the skull. Look at the ears, nose and mouth for signs of bleeding from a head injury. Inability to move either arms or legs properly or unequal size of the pupils may be an indication of injury.

Follow these guidelines in dealing with possible traumatic injury:

1. *Apply direct pressure to the bleeding sites.*

2. *If head injury is suspected, do not move patient except on a stretcher or board, keeping the head as rigid as possible in relation to the rest of the body.*

3. *Call for an ambulance or other professional help, if necessary.*

4. *Once in the emergency room, perform a thorough history and physical examination.*

5. *Take appropriate x-rays.*

6. *Observe the patient for head injuries.*

Methyl alcohol poisoning

Sometimes homeless alcoholics living in a skid-row environment will drink canned heat (Sterno), paint thinner, bay rum, or a harmful hair tonic containing methyl alcohol (wood alcohol). The "squeeze," usually mixed with an inexpensive wine or with a carbonated drink, may cause irreversible blindness, brain damage, or death. The important symptom is a sudden onset of impaired vision.

In the case of wood alcohol poisoning, a life-threatening emergency, the patient should be taken immediately to an emergency room.

Follow these guidelines in dealing with methyl or wood alcohol poisoning:

1. *Protect the patient's eyes from light.*

2. *Perform gastric lavage, with sodium bicarbonate (1 to 3 percent).*

3. *Give an intravenous injection of sodium bicarbonate (5 percent) not exceeding 6 ml per kilogram of body weight slowly over a period of at least 30 minutes.*

4. *For cerebral edema, give intravenous dextrose (50 cc of 50 percent solution).*

Pathologic intoxication

In this uncommon condition, the patient acts wildly uninhibited and frequently assaultive; yet the history reveals that he drank only a small amount of alcohol, usually one or two ounces. Nonetheless, he is to be treated as an assaultive drunk. Pathologic intoxication is thought to be related to a seizure equivalent, as is Jacksonian epilepsy. In addition to follow-up referral, arrange a neurologic consultation.

SUGGESTED READINGS

Gilbert, J. A. L. "Emergency Hospital Alcohol and Drug Admissions in the Province of Alberta." In *Proceedings of the 30th International Congress on Alcoholism Drug Dependence*, edited by Eva Tongue and Zsuzsanna Adler. Lausanne, Switzerland: International Council on Alcohol and Addiction, 1972.

Kaim, S. C., and Klett, C. J. "Treatment of Delirium Tremens, A Comparative Evaluation of Four Drugs." *Quarterly Journal of Studies on Alcohol* 33(1972):1065-72.

Knott, David H.; Beard, James D.; and Fink, Robert D. "Acute Withdrawal from Alcohol." *Emergency Medicine* 6(1974):87.

Mayfield, Demmie G., and Montgomery, Dan. "Alcoholism, Alcohol Intoxication, and Suicide Attempts." *Archives of General Psychiatry* 27(1972):349-53.

National Institute of Mental Health, National Institute on Alcohol Abuse and Alcoholism. *Proceedings: On Alcoholism Emergency Care Services.* Department of Health, Education, and Welfare Publication No. (HSM) 73-9024. Washington, D.C.: U. S. Government Printing Office, 1972.

Rothstein, Emil. "Prevention of Alcohol Withdrawal

Seizures: The Roles of Diphenylhydantoin and Chlordiazepoxide." *American Journal of Psychiatry* 130(1973):12.

Siegel, Harvey H. *Alcohol Detoxification Programs.* Springfield, Ill.: Charles C. Thomas, Publisher, 1973.

Taubenhaus, Leon J. "The Neglected Alcoholic." *Emergency Medicine* 6(1974):97.

V

Acute Reactions from Drug Abuse Problems

John M. Davis, M.D.
John A. Benvenuto, Jr., M.D.

THE PROBLEM

Overdoses of psychotropic drugs cause many health and mental health emergencies. These agents which act on the mind and influence behavior include not only narcotics and other illegal substances, but also prescribed medications such as tranquilizers and sedatives and even over-the-counter drugs like Sominex. The overdoses may occur as a suicide attempt, by accident during periods of confusion or alcoholic intoxication, or simply from unsupervised self-medication. A related tragedy is the accidental poisoning of young children by drugs prescribed for adults in the family. This chapter describes how to recognize and treat overdoses of five different classes of psychotropic drugs: sedatives, stimulants, opiates, psychedelic agents, and volatile inhalants. But before discussing these subjects we shall consider what must always be the first line of defense against this problem—prevention.

The prescribing physician has the primary responsibility of preventing patients from acquiring large amounts of dangerous drugs. Any prescribing of large drug quantities to disturbed patients on an outpatient basis is unwise and unjustifiable. Unfortunately, the potentially lethal dose of some drugs is much lower than many physicians realize. For example, patients with depression are known to be high risks for suicide. In prescribing anti-depressant therapy, the physician should be aware that an overdose—consisting of a normal 10- to 14-day supply of the drug—can be fatal. Consequently, he must decide whether to treat seriously depressed individuals as outpatients. If a responsible relative cannot supervise a drug's administration, admission to a hospital may be preferable. Another problem is that chronic patients receiving long-term drug treatment frequently fail to take the medication regularly. This failure not only deprives them of the drug's therapeutic benefit, but also allows them to accumulate potential supplies for an overdose attempt.

The first rule of prevention is to use caution and common sense in prescribing psychotropic drugs. They are not harmless compounds, especially the newer tranquilizers and anti-depressants about which basic information on toxicity is still being gathered.

Even when a physician makes every effort to prescribe drugs conscientiously, suicide attempts are still possible. Patients can mislead their doctors, and no physician should be so naive as to assume this cannot happen to him. Moreover, patients with chronic anxiety or depression may seek care from two physicians at one time, receiving drug therapy from each.

Impulsive suicide attempts might be discouraged by packaging psychotropic drugs individually. A hundred tablets are easily poured from a bottle and swallowed; it takes more time to take the same number from individual foil wrappers. Also, the use of "child-proof" bottles for drugs offers a hopeful note in reducing accidental drug deaths of children.

A crisis associated with psychotropic drugs may take one of several forms. A patient might be discovered in a comatose or heavily sedated state by a friend, relative, or policeman. Another patient might be highly excited, agitated, or delirious. Or a patient could exhibit psychotic behavior and be out of contact with reality. In many instances, serious physical signs—perhaps hypotension, shock, pulmonary edema, or respiratory failure—may dominate the clinical picture, thus obscuring the underlying cause of the problem.

Often the emergency team can pinpoint drug overdose as the cause of a crisis simply from the history given by a patient. He may admit to drug abuse or say that he has taken medications in a suicide attempt. Important information can also come from relatives or friends, especially when the patient is unable to communicate. Sometimes a suicide note or an open bottle of medication is found at the scene. In these circumstances, if the patient is heavily sedated or comatose, the crisis worker should assume, at least tentatively, that a drug overdose is responsible for the condition. Also remember that drug poisoning frequently occurs in conjunction with alcohol intoxication.

Another source—the patient's local physician—can assist in determining whether drug overdosage is a likely cause of the crisis. He is usually aware of the patient's background and emotional status; above all, he knows which drugs have been prescribed.

ASSESSMENT OF THE CRISIS

The first step in all drug overdosages is to assess the seriousness of the poisoning. The crisis can be classified as one of the following: (1) life-threatening, requiring immediate measures to prevent death; (2) serious, requiring immediate hospitalization for treatment or evaluation; (3) potentially serious, requiring medical care or observation, but not necessarily hospitalization; (4) not immediately dangerous, requiring initial evaluation and then referral to a clinic or other facility.

Coma, respiratory depression, and circulatory failure present the main life-threatening emergencies. Treatment for these dangerous complications must begin as soon as the patient is seen. Classifying the other levels of severity is more difficult. For example, a patient may be somnolent, but in no distress when he is first examined and then may rapidly lapse into a deep coma. What appeared to be a potentially serious problem suddenly becomes a life-threatening emergency. Because the clinical course of drug poisonings is unpredictable, the crisis worker is wise to regard every case as serious unless there is clear evidence to the contrary.

There are some situations, however, where drug ingestion can properly be classified as not immediately dangerous. For instance, if a patient takes five pills that are not very potent in front of his family as a suicide gesture, the problem should not be managed as a medical emergency. In such cases the suicide gesture is more appropriately viewed as a cry for help, necessitating referral to a mental health clinic or other counseling service. If such gestures are ignored, the patient may escalate his suicidal attempts or unknowingly ingest more dangerous drugs.

With the exception of the patient just described, the crisis worker should adopt an *overcautious* attitude in assessing drug overdoses. Every incident should be considered serious until proven otherwise. Take the patient to a medical facility if you suspect his condition might be serious. Even when the poisoning does not seem serious, keep the patient under observation for any changes until the drug effects have worn off. *Deaths occur when the seriousness of the poisoning has been underestimated.*

There is often a tendency in emergency mental health situations to deny or underestimate the seriousness of the medical condition. Personnel with mental health training may see the problem from a psychiatric rather than medical viewpoint and may overlook the physical gravity of a drug poisoning.

Many patients will deliberately take overdoses of drugs and then seek help, even though they are not medically ill at the time. They simply tell their spouse, a policeman, or an emergency worker, "I have just taken pills to kill myself." Because the patient does not seem acutely ill or does not exhibit the symptoms of drug poisoning, the potential danger of the drug ingestion is often minimized or overlooked. Remember, however, it may take several hours—as many as 8 to 24—for a seemingly normal patient to lapse into coma and then die from a drug overdose. Ironically, it is not uncommon for a patient to be sent home from an emergency room because he appears stable, only to die 12 hours later of the drug overdose that brought him to the hospital.

IMMEDIATE MANAGEMENT

Follow these guidelines in dealing with a possible overdose crisis:

1. *If the patient is comatose, establish*

and maintain an open airway and prevent aspiration of vomitus or foreign material.

2. *Induce vomiting particularly if the drug has been ingested within the past two hours.* This course of action depends, however, on where the crisis occurred. If the patient can be brought to a hospital within minutes, this measure is unnecessary for the emergency worker to perform. On the other hand, in an isolated setting where medical care is not promptly available, this treatment is useful. Of course, if the drug has been taken intravenously or by inhalation (sniffing), induced vomiting is meaningless. Nor should vomiting be induced in stuporous patients who may become comatose within minutes; the danger of aspiration of vomitus is too great.

3. *Attempt to identify what medication was taken and, if possible, how much.* Look for pill bottles and check if they are empty. Note and record the prescribing physician's name on the bottle. This information will be useful in determining how to treat the patient since some drugs have specific antidotes or antagonists.

4. *Ask everyone at the scene if they know the person, his friends, or his relatives.* Do they know anything about his medical history? Is he a known drug user? Is he a diabetic? Does he have epilepsy? These facts can help in differentiating drug-induced coma from other medical illnesses.

5. *Arrange for prompt and safe transportation to the hospital.* If the patient is comatose, has respiratory depression or circulatory collapse, or is extremely agitated, he should be closely attended en route. Oxygen and other life-support measures should be available.

6. *If the patient becomes increasingly excited and approaches or reaches a delirious phase, be firm, but friendly in dealing with him.* Some patients will be in an excited phase when the emergency team arrives. This is a common problem with overdoses or amphetamines, antidepressants, and over-the-counter medications containing scopalamine (e.g., Sominex). This excitement period, often a prelude to coma, may last for several hours. If necessary, make proper efforts to restrain the patient and to protect him from himself and try to obtain help, especially en route to the hospital.

EMERGENCY ROOM CARE

The treatment of drug overdoses involves three basic methods: (1) prevention of further absorption, if possible, (2) supportive therapy, and (3) specific antidotal measures. Table 5-1 outlines these methods and possible treatment.

Prevention of further absorption is useful only with poisoning from recently ingested drugs. In the case of conscious patients, induced vomiting—shown to be more effective than gastric lavage—should be attempted when it is possible. But the method should not be used in unconscious patients who may aspirate the vomitus. Another technique for blocking absorption involves the use of activated charcoal, a substance which binds many drugs and can be effective in reducing further absorption. It should be instilled in the stomach with a lavage tube following drug-induced vomiting or gastric aspiration. The use of cathartics to promote excretion of any drug residual is of unproven value. These three conservative measures, combined with careful observations, are usually sufficient in mild drug poisonings.

In more severe cases, the most important aspect of care is supportive treatment. The management of complications associated with large overdoses like coma, shock, or respiratory failure requires skilled medical care. It is important to monitor cardiac function, blood pressure, central venous pressure, respiration, temperature, renal output, level of consciousness, and other parameters of body function. The methods of treatment depend on many factors, with clinical judgment playing an important role.

The toxic effects of certain drugs can be

TABLE 5-1. Treatment of Drug Overdoses

	Basic Method*	Possible Treatment
1.	Prevention of further absorption	induced vomiting gastric lavage cathartics
2.	Supportive treatment of complications	
	Coma	prevention of complications
	Shock	administration of fluids vasopressors steroids
	Respiratory depression or failure	maintenance of clear airway oxygen administration mechanical assistance prevention of complications like pneumonia or atelectasis
	Temperature control	management of hyperthermia or hypothermia
	Renal problems	diuretics preservation of adequate output fluid and electrolyte balance control of convulsions with short-acting barbiturates or diazepam (Valium)
3.	Specific antidotal treatment	promotion of drug excretion antagonistic action biochemical competition

*Under Method 2 (Supportive Treatment), treatment is listed for particular complications like coma or shock.

counteracted by administering agents which have specific antagonistic action (e.g., morphine antagonists). Another antidotal measure involves forced diuresis along with alkalinization of the urine for phenobarbital or acidification of the urine for amphetamines.

SPECIFIC DRUGS AND THEIR TREATMENT

Opiates and Narcotic Analgesics

This group of drugs, the opiates and narcotic analgesics, includes the following:

- Heroin (smack, stuff, scag, dynamite)
- Morphine (white stuff, hard stuff, M, morph)
- Methadone (dolly and dollies)
- Dilaudid (dillies)
- Opium (poppy, black stuff, tar)
- Meperidine (Demerol)
- Paregoric (P.G., P.O., blue velvet)
- Codeine (pop, schoolboy, turp)

While opiates and narcotic analgesics produce euphoria, lethargy, sedation, and pain relief, they may at the same time markedly decrease respiration. An overdose of these drugs can cause death from respiratory failure.

These substances—of which heroin is the most frequently abused—can be injected, ingested orally, or, less frequently, inhaled. The duration of effect varies from 4 to 10 hours. Highly addicting, they can produce tolerance and psychological dependence. Withdrawal symptoms are uncomfortable and can be severe, though they are not usually life-threatening. When opiates and narcotics are sold "on the street," they are frequently altered with other substances so that the actual dose and specific drug is unpredictable. What makes a lethal dose of opiates and narcotics varies according to the patient's age, physical condition, and tolerance to the drug. For example, the risk is greatly increased in the asthmatic patient.

Signs and symptoms of overdose. Symptoms of overdose are related to the amount of drug taken and result from altered function of the autonomic nervous system. The effects of overdose on the central nervous system include the following. Initially, the patient usually exhibits drowsiness (nodding). Periods of euphoria and excitation may be noted during the early stages. With large overdoses, coma can occur. The deep tendon reflexes are depressed and a positive Babinski sign is often present.

The respiratory system is also affected. The rate of respiration is decreased. Cheyne-Stokes breathing may be observed. Death due to apnea may occur 6 to 12 hours after the overdosage.

With respect to the cardiovascular system, the pulse rate and blood pressure are significantly decreased in most instances. Shock may follow. Some patients—particularly heroin or methadone users—may develop acute pulmonary edema.

Itching of the skin is a prominent symptom of overdose, and flushing of the skin is often observed. Needle marks on the skin are *not* a reliable sign since the marks may be cleverly hidden or the drugs may be taken by other routes. The pupils of the eye usually become constricted after narcotic administration, but this is not a dependable diagnostic sign because it varies with individual drugs. With massive overdoses, the pupils may actually be dilated (terminal mydriasis). Loss of appetite, nausea, vomiting, and especially constipation are frequent symptoms.

In the laboratory, opiates and narcotic analgesics can be detected in both blood and urine if the samples are obtained within 8 to 10 hours of the last dose.

Treatment of overdose. In treating an overdose, if there is any evidence of respiratory depression, circulatory failure, or a decreased level of consciousness, life-supporting measures must be initiated immediately. Follow these general guidelines in dealing with opiates and narcotics:

1. ***Clear and establish an airway.***

2. ***Administer oxygen and 5 percent CO_2.*** Some type of ventilatory assistance may be required. The method will depend on the severity of the respiratory depression.

3. ***Support the blood pressure and circulation by means of intravenous fluids and vasopressors, if needed.***

4. ***Determine the level of consciousness repeatedly and attempt to keep the patient aroused.***

5. ***Gastric lavage can be utilized, but only if it has been established that the drug was taken recently and by mouth (not by injection).*** Use saline or another isotonic fluid. After lavage, 15 to 30 grams of sodium sulfate in water (½ to 1 ounce) may be instilled in the stomach for cathartic purposes.

Specific treatment involves the use of narcotic antagonists and respiratory stimulants. Prompt improvement in a patient's clinical condition after the administration of a narcotic antagonist is usually diagnostic of a narcotic overdosage. Lack of a clear response after several trials generally indicates the presence and predominance of other depressant drugs, usually sedatives. Antagonists should be used only when respiratory depression is present.

The drug of choice is naloxone (Narcan), the usual dose being 0.4 mg (1 ml). Intravenous administration is preferable for rapid response, but it also may be given intramuscularly. The calculated dosage is 0.05 mg per kilogram of body weight. A positive response is almost immediate. If the patient's respirations do not improve, the dose may be repeated every 3 minutes for two more times.

Nalorphine (Nalline) and levallorphan (Lorfan), while also effective, are less desirable because—unlike naloxone—they may actually increase respiratory depression if other sedatives are present. Recommended average doses for adults are: Nalline (5 to 10 mg) or Lorfan (1 mg) administered intravenously one to three times (every 15 minutes) as indicated by the patient's response. Since the possibility of further respiratory depression must always be considered, it is safer not to repeat these drugs (unlike naloxone) if the first trial is not successful.

These specific narcotic antagonists may dramatically increase respiration without improving consciousness. The crisis worker should be alerted to the possibility that the patient may become less cooperative when consciousness does return.

In all cases of treatment with narcotic antagonists, patients should be kept under observation for 12 to 24 hours, even if the crisis seems resolved. The activity of these antagonist drugs is of short duration, but long-acting narcotics may last more than 24 hours. There are numerous cases of a patient being discharged in an alert and stable condition and being found comatose 2 or 3 hours later when the effects of the short-acting antagonist had lapsed.

Enlisting respiratory stimulants involves caution, too. For example, doxapram (Dopram), a respiratory stimulant, may be used in the treatment program only if certain specific conditions are satisfied. First, establish clearly that the respiratory depression was produced by a recent overdose of narcotics. Second, never administer this agent without first using a narcotic antagonist; give Dopram only after the antagonist. Third, do not use the drug if a lengthy respiratory depression has created acidosis. Dopram will greatly intensify the acidosis by increasing the metabolic rate in conjunction with a temporary hypertensive effect. Fourth, this respiratory stimulant is contraindicated if pulmonary edema, atelectasis, or pneumonia is involved in the respiratory depression.

If none of these contraindications exist, Dopram can be a very useful, though temporary, agent. By acting rapidly to stimulate deep respirations for several minutes, it allows critical time for specific treatment to be started. When Dopram is used, a brief increase in consciousness as well as a moderate elevation in blood pressure may occur.

If pulmonary edema is present, administer furosemide (Lasix) or ethacrynic acid (Edecrin). Positive pressure breathing may also help this situation.

If the patient fails to respond to the above measures, you should actively investigate other causes of coma and respiratory depression while continuing the support procedures. Do not rule out unlikely circumstances. For instance, a known addict might have meningitis or be in diabetic coma.

Do not use central nervous system stimulants when narcotic overdosage is suspected. Unlike narcotic antagonists or respiratory stimulants, these drugs have no effect on the narcotic depression. In fact, they may confuse the clinical picture.

Withdrawal. An adult patient's physical dependence on opiates and narcotics can introduce signs and symptoms of withdrawal. The clinical picture depends on the degree of physical dependence and ranges from anxiety to a severe condition resembling delirium tremens. Generally the withdrawal state is not a dangerous condition; but—in occasional situations of extreme dependence—hallucinations, convulsions, and coma may occur.

Withdrawal symptoms first appear about 8 hours after the last use of drugs and increase to a peak in 36 to 72 hours, after which they generally subside. The most common complaints are agitation, sleeplessness, chills, muscular discomfort, diarrhea, nausea, and vomiting. These symptoms are usually mild at the beginning, but get worse over the next day or so; this sequence is often diagnostic of withdrawal states. Physical examination may reveal tachycardia, elevated blood pressure, rapid respiration, and temperature elevation. Runny eyes and nose, a gooseflesh appearance, and repeated yawning are also frequently observed.

Withdrawal may require treatment. Generally, symptomatic treatment is sufficient. Long-acting sedatives, such as phenobarbital, or a minor tranquilizer can be given for agitation and anxiety. Chloral hydrate, at bedtime, is useful for insomnia. If vomiting is severe or persistent, prochlorperazine (Compazine) is usually effective. Muscle pain can be relieved with aspirin. When the withdrawal state cannot be controlled with symptomatic measures, more specific therapy is required. This involves substituting the narcotic used with an elixir of methadone, such as Dolophine, in low dosages of 10 to 30 mg twice a day. In severe cases, hospitalization may be necessary for controlled withdrawal and support.

The infant of an addicted mother can also suffer withdrawal because narcotics are transferred across the placental membrane. Indeed, the incidence of passive addiction in infants is on the increase. In most cases the condition is diagnosed and treated in the newborn nursery. Occasionally, however, an infant in withdrawal may reach an emergency medical room.

The severity of the infant's condition—which is the counterpart of the syndrome as seen in adults—generally parallels the extent of the mother's physiologic dependency. However, in contrast to adults, significant mortality and morbidity occur even in treated cases. Such infants should be hospitalized for controlled treatment.

The infant will show multiple signs of central nervous system irritability—including hyperactivity, a shrill cry during waking periods and, not uncommonly, respiratory distress and convulsions. Vomiting, diarrhea, and dehydration as well as frequent periods of tremors, flushing, and fever may also be present. These infants usually have a low weight for their gestational age and frequently also show the effects of inadequate maternal prenatal care.

Infants with withdrawal findings should be hospitalized for treatment for a gradual withdrawal regime.

Other medical conditions related to narcotic abuse. Because the narcotic life-style is frequently associated with poor health maintenance and care, the drug abuser often has significant medical problems resulting from or concurrent with his abuse. Once the initial emergency condition has been treated, the patient should be examined for the following conditions prior to discharge: (1) trauma and body injury, particularly to the head; (2) localized infections, abscesses, and hematoma at the sites where substances may have been injected; (3) pneumonia; (4) severe allergic reactions to the variety of injected foreign matter; (5) acute septicemia, possibly with endocarditis ("cotton fever"); (6) hepatitis; and (7) passive infant addiction in pregnant addicts.

Central Nervous System (CNS) Depressants

This class includes barbiturates, nonbarbiturate sedatives, minor tranquilizers and, in a broader sense, major tranquilizers, and lithium. These depressants produce generalized and progressive depression of the central nervous system (CNS). The depression is characterized by lethargy, sedation, and sleep, but the depressive effects may be preceded by a varying period of excitation. Persons abusing these substances frequently seek the effect of disinhibition. Excessive dosages lead to coma and death from respiratory failure. The effects of most CNS depressants are additive so that repeated use can lead to physical and psychological dependence. These substances are usually ingested, but they can be injected. Most of the drugs in this category have cross-tolerance and cross-dependence, i.e., one drug can be substituted for another to forestall withdrawal symptoms.

By far, the most common and dangerous pattern of use is the combination of barbiturates and alcohol, which can easily produce a lethal overdose. Withdrawal from these drugs is also dangerous, unlike narcotic withdrawal, and the withdrawal symptoms are characteristically different. Each of the drugs will be considered separately in the following pages.

Barbiturates

The most frequently used drugs in suicide attempts and the most common cause of drug fatalities are barbiturates. In addition, barbiturate overdoses are often taken by accident because of confusion or alcoholic intoxication. These dangers, coupled with the threat of barbiturate addiction, should make physicians extremely cautious about prescribing barbiturates. It is advisable to limit each prescription to *a total of no more than 1 gram of barbiturate*—the equivalent of 10 hypnotic doses. Even this amount—particularly in combination with alcohol—can produce a coma and be fatal in the absence of prompt medical care. With larger doses, death can occur, even with treatment of the poisoning. The potentially lethal dose of short-acting barbiturates like amobarbital (Amytal), pentobarbital (Nembutal), or secobarbital (Seconal) is 3 grams. Long-acting barbiturates like phenobarbital (Luminal) are generally less toxic (6 to 9 grams). The clinical picture and prognosis depend largely on the concentration of barbiturate in the blood. When the serum level exceeds 2 to 3 mg/100 ml with short-acting barbiturates or 8 to 12 mg/100 ml with long-acting agents, dialysis or a similar other method to remove the drug from the system may be considered.

Signs and symptoms of overdose. In a barbiturate overdose situation, the patient may be very drowsy and speak indistinctly or he may be stuporous or profoundly comatose—depending on the extent of the overdose. Respiration is usually slow and labored because of medullary depression. The blood pressure is generally low and shock may be evident. Renal function is frequently depressed and acute renal failure may develop. Occasionally, false localizing neurological findings—such as absent deep tendon reflexes or a positive Babinski sign—may prompt the emergency team to assume that the patient has experienced a stroke, especially if a definite history of barbiturate ingestion is unobtainable.

Since barbiturate overdose symptoms resemble those for other types of poisoning, the crisis worker must be alert to deceptive appearances. The patient, seemingly in an alcoholic stupor or with signs of opiate overdosage, might have taken an overdose of barbiturates. Furthermore, a second problem can exist: illicit opiates are sometimes "cut" with barbiturates so that both forms of toxicity may be simultaneously present.

Laboratory methods are available for the quantitative assay of barbiturates in the blood. These determinations are helpful in confirming the diagnosis and, to a lesser degree, in planning the therapy.

Treatment of overdose. Except in instances of huge overdoses, most patients will recover with supportive care alone: maintenance of a clear airway, oxygen administration and, if needed, ventilatory assistance; correction of hypotension; proper hydration and electrolyte balance; preservation of renal function; control of body temperature; and conscientious nursing care to prevent complications, particularly in comatose patients.

If measures are necessary beyond general supportive care, follow these specific guidelines in dealing with barbiturate overdose:

*1. **If the overdose was taken recently, try to prevent further absorption of the drug.*** Use only simple aspiration without lavage because full-scale lavage can wash more drug into the system.

2. *The urinary excretion of some barbiturates such as phenobarbital can be increased by forced diuresis and by alkalinization of the urine (to a pH of greater than 7.8).* However, the effectiveness of this treatment varies with different drugs. For instance, forced diuresis and alkalinization of urine are valuable for phenobarbital overdoses, but less so for other barbiturates. Also, alkalinization is not helpful in treating poisonings from short-acting barbiturates. Since barbiturates stimulate the production of anti-diuretic hormone (ADH), forced diuresis can be done by the combined use of furosemide (Lasix) and mannitol. Alkalinization is achieved with sodium bicarbonate.

3. *In cases of severe barbiturate poisoning, supportive care together with the treatment just described may not be sufficient so that dialysis becomes necessary.* Hemodialysis is claimed to be 30 times more effective than forced diuresis in removing barbiturates from the body. However, it is also claimed that conservative therapy methods produce equal results.

Non-barbiturate sedatives

These hypnotics include the following:

- Doriden
- Quaalude
- Placidyl
- Noludar
- Chloral hydrate

They can be just as dangerous as barbiturates, if not more so. While these drugs are not barbiturates, any distinction is meaningless from a clinical standpoint since they produce similar symptoms. Overdoses of such sedatives can lead to coma, respiratory depression, and death.

Glutethimide (Doriden) is of special concern because it is more toxic than bartiburates. The fatal dose—about 10 grams—is only 10 or 20 times the usual nightly dose. Since diagnosing and treating overdoses of the other non-barbiturate hypnotics are the same as for barbiturate poisoning, the following discussion is limited to glutethimide toxicity.

Signs and symptoms of overdose. The clinical picture of glutethimide poisoning resembles that of barbiturate overdosage, but the atropine-like effect of glutethimide produces additional findings: dilated pupils, urinary retention, dry mouth, and atony of the bowel. More seriously, laryngeal spasm and sudden apnea may occur. Furthermore, coma with glutethimide lasts longer than with barbiturate poisoning, with the respiratory distress often overshadowed by cardiac failure.

In the laboratory, blood levels of glutethimide correlate poorly with coma or other serious manifestations of overdoses; they should not be considered prognostic determinants.

Treatment of overdose. Supportive measures for treating this problem are the same as for barbiturate overdoses. Bear in mind, however, the clinical course is unpredictable; sudden deterioration occurs unexpectedly in some patients.

In specific treatment procedures, forced diuresis and alkalinization of urine are of little value, nor do they enhance excretion of the drug. The effectiveness of dialysis is limited by the protein binding of the drug and by its storage in body fat. It has been suggested that lipid dialysis may be beneficial, but the value of this technique has not been clearly confirmed.

Minor tranquilizers

Minor tranquilizers include the following:

Benzodiazipine Derivatives
- Chlorodiazepoxide (Librium)
- Diazepam (Valium)
- Oxazepam (Serax)

Meprobamate
- Equanil
- Miltown

Benzodiazipine derivatives are the most frequently used minor tranquilizers or anti-anxiety agents. Relatively benign in their dosage toxicity, the derivatives generally produce no more than drowsiness or ataxia, though a mild, short-lived coma may occur rarely. Even with huge overdoses—for example, greater than 2000 mg of Librium—patients have survived. For a generally uncomplicated clinical course, only supportive care is needed. In fact, overzealous treatment may produce more serious complications than the effect of the overdose itself. But when minor tranquilizers are taken together with other more serious drugs, the problem becomes complex. Meprobamate—for example, Equanil or Miltown—intoxication is more dangerous than the benzodiazipines. Sixteen fatal cases have been reported by Davis et al.[1]

Signs and symptoms of overdose. Overdoses of meprobamate are characterized by coma, hypotension, slow pulse rate, and low body temperature. These effects are partly due to the drug's muscle-relaxing properties. Occasionally, paradoxical excitement and seizures may be noted. The most serious complications are shock, pulmonary edema, and atelectasis, although acute tubular necrosis can develop from prolonged hypotension.

Meprobamate can be detected and measured in the urine and blood, although neither test is commonly performed. Blood levels of about 10 mg/100 ml are thought to be associated with deep coma.

Treatment of overdose. Managing an overdose of meprobamate is similar to the treatment for barbiturates. In most cases, a conservative approach of nursing care and surveillance leads to a complete recovery. Severe neurological depression or hypotension, however, requires additional measures, including mechanical assistance for respiration.

The excretion of meprobamate can be significantly increased by forced osmotic diuresis—using 20 percent mannitol intravenously at a rate of 50 ml per hour. The rate of disappearance of meprobamate from the blood is three to seven times faster than that of barbiturates or glutethimide (Doriden). This is noteworthy in terms of the incidence of complications and the likelihood of death.

Major tranquilizers

Major tranquilizers include the following:

Phenothiazine Derivatives
- Chlorpromazine (Thorazine)
- Acetophenazine (Tindal)
- Fluphenazine (Prolixin and Permitil)
- Promazine (Sparine)
- Prochlorperazine (Compazine)
- Perphenazine (Trilafon)
- Serentil
- Thioridazine (Mellaril)
- Trifluoperazine (Stelazine)

Thioxanthene Derivatives
- Chlorprothixine (Taractan)
- Thiothixene (Navane)

Butyrophenone Derivative
- Haloperidol (Haldol)

These tranquilizers, used primarily for the treatment of psychotic disorders, are less lethal than opiates, barbiturates, and non-barbiturate sedatives. Most antipsychotic agents are phenothiazine derivatives, chlorpromazine (Thorazine) being the prototype. While poisoning does occur, death from overdose is almost unknown in adults and rare in children.

In clinical practice, the total dose of chlorpromazine can range from as low as 150 mg per day to as much as 4,000 mg per day for severe psychotic states. This indicates a wide margin of safety. Nevertheless, scattered reports have been made of sudden death during prolonged high dosage phenothiazine therapy

---

1. J. M. Davis, E. Bartlett, and B. A. Termini, "Overdosage of Psychotropic Drugs: A Review. I. Major and Minor Tranquilizers." *Diseases of the Nervous System* 29(1968):157.

among patients in mental hospitals. Presumably, these fatalities resulted from drug-induced cardiac arrhythmias, although this effect is not clearly understood. On the other hand, suicide attempts with chlorpromazine seem to carry a relatively benign prognosis. Thioridazine (Mellaril) also appears safe in this regard. Even less dangerous in suicide attempts are the piperazine side-chain phenothiazines, such as trifluoperazine (Stelazine) and perphenazine (Trilafon); no deaths from these drugs have been reported in adults and few in children. Haloperidol (Haldol) overdoses have produced no reported fatalities.

Signs and symptoms of overdose. Major tranquilizers can produce sedation, drowsiness, or light coma. The blood pressure may fall and the pulse rate increases; in some cases, hypothermia occurs. These effects, however, are seldom lethal. In addition, many patients develop symptoms caused by extrapyramidal tract stimulation: twitching, generalized muscle contractions (dystonia); rigidity of the neck muscles (torticollis) or extremities; and oculogyric crisis. These discomforting symptoms may stem from an extrapyramidal side effect, which can occur from small doses as well as excessive dosage associated with suicide attempts or accidental poisonings. It should be kept in mind that phenothiazines are frequently used as antiemetic agents and, further, that the extrapyramidal side effect may also occur with these drugs. Seizures can also occur.

When there is uncertainty about the diagnosis, laboratory methods are available for detecting phenothiazines in the urine.

Treatment of overdose. Follow these guidelines in dealing with overdoses of major tranquilizers:

1. *Since patients with phenothiazine or other major tranquilizer poisoning rarely become deeply comatose or develop respiratory or cardiac failure, overdoses of these drugs are not as serious as those involving opiates or barbiturates.* Supportive measures will be required for some patients, however. Prolonged hypotension can lead to acute tubular necrosis. If blood pressure support is necessary, use levarterenol (Levophed). Epinepherine should never be used because it will produce further fall in blood pressure.

2. *Cardiac monitoring may be required, particularly if an arrhythmia is evident from a physical examination or a routine electrocardiogram.* In one case, a cautious resident physician decided to admit a patient for observation following thioridazine (Mellaril) ingestion. Shortly after admission the patient developed a lethal arrhythmia and was resuscitated. The action saved the patient.

3. *Gastric lavage, with the addition of charcoal and exchange resins, can be useful—even late in the course—by absorbing any drug remaining in the stomach or bowel.*

4. *Forced diuresis or hemodialysis is not effective in increasing the elimination of the drug since these agents are bound to proteins in the blood.*

5. *Extrapyramidal symptoms can usually be anticipated.* Treatment consists of either (1) intravenous or intramuscular benztropine (Cogetin) in 2-mg doses or (2) an intravenous antihistamine, such as diphenyldramine (Benadryl), given intravenously in a dose of 50 mg. Symptoms will usually be controlled by either method within 1 minute after intravenous administration or 5 to 15 minutes after intramuscular use.

6. *If seizures occur, treat them in the manner prescribed for seizures resulting from withdrawal from CNS depressants (see page 93).*

Lithium

Lithium includes the following:

- Eskalith

- Lithane
- Lithonate

Used to control the manic phase of manic-depressive psychosis, lithium is just beginning to have wide use as a psycho-pharmacological agent. Although the true incidence of poisoning is still uncertain, it is well known that lithium has a very narrow margin of safety; therapeutic doses do approach the toxic range. The drug's greatest danger is the adverse effects which overdoses can have on the central nervous system.

Signs and symptoms of overdose. In a lithium overdose situation, the level of consciousness is usually impaired, with coma frequently developing. Other neurological findings include hypertonic or rigid muscles with hyperactive deep tendon reflexes; muscle tremors or fasciculations; spontaneous attacks of hyperextension of the extremities, often accompanied by wide opening of the eyes, grunts and grasping; and epileptic seizures. Transient asymmetrical neurological findings can occur. In addition to these central nervous system signs, pulmonary complications are seen in the form of pneumonia or atelectasis.

Lithium levels in the blood can be measured by a simple photometric method. Serial determinations should be made during the course of treatment because a close correlation exists between blood levels and toxicity. Levels of less than 2.0 mEq/liter are usually safe, while levels above 2.5 mEq/liter are associated with severe reactions.

Treatment of overdose. The two most important concerns in treatment of lithium overdosage are the management of coma and the prevention of pneumonia. Survival depends mainly on the quality of nursing care. Follow these guidelines in dealing with lithium overdosage:

1. No specific antidote for lithium poisoning (other than dialysis) is known. Neither sodium chloride nor potassium chloride has proved effective in producing rapid clinical improvement or in reducing blood lithium levels.

2. Use aminophylline, osmotic diuretics (mannitol or urea) and sodium lactate to promote lithium excretion, if necessary.

3. With severe toxicity, dialysis is indicated. But proceed cautiously because serum lithium levels may rebound after discontinuance of the dialysis due to redistribution of lithium from tissue stores.

Withdrawal from CNS depressants

Many CNS depressants (including barbiturates, non-barbiturate sedatives, and minor tranquilizers) have addictive properties; consequently, abrupt cutoff of these drugs could produce withdrawal symptoms. Unlike narcotic withdrawal which is seldom dangerous, withdrawal from these depressants can be potentially lethal. Most patients who develop this withdrawal syndrome should be hospitalized for treatment. The anti-psychotic drugs and lithium do not present withdrawal symptoms.

There is often a history of prior use of the drug and it is reasonable to assume that the last dose was taken up to 48 to 72 hours before the appearance of symptoms. The clinical picture varies with the dosage and the length of prior use. Symptoms can range from anxiety and sleeplessness through agitation to delerium. The most dangerous features of withdrawal are postural hypotension, high fever, and major convulsions.

Administering supportive treatment is difficult because of the severity of symptoms (e.g., agitation and convulsions) and because of the profound sleep and dream disturbances accompanying the process.

Follow these guidelines in dealing with CNS depressant withdrawal:

1. In the emergency situation—when tremors, convulsions, hyperpyrexia, and postural hypotension are present—phenobarbital can be injected intramuscularly in a dose of 200 mg.

This is almost always effective and can be repeated later if necessary. The barbiturate phenobarbital is a well-accepted drug for replacement because of its well-maintained dose level and of its relatively high margin of safety.

2. *An alternative emergency procedure is to administer diazepam (Valium) intravenously to control convulsions or a preconvulsive state.* The injected dose of Valium is usually 5 to 10 mg (1-2 ml). It should be injected slowly, taking at least 1 minute for every 5 mg.

3. *Once the crisis is under control, phenobarbital is then given orally as a substitute for the previous drug.* The dosage must be titrated to alleviate symptoms. Gradually this substitute is withdrawn by decreasing the oral phenobarbital by 30 mg each day.

CNS Stimulants and Anti-Depressants

Three general classes of drugs are used as anti-depressants: (1) psychomotor stimulants, (2) tricyclic anti-depressants, and (3) monoamine oxidase inhibitors. Because the actions, side effects, and withdrawal symptoms differ to some degree, each class will be considered separately.

Psychomotor stimulants

These stimulants include the following:

- Amphetamine (Benzedrine)
- Dextroamphetamine (Dexedrine)
- Methamphetamine (Desoxyn)
- Phenmetrazine (Preludin)
- Methylphenidate (Ritalin)

The illegally used drug cocaine (snow) also produces psychomotor stimulation.

Agents in this class are often taken to combat fatigue and sleepiness, or to provide a feeling of exhilaration and increased energy. As they act on the central nervous system, these stimulants produce symptoms of sympathetic nervous system stimulation. The doses can vary widely, with effects ranging from mild excitation to severe psychotic episodes which follow prolonged high doses or intravenous use. Tolerance to these drugs develops rapidly so that psychological dependence is not uncommon. On the other hand, true physical dependence with a distinct abstinence syndrome has not been clearly demonstrated to date. It is known, however, that stimulation and excitation are shortly followed by a stage of physical and mental depression ("crashing"). Because of these qualities, intermittent use is most common. The duration of effects lasts from 4 to 24 hours, depending upon the substance. Most of the drugs in this group are taken orally, but the sniffing of cocaine and intravenous use of amphetamines occur frequently. These latter routes may produce death. In fact, amphetamines have a relatively wide safety margin—with only a few deaths attributed to overdoses. In these cases the lethal dose varied greatly. Survival, for example, has been reported after a massive 500-mg dose of amphetamines. Death can also occur with cocaine overdosage. Although the lethal dose of cocaine is unknown, it is probably about 1.2 grams.

Signs and symptoms of overdose. Among the symptoms which amphetamines produce, the most prominent involve the central nervous system. Patients may describe signs of wakefulness, irritability, agitation, or belligerence, often alternating with euphoria, excessive confidence, confusion, or panic. With prolonged high-dosage use, convulsions and hallucinations—auditory, visual, and tactile—may occur. During the depression period which follows, suicidal behavior may be present. Gastrointestinal symptoms—including dry mouth, nausea, vomiting, diarrhea—can occur. Patients with coronary disease often experience angina. Arrhythmias, too, are noted. Hyperthermia (temperatures of 104° to 110°F) can occur, necessitating immediate cooling with ice packs.

Patients with cocaine intoxication are usually confused, paranoid, anxious, excited, or delirious. Convulsions are common. The cocaine may produce circulatory collapse. When death does occur, it usually results from the depression of vital medullary centers and from respiratory failure. Adequate oxygenation is important in treatment.

Recently developed laboratory techniques allow identification of these drug substances from urine specimens.

Treatment of overdose. Follow these guidelines in dealing with an overdose of psychomotor stimulants:

1. *The first concern is to reassure and calm the agitated or paranoid patient.* Put him in a quiet place where he can be observed, but also have minimal interaction. If active treatment is necessary, try to lessen the chance of paranoid reaction by informing the patient before each step.

2. *Be prepared to deal with patients who often become panicky and who actively resist all treatment efforts.*

3. *If the history or symptoms indicate a large and relatively recent overdose, try gastric lavage or inducement of vomiting because a number of these drugs have delayed gastrointestinal emptying time.*

4. *In severe cases of amphetamine overdose, give ammonium chloride to acidify the urine and increase urinary excretion.* Forced osmotic diuresis may also be used. Dialysis can be used in severe cases.

5. *If severe aggressive behavior or life-threatening symptoms are observed, one of several medications may be employed to combat the crisis: haloperidol (Haldol) or chlorpromazine (Thorazine).*

Pharmacologic reasons support the choice of haloperidol (Haldol) as a treatment for pure amphetamine intoxication. The customary dose is 1 to 5 mg intramuscularly; it can be repeated in 60 minutes, if necessary. Since haloperidol may be a specific antidote for any of the pharmacologic actions of amphetamines, it is indicated in many cases of known amphetamine ingestion.

An alternative drug proposed for treating pure amphetamine overdose is chlorpromazine (Thorazine). The customary dose in this circumstance is 25 to 50 mg, given intramuscularly, with repeat doses of 25 to 50 mg every 2 hours when clinically indicated. Patients receiving chlorpromazine must be monitored for hypotensive reactions. There is some concern that Thorazine may actually intensify psychotic symptoms if other psychomimetic agents are involved in the poisoning. Specifically, chlorpromazine is said to aggravate STP (or anticholinergic) poisoning.

Therefore, when the exact agent causing the poisoning is unknown, it is often advisable to use either no medications or diazepam. Diazepam (Valium) can be used either orally or intramuscularly to control marked agitation. The initial dose is usually 20 to 25 mg, supplemented by additional doses of 5 to 10 mg every 2 hours, according to the clinical response.

Withdrawal. Abrupt termination after prolonged chronic use or large single doses can produce withdrawal symptoms within 2 to 12 hours, depending on the substance. Initially there may be lethargy alternating with periods of easily provoked aggressive behavior, then exhaustion, followed by a deep sleep lasting as long as 2 days. After awakening, the patient may experience varying degrees of sleep disturbance along with retarded or agitated depression associated with suicidal tendencies. This emotional and somatic depression may last for several weeks.

Follow these guidelines in dealing with withdrawal from psychomotor stimulants:

1. *In cases of moderate severity, observation and supportive measures—such as balanced food and fluid intake and rest—are sufficient to*

manage the problem. Sedatives for sleep disturbances may be used.

2. *In cases of prolonged, heavy abuse, a regime of gradual withdrawal with decreasing doses of amphetamines over 10 days to 2 weeks will prevent restlessness, disquiet, and "crashing."* Diazepam (Valium) in oral doses of 20 to 25 mg is effective for agitation and anxiety following acute withdrawal.

3. *If the post-withdrawal depression is severe or protracted, prescribe tricyclic anti-depressants such as imipramine (Tofranil) or amitriptyline (Elavil).* Do not forget to keep these patients under surveillance for any suicidal tendencies during their cycles of deep depression.

Tricyclic anti-depressants

These anti-depressants include the following:

- Imipramine (Tofranil)
- Amitriptyline (Elavil)
- Desipramine (Norpramin and Pertofrane)
- Nortriptyline (Aventyl)
- Protriptyline (Vivactil)
- Doxepin (Sinequan)

These drugs are effective in treating moderate and severe depressive illness. Since suicidal tendencies are high in depressed patients, the risk of deliberate overdosage must always be considered. Many adverse reactions are associated with their overdose, several of which can lead to death. In one study the average fatal dose of imipramine (Tofranil) was 3619 mg—the equivalent of 14 days of treatment at usual doses. In general, the lethal dose is 10 to 30 times the normal daily dose.

Signs and symptoms of overdose. The clinical symptoms of tricyclic anti-depressant poisoning differ significantly from the general depression of CNS activity caused by barbiturates. For example, clouding of consciousness and confusion is not always the case in early cases; instead, agitation, delirium, or hypomania may be evident. As a matter of fact, deaths have occurred from cardiac arrhythmias without any marked depression of consciousness. However, in severe cases, drowsiness and disorientation are usually noticeable within a few hours. These symptoms can progress to coma, accompanied by respiratory and vasomotor depression. Hyperreflexia may precede the development of hypotonia. Grand mal seizures are not uncommon. In addition to the CNS effects, tachycardia and hypotension usually develop, often in association with arrhythmias or heart block. Temperature regulation is also disturbed, with hypothermia more common than hyperthermia. Peripheral anticholinergic signs also occur like hot, dry skin; dilated pupils; and tachycardias.

Death usually results from arrhythmias. Evidence points to tricyclic drugs having a direct toxic effect on the myocardium. The effect results in decreased cardiac output, a fall in blood pressure, and a variety of extremely dangerous arrhythmias, e.g., ventricular tachycardia and ventricular fibrillation. Prevention and control of the arrhythmia is most important in treatment.

For confirmation of symptoms urinary screening methods from the laboratory are currently available.

Treatment of overdose. Since the direct cause of death from tricyclic drug overdoses is usually cardiovascular collapse, every effort must be made to reduce the heart's work load and prevent or control the arrhythmias. Intensive medical care and continuous cardiac monitoring are important. The management of coma and respiratory failure presents less of a problem with these drugs than with barbiturates or opiates. Coma is seldom deep so that most patients are easily arousable.

Follow these guidelines in dealing with tricyclic anti-depressant overdoses:

1. *Initiate continuous cardiac monitoring.*

2. *One approach to prevent or control the cardiovascular complications of overdoses is to counteract rapid heart rates—caused by the anticholinergic action of the tricyclic antidepressants—with antagonistic drugs.* Good results have been reported with pyridostigmine (Mestinon), using 1 mg every 4 hours. However, an intravenous dose of 1 to 4 mg of physostigmine (Esserine) appears to have a broader action, controlling both central and peripheral anticholinergic effects. It reverses the anticholinergic component of the tricyclics. This agent is capable of reducing the heart rate and improving cerebral function; it can reverse coma from tricyclic compounds as well as other anticholinergic agents such as atropine and scopalamine, which also act as central nervous system depressants. Its short duration of action of only a few hours, though, make repeated doses necessary. Since overdose of physostigmine produces a cholinergic crisis, it should only be used by someone familiar with its pharmacology and should be used only for severe tricyclic poisoning.

3. *Once the poisoning is identified, 200 to 300 mg Dilantin can be administered intravenously, followed by doses of 100 mg every 4 to 6 hours.* Diphenylhydantoid (dilantin) has been used successfully to prevent both cardiac arrhythmias and cerebral dysfunction. Since plasma Dilantin levels above 10 nanograms per liter are necessary, oral usage is inadvisable. Also, rapid intravenous injections of Dilantin are dangerous. Therefore, the drug should be given in increments of 50 to 100 mg over 5-minute periods until a response is obtained or the total dosage reaches 300 mg (in an average-sized person), or, more exactly, a plasma level of 18 nanograms per milliliter. The rate of injection should not exceed 50 mg per minute. Cardiac monitoring is essential with intravenous Dilantin therapy.

4. *Propranolol is sometimes useful.*

5. *If ventricular arrhythmias develop, lidocaine should be used.* The value of digitalis in this setting is uncertain.

6. *Convulsions or established status epilepticus can usually be managed with intravenous diazepam (Valium) in doses of 5 to 10 mg.* At times, paraldehyde may also be needed. A 5-mg intramuscular dose of diazepam, as well as phenobarbital, has been suggested to prevent seizures.

7. *Although no effective way to increase the elimination of tricyclic drugs from the body is yet known, activated charcoal or ion exchange resins can be used in a gastric lavage mixture to absorb any of the drug still in the bowel.* The traditional methods of hemodialysis, peritoneal dialysis, or forced diuresis are of little value.

8. *Since prolonged hypotension may lead to acute tubular necrosis, if urinary output is diminished in the early stages of the poisoning, mannitol can be attempted.* However, this osmotic diuretic increases venous pressure and may intensify cardiac complications.

9. *If agitation, hypomania, and paranoid behavior are observed when the patient regains consciousness, a minor tranquilizer such as diazepam (Valium) can generally control most of these symptoms.* These problems are usually transitory so that a conservative approach to their management is recommended. In theory, phenothiazines should not be used at this stage because, having a structure similar to the tricyclic compounds, they can produce arrhythmias in their own right. Physogligine is useful when anticholinergic symptoms are present but should only be used in very severe cases.

10. *Even when the immediate crisis appears controlled, surveillance should be continued.* Presumably, the cardiac dysfunction produced by the tricyclic drugs may persist after the period of coma. Deaths have even been reported several days after apparent recovery. Cardiac

monitoring should be continued for several days and the patient should be kept in bed. Supervision is important during the patient's gradual return to full physical activity. It is not unusual for arrhythmias to develop 12 to 24 hours after the patient has come out of a coma.

Monoamine oxidase inhibitors

Monoamine oxidase inhibitors include the following:

- Phenelzine (Nardil)
- Tranylcypromine (Parnate)
- Isocarboxazid (Marplan)
- Nialamide (Niamid)

Deaths due to *monoamine oxidase (MAO) inhibitors* have been reported much less frequently than those due to the tricyclic compounds, possibly because the former agents are used less in treating depression. MAO inhibitors produce many side-effects, even with customary therapeutic doses. Most important, their interaction with exogenous amines—mainly tyramine—in food or drugs causes sudden, severe hypertension. These hypertensive crises are precipitated by cheese and foods capable of releasing large amounts of norepinephrine as well as by drugs like ephedrine or "cold medications." Lethal doses vary considerably. For example, with tranylcypromine (Parnate), death has been reported with a dose of 170 mg while a patient who ingested 350 mg survived.

Signs and symptoms of overdose. In addition to hypertension, patients often develop anxiety, agitation, hyperactivity, and hallucinations. Hypertermia with excessive sweating is often noted with overdoses. The temperature may register within the 105° to 110°F range, constituting a medical emergency and necessitating immediate treatment with ice packs and other cooling measures. There is often a delay of up to 12 hours after the tablets have been ingested before symptoms of overdose occur. During this time the patient is relatively asymptomatic. Indeed, patients have been presented to the emergency room during this lag period and have been sent home because they showed no symptoms. Later, the symptoms became apparent, and the patients died.

Detection methods for MAO inhibitors are not generally available.

Treatment of overdose. Overall, if no other drugs have been taken in conjunction with MAO inhibitors, it is best to manage these cases conservatively.

Follow these specific guidelines in dealing with an overdose of MAO inhibitors:

1. *If tranquilizers are needed to control anxiety, agitation, and other symptoms, give only small doses.* Bear in mind that MAO inhibitors also inhibit the enzymes which metabolize these other drugs. Chlorpromazine may be useful, but should be used cautiously.

2. *Acidification of urine and forced osmotic (mannitol) diuresis will enhance the excretion of tranylcypromine (Parnate) and phenelzine (Nardil).* With severe overdoses, hemodialysis may be useful.

3. *Hypertensive crises are best managed with alpha-blocking agents Regitine.* Never use reserpine to control this type of hypertension. Since reserpine depends on monoamine oxidase for its hypotensive action, its use may make the situation worse.

4. *Patients with MAO inhibitor overdosage should not receive meperidine (Demerol) or tricyclic anti-depressants.* The drugs interact—probably through the medium of brain serotonin—to produce extremely high temperature elevations. Patients who have taken an overdose of MAO inhibitors and also an overdose of meperidine (Demerol) or a tricyclic anti-depressant can develop an overdose syndrome very similar to that exhibited with an overdose of MAO inhibitors alone, namely, hyperpyrexia with temperatures of 105° to

110°F. This condition constitutes an acute medical emergency; the patient's body temperature should be cooled to the normal range with ice packs and other cooling methods immediately. Chlorpromazine administered intramuscularly may also be helpful.

Hallucinogens and Psychedelics

This category of natural and synthetic drugs is broad:

- Lysergic acid diethylamide (LSD)
- Mescaline or peyote (buttons, cactus)
- Psilogybin (magic mushrooms)
- Dimethyltryptamine (DMT or businessman's trip)
- Phencyclidine (PCP, peace pill, Sernyl)
- Dimethoxymethylamphetamine (STP, DOM)
- Cannabis/marijuana/hashish (grass, THC, weed, gold)
- Nutmeg and mace (spice, musket balls)
- Morning glory seeds (heavenly blue, flower power)

Such a large group produces a wide range of symptoms—with emphasis on the psychological and perceptual rather than the physical. In fact, a severe reaction is generally viewed as an acute drug abuse problem or a toxic reaction rather than as a true overdose.

How durable, potent, and intense the effect is varies markedly with each drug and with the individual user. One person can even experience wide variations at different times. The range of drug action within this class can be as short as an hour to as long as 48 hours. These drugs are usually ingested or inhaled, but some may be injected.

Tolerance is believed to develop with some of these drugs, particularly LSD. Psychological dependence occurs in some highly suggestible individuals, but any specific physical dependence and abstinence syndrome has not been demonstrated.

While drugs of this class act predominantly on the central nervous system, autonomic nervous system effects can complicate the picture. In general, though, they produce a clinical picture of delirium with hallucinations, and illusions, with frequently bewildering disturbances in perception and proprioception. The drugs are difficult to identify or differentiate by sight so that the user is often unaware of which one he has actually used. This adds to the characteristic unpredictability of effects in this drug class. Consequently, overdose or toxic reaction to specific drugs is not easily diagnosed.

Signs and symptoms of overdose. There are no specific physical signs indicative of a toxic reaction to psychedelic drugs. Although some patients may exhibit dilated pupils, alterations in blood pressure, increased heart rate, impaired coordination, and possibly nausea and vomiting, these signs are too vague for diagnosis. Therefore, a history of hallucinogenic drug use by the patient is essential to diagnosis.

Symptoms described by the patient can range from euphoric expansiveness and flight of ideas to illusions and hallucinations, usually visual rather than auditory. A crisis situation is often created when the patient begins to feel that the experience is out of control and unending. He reports fearfulness, agitation, depersonalization, terrifying hallucinations and severe or violent panic—signs resembling an acute psychotic-like reaction. This severe condition can lead to desperate behavior, including suicidal.

At present, there are no generally available or reliable laboratory tests for detecting this class of drugs.

Treatment of overdose. In most cases, the best treatment is simply careful reassurance and emotional support or what is called "talking-down." This technique counteracts the patient's feeling that his reaction is hopelessly out of control. It can help the patient whose toxic reactions have not yet become overaggressive psychotic behavior and who is not having convulsions or is not in a coma. If he has progressed beyond that point, more specific measures are necessary. Through "talking down," the emergency team can (1) enable the patient to see that this experience is due only to the drug rather than to mental illness and that it will end when the drug wears off, without harming him, and (2) to provide a quiet pleasant environment while the patient is being helped to restructure his thinking and perceptions.

A busy emergency room setting is apt to be upsetting. For the patient reacting from hallucinogens or psychedelics a less hectic environment is necessary, with someone who will maintain a caring attitude—possibly the patient's friend—in attendance at all times. Establish a trusting contact which will assist him in reestablishing his body limits by gently holding or touching the patient. Rough handling must be avoided; it will simply increase the sense of panic.

Encourage the patient to talk about what he is experiencing—as a counteraction to his sense of isolation—and make his perceptions seem less bizarre. To increase the patient's sense of structure, the therapist should try to help him focus his speech and avoid flights of ideas. Make frequent statements that orient the patient to time, place, and person. Often, street-wise friends or experienced emergency service personnel who are not upset by the bizarre quality of "psychedelic" behavior can prove helpful in these situations. Finally, assure the patient that the treatment relationship is confidential.

If the reassuring supportive treatment has been unsuccessful or if the patient has progressed to a psychotic or overaggressive state, psychopharmacologic agents can help—not as the sole therapy, but in conjunction with the "talk-down" approach.

Follow these guidelines in dealing with hallucinogens or psychedelics beyond the "talk-down" technique:

1. Diazepam (Valium), 10 to 20 mg orally, is the safest drug to use for a patient's aggressiveness or uncontrolled anxiety. The same dosage may be given intramuscularly—but at the risk of alarming the patient by using a needle and a syringe. Nonetheless, parenteral diazepam is very effective and it should be used if necessary.

2. Avoid other sedatives and tranquilizers such as the barbiturates or chlorpromazine (Thorazine). Since many of the abused drugs are mixed or substituted with other chemicals, the effects of Thorazine or barbiturates could precipitate a severe hypotensive crisis. Patients frequently know about this effect from "street talk"; this knowledge may explain why they struggle against parenteral medications—out of the fear that they are being given Thorazine.

Inhalants and Volatile Hydrocarbons

The drugs in this class include:

- Glue
- Gasoline/petroleum distillates
- Carbon tetrachloride solvents
- Freon/aerosol propellants
- Amyl nitrate (poppers, pearls)

They are abused mainly by children and adolescents. Except for amyl nitrate, these agents are rarely used by adults, although incidental exposure to these compounds can occur in industrial settings.

Drugs in the group produce central nervous system effects which appear rapidly, resembling intoxication from alcohol. Acting as a temporary toxic to the liver and kidneys, they are periodically responsible for tragic "sudden sniffing deaths" (SSD) in children. SSD can bring almost instantaneous death in children who have inhaled volatile hydrocarbons. Typically, the tragedy follows a brief period of strenuous exertion, like running or jumping. Sometimes, just a few deep inhalations trigger the event. The actual mechanism of death is probably ventricular fibrillation. SSD is not the same as death by asphyxiation, which usually results from the practice of sniffing the solvent from a plastic bag.

Signs and symptoms of overdose. An overdose or toxic reaction to this drug group resembles alcohol inebriation: dizziness, a sense of well being, and distortions of visual and space perception. Increased exposure adds a loss of appetite, ringing in the ears, feelings of depression, hallucinations, and occasionally amnesia. There is slurred speech, poor muscular control, nausea, vomiting, and increased salivation. Occasionally, a form of peripheral neuropathy occurs, with numbness in the hands and feet. The most characteristic sign—the odor of the substance on the patient's breath—may last for several hours if use has been heavy.

Treatment of overdose. Follow these guidelines in dealing with an overdose or toxic reaction to inhalant or volatile hydrocarbons:

1. In early treatment of severe solvent toxicity, use respiratory support to combat hypoxia. Observe the patient for pulmonary edema, and monitor his condition for disturbances of cardiac and renal function.

2. There are no specific antidotes for this type of toxicity.

3. Attempt to lessen or delay further absorption of the substances by washing the mucus membranes of the nose and mouth if the substances have been inhaled and by administering milk, water, or activated charcoal if ingested.

4. After the acute stage has passed, evaluate the renal and liver functions to determine whether permanent damage has occurred.

SUGGESTED READINGS

Carroll, B. J. "Barbiturate Overdosage: Presentation with Focal Neurological Signs." *Medical Journal of Australia* 1(1969):1133-35.

Davis, J. M.; Bartlett, E.; and Termini, B. A. "Overdosage of Psychotropic Drugs: A Review. I. Major and Minor Tranquilizers." *Diseases of the Nervous System* 29(1968):157-64.

Decker, W. J., and Corby, D. G. "Activated Charcoal as a Gastrointestinal Decontaminant. Experiences with Experimental Animals and Human Subjects." *Clinical Toxocology* 3(1970):1-4.

Goldstein, L. I. "Emesis versus Lavage for Drug Ingestion." *Journal of the American Medical Association* 208(1969):2162.

Matell, G., and Thorstrand, C. "A Case of Fatal Nialamid Poisoning." *ACTA Medica Scandinavica* 181(1967):79-82.

Nymark, M., and Rasmussen, J. "Effect of Certain Drugs upon Amitriptyline-Induced Electrocardiographic Changes." *ACTA Pharmacologica et Toxicologica* 24(1966):148-56.

Rasmussen, J. "Poisoning by Amitriptyline, Imipramine, and Nortriptyline." *Danish Medical Bulletin* 12(1966):202-203.

Robertson, J. C. "Recovery after Massive MAOI Overdose Complicated with Malignant Hyperpyrexia, Treated with Chlorpromazine." *Postgraduate Medical Journal* 48(1972):64-65.

Slovis, T. L., et al. "Physostigmine Therapy in Acute Tricyclic Antidepressant Poisoning." *Clinical Toxocology* 4(1971):451-59.

Teitelbaum, D. T., "Poisoning with Psychoactive Drugs." *Pediatric Clinics of North America* 17 (1970):557-67.

VI

Suicide Prevention

Norman Farberow, Ph.D.
Robert E. Litman, M.D.

THE CRISIS

Every year, suicide accounts for more than 20,000 deaths in the United States, making it the eleventh leading cause of death. It ranks second as a cause of death for adolescents and college students.

Although this death rate has remained relatively stable during the past decade, suicide attempts, suicide threats, drug overdosages, and other forms of self-destructive behavior have increased dramatically. At a large general hospital in Los Angeles, for example, five percent of *all* admissions are now due to self-administered injuries. A night rarely goes by in any emergency department without its workers encountering a suicide attempt.

The most common form of attempted suicide is the ingestion of a sedative or hypnotic drug. Suicide attempts by methods other than drug ingestion—such as hanging, wrist-cutting or other body mutilation, gas inhalation, gunshot wounds, and jumping from high places—are less frequent.

In addition to actual suicide attempts, other persons are referred or brought to hospitals and mental health centers because they have threatened suicide or because they have demonstrated some form of self-destructive behavior, such as running into highway traffic or threatening to jump from a bridge.

Suicidal behavior is also encountered in conjunction with other crises. Alcohol, drug abuse, family crises, acute psychotic reactions—in fact most of the crises considered in this book—can be associated with a special risk for suicide. Indeed, in many of these situations, suicidal intent represents the underlying problem—a fact which you as a member of an emergency team must recognize and evaluate.

Regardless of how the suicidal behavior is manifested, the basic question is, "Why suicide?" There is no single or easy answer to this question. The complex motivations, weaknesses, and strengths that determine all types of human behavior apply also to suicide. Consequently, there are many different roads that individuals may take in reaching a decision to commit suicide. Usually the process is long, and often it is complicated by other physical and emotional symptoms of distress. Despite this multiplicity of causes and patterns, suicidal behavior can usually be related to a few primary motivations.

Loss of Communication

In general, suicidal reactions are associated with feelings of hopelessness and helplessness, often related to the separation or loss of a significant or valued relationship. Suicidal behavior can perhaps best be understood as an expression of intense feelings when other forms of expression have failed. The expression of feelings can range from poignant cries for help to desperate statements of despair. A suicidal person is driven to this act because he feels unable to cope with a problem and believes that others are not perceiving or responding to his need. The suicidal behavior thus becomes a claim for the attention he feels he has lost. Suicidal thoughts may be expressed verbally or by actions. The person may say, "I no longer want to live" or "I am going to kill myself," or he may act by procuring sleeping pills or a gun. Either directly or indirectly, the communication is frequently aimed at a specific person—"the significant other." An indirect communication poses the problem of recognizing the intent of the disguised message and understanding its real contents. If you are aware of the communicative aspects of suicidal behavior, you will be better able to evaluate the situation and to respond helpfully.

Ambivalence about Life and Death

Only a small number—perhaps 10 percent—of people who threaten or attempt suicide actually succeed. Emergency teams often find this hard to understand; in fact, they frequently express a feeling of contempt for suicide attempters. "He's such a failure; he can't even do a good job of killing himself." The general explanation for an incomplete or partially effective suicidal act is that the individual was filled with contradictory feelings about living and dying. Psychiatrists call this state "ambivalence." Crisis workers should realize that ambivalence is a universal human trait, not a weakness. Everyone experiences ambivalence over decisions at one time or other, especially in choosing a career, spouse, or place to live. Certainly the choice of a place and time to die is no exception. Indeed, in making the decision of whether to live or die one would expect to find even more than the usual amount of ambivalence. This psychological characteristic accounts for the sometimes puzzling fact that a person will take a lethal or near-lethal action and then counterbalance it with some provision for rescue. It is common for a patient to express his contradictory feelings with words of "I'm sorry you saved me; I'm glad I'm alive." The very fact that every person is divided within himself over decisions provides the chance for successful crisis intervention with a suicidal patient. By making constructive use of the patient's wish to live, suicide may be averted.

Effects of Suicidal Behavior on Others

Suicidal behavior can further be understood in terms of its effect upon those receiving the communication. For example, a suicidal attempt may arouse feelings of sympathy, anxiety, anger, or hostility on the part of family or friends and therefore serve to manipulate relationships. The crisis worker may experience similar feelings unless he can anticipate and counteract these reactions in himself. The crisis worker must resist the desire to be omnipotent. No one is really omnipotent just as no one can solve all the problems and meet all of the demands of every patient. This is particularly true in dealing with intensely dependent patients who often attribute tremendous powers to the potential rescuer.

Many suicidal situations will arouse within the worker feelings of anxiety and self-doubts of his adequacy to handle crises of this type. While a moderate level of anxiety is appropriate, too much may seriously hamper the helping effort, especially if it is transmitted to the patient who, at this point, is depending upon the worker to help him solve his problems. Already helpless and lost, the suicidal person who perceives excessive anxiety in the worker, may lose hope of being helped. As in all forms of crisis intervention, the suicide prevention worker develops confidence and poise with training and experience.

ASSESSMENT OF THE CRISIS

The first task of the emergency team after a patient's suicide attempt is to determine whether his physical state is in immediate danger. If an individual has already swallowed a large number of sleeping pills, your first concern must center on the drug's physical effects rather than on the motivation or significance of the act.

This discussion, however, will focus on how to evaluate the suicidal potential of those who threaten to commit suicide or who have made an unsuccessful attempt.

Evaluation of Suicidal Potential

Before describing factors influencing the probability of suicide, we need to consider the crisis worker's own attitudes towards suicide and death since these feelings affect the interview and evaluation process. Death is a part of life and living, but in our culture it has always been surrounded by powerful taboos. These taboos and the feelings they can arouse in the worker might very well interfere in the interaction with the patient. To be effective, the crisis worker must be sensitive to his own feelings about death and suicide and, regardless of his personal attitudes, must avoid any moralistic judgments about what has happened. Your professional point of view must be that death is to be prevented, if possible. Often you will be placed in the position of actually debating life and death questions with upset people. Although you must recognize the existence and merits of other viewpoints, your role as crisis worker is to represent life and the opportunity for assistance to distressed, helpless people.

From your first conversation with a suicidal individual, you immediately assume some responsibility for preventing the suicide. In working out some plan for prevention, you must first determine the individual's suicidal potential, i.e., the degree of probability that the person may kill himself in the immediate or near future. In some individuals the suicidal potential will be minimal, while in others it will be immediate and great. You must decide the degree of risk for each patient.

You should be aware that the prediction of suicide is by no means an exact science at the present time.[1] Even the most experienced interviewer can be misled in assessing a problem. Nevertheless, certain criteria allow suicidal potential to be evaluated with responsible assurance. Effective assessment depends on obtaining detailed information about each of the items described in the following paragraphs. While the patient may supply some of these facts himself,

1. For detailed information concerning the current status of various methods and approaches to the evaluation of suicide, see A. T. Beck, H. L. P. Resnik, and D. J. Lettieri, eds., *The Prediction of Suicide,* (Bowie, Md.: The Charles Press, 1974).

families and other interested persons are also valuable sources.

Factors Influencing Suicidal Potential

Age and sex

One factor is a patient's age and sex. Statistics indicate that women attempt suicide more often than men, but that men commit suicide more often than women. In other words, men complete the act more frequently than do women (usually because of different motives and the more lethal methods of suicide they have chosen). It is also known that the rate for completed suicide rises with increasing age. Consequently, an older male presents the greatest threat of actual suicide and a young female, the least. Within this framework, then, age and sex offer a general, though by no means a clear-cut, basis for evaluating suicidal potential. You should remember that young women and young men do indeed kill themselves, even if their original aim was to manipulate other people. Each case requires individual appraisal.

Suicide plan

A second factor is the suicide plan. How an individual plans to take his life is one of the most significant criteria in assessing suicidal potentiality. In appraising a patient's suicide plan, you should consider three main elements:

1. How relatively *lethal* is the method? A person who intends to commit suicide with a gun, by jumping from a high building, or by hanging is a far greater risk to kill himself than someone who plans to take pills or cut his wrists. Since the latter methods are amenable to treatment or resuscitation, they are less lethal than the irrevocable consequences of, say, putting a gun to one's head, which is the most lethal of all methods.

2. How *available* are the means? It must be determined if the method of suicide the individual has considered is in fact available to him. For example, an actual threat to use a gun in hand obviously is more serious than the same threat without a gun.

3. How *specific* is the suicide plan? If the patient has spent time thinking out details and specific preparations for his death, his suicidal risk is markedly increased. Changing a will, writing notes, collecting pills, buying a gun, and setting a time or place for suicide suggest a high risk. When a patient's plan is obviously confused or unrealistic, you need also to consider the possibility of an underlying psychiatric problem. A psychotic person with the idea of suicide is a particularly high risk because he may make a bizarre attempt based on his distorted thoughts. Find out if the patient has a past history of any emotional disorder and whether he has ever been hospitalized or received other mental health care.

Stress

A third factor is stress. Find out about any stress which may have precipitated the suicidal behavior. The patient's response to the question "Why do you want to kill yourself at this time?" is usually revealing. The most common precipitating stresses are losses, such as the death of a loved one; divorce or separation; loss of job, money, prestige, or status; loss of health through sickness, surgery, or accident; loss of esteem because of threat of prosecution or criminal involvement. Not all stresses are due to bereavement. Sometimes increased anxiety and tension are a result of success, such as promotion on the job and increased responsibilities.

Learn to evaluate stress from the patient's point of view rather than from your own or what you think is society's point of view. What you might consider minimal stress can be perceived by the patient as severe. The relationship existing between stress and symptoms (see fourth factor below) is useful in evaluating prognosis. In general, if both stress and symptoms are severe, the action response of the worker must be strong. Conversely, if symptoms are severe, but stress is low, either the facts you have are incomplete or the person is chronically unstable and has a history of similar crises.

Symptoms

A fourth factor influencing suicidal potential is the presence of various emotional symptoms. The most common and most important suicidal symptoms relate to depression. By careful questioning you can determine the presence of a depressive state. Typical symptoms of severe depression include: loss of appetite, weight loss, inability to sleep at night, loss of interest, social withdrawal, apathy and despondency, severe feelings of hopelessness and helplessness, and a general attitude of physical and emotional exhaustion. The crisis worker must be sensitive to these signs and symptoms because the risk of suicide is high in depressed patients.

Other patients may exhibit agitation through symptoms like tension, anxiety, guilt, shame, poor impulse control and/or feelings of rage, anger, hostility, or revenge. Alcoholics, homosexuals, and drug addicts (among whom agitation is common) tend to be high suicidal risks.

The person who is both agitated *and* depressed is particularly a risk. Unable to tolerate the pressure of his feelings, the individual in a state of agitated depression shows marked tension, fearfulness, restlessness, and pressure of speech. He eventually reaches a point where he must act in some direction to relieve his feelings. Often he chooses suicide.

Suicidal symptoms may also occur with psychotic states. The patient may have delusions, hallucinations, misinterpreted sensory impressions, loss of contact, disorientation, or highly unusual ideas and experiences. As a baseline for judging psychotic behavior, use your own sense of what is real and appropriate.

Resources

A fifth factor in determining suicidal risk is resources. The patient's environmental resources are often critical in deciding how you will manage the immediate problem. Inquire about resources which can be used to support him through the suicidal crisis: family, relatives, close friends, employers, physicians, or clergymen. If the patient is already under the care of a professional therapist or is known to some mental health agency, first try to contact the therapist or agency. Consider the patient's work as a possible resource, especially if it can provide him with self-esteem and gratifying relationships. Keep in mind that the patient's financial status influences the availability and location of immediate physical and psychological care.

The choice of various resources is sometimes affected by the fact that the patient and family might try to keep the suicidal situation a secret, even to the point of denying its existence. As a general rule this attempt at secrecy and denial must be counteracted by dealing with the suicidal situation openly and frankly. It is usually better, both for the crisis worker and the patient, when the responsibility for a suicidal patient is shared by as many people as possible. This joint effort provides the patient the feeling he lacks—that others are interested and ready to help him.

Where there are no apparent sources of help or support, the crisis situation should be considered more ominous. The same conclusion holds true when available resources have been exhausted or family and friends have turned away from the suicidal patient. In most instances, however, people will respond to crises if they are given an opportunity.

Life style

A sixth factor in assessing suicidal risk is the way the patient has functioned in the past—his life style. In this regard, two basic questions must be answered: (1) Has his style of life been stable or unstable? (2) Is the suicidal behavior acute or is it chronic?

The stable person will describe a consistent work record, sound marital and family relationships, and no history of previous suicidal behavior. The unstable personality may have had severe character disorders, borderline psychotic behavior, and repeated difficulties with major situations like interpersonal relationships or employment.

A suicidal person responding to acute stress—such as the death or loss of someone he loves, bad news, or loss of a job which has thrust him into an unfamiliar status—presents a special concern. The risk of early suicide among this group is high; on the other hand, the opportunities for successful therapeutic intervention are correspondingly greater. Experience has shown that if the suicidal danger can be averted for a relatively short period of time, persons in acute crises tend to emerge from the suicidal crisis without great danger of recurrence.

In contrast, persons leading chronic "careers" of self-destruction may be helped through one emergency, but the suicidal danger can be expected to return at a later date. In general, if a patient has made serious attempts in the past, his current suicidal situation should be rated more dangerous. Although persons with chronic suicidal behavior benefit temporarily from crisis management, the emphasis needs to fall more on continuity of care and the maintenance of relationships. Examples of persons leading "careers" of suicide are: chronic alcoholics, persons with both unstable personal lives and histories of repeated suicide attempts, and those who habitually abuse sleep medications.

Acute suicidal behavior may be found in either a stable or an unstable personality; however, chronic suicidal behavior occurs only in an unstable person. In dealing with a stable person undergoing a suicidal crisis (usually in reaction to a specific stress), you should be highly responsive and active. With an unstable person, you need to be slower and more thoughtful, reminding the patient that he has weathered similar crises in the past. Your main goals will be helping thim through another crisis as order is restored and assisting him in reconstituting an interpersonal relationship with a stable person or resource.

Communication

The seventh factor is communication. The communication aspects of suicidal behavior have great relevance in the evaluation process. The most important question is whether or not communication still exists between the suicidal person and others. When communication with the suicidal patient is completely severed, it indicates that he has lost hope in any possibility of rescue.

The form of communication may be either verbal or nonverbal; its content, direct or indirect. The suicidal person who communicates nonverbally and indirectly makes it very difficult for the recipient of the communication to recognize or appreciate the suicidal nature of these "action communications." Moreover, this type of communication in itself implies a lack of clarity in the interchange between the suicidal person and others. At the same time it raises a danger that the patient may "act out" his suicidal impulses. One of your primary goals as a crisis worker is to open up and clarify communication among everyone involved in the suicidal situation.

The patient's communication may be directed toward one or more significant persons within his environment. He may express hostility, accuse, blame, or demand openly or subtly that others change their behavior and feelings. His communication may express feelings of guilt, inadequacy, and worthlessness or indicate strong anxiety and tension.

Reactions of "significant other"

When the communication is directed to a specific person, the reaction of the recipient—the "significant other"—becomes the eighth important factor in evaluating suicidal danger. You must decide if the "significant other" can be an important resource for rescue, if he is best regarded as nonhelpful, or if he might even be injurious to the patient's welfare.

The nonhelpful "significant other" either rejects the patient or denies the suicidal behavior itself by withdrawing, both psychologically and physically, from continued communication. Sometimes this other person may resent the patient's increased demands, insistence on gratification of dependency needs, or dictum to change his own behavior. In other cases, the "significant other" may act helpless, indecisive, or ambivalent, indicating that he does not know what the next step is and has given up. His reaction of hopelessness gives the suicidal person a feeling that aid is not available from a previously dependable source. The feeling can increase the patient's own hopelessness.

By contrast, a helpful reaction from the "significant other" is one in which the person recognizes the communication, is aware of the problem, and seeks help for the patient. This indicates to the patient that his communications are being heard and that someone is doing something to provide help.

Medical status

The ninth factor in determining suicidal potential is medical status. Since the state of the patient's health may have an important bearing on suicidal behavior, the crisis worker should specifically inquire about concomitant medical problems. For example, a person suffering from a chronic, debilitating illness may experience a considerable change in self-image and self-concept, both of which serve to influence his feelings and behavior. For a chronically ill person, the relationships with his physician, family, or the hospital staff will be most meaningful. It is encouraging if the patient continues to recognize these people as resources for help.

A patient having ungrounded fears of a fatal illness like cancer or a brain tumor is often preoccupied with death and dying. His history may indicate many unsuccessful experiences with doctors or a pattern of failure with previous therapy. These symptoms are important because their effect on the "significant others" as well as on physicians is to exhaust both as resources for the patient.

Summary

Of the nine factors for determining suicide potential, only one should be considered especially dangerous or alarming: having a specific plan for suicide involving a very lethal method. Generally, the evaluation of suicidal potential should be based on the general pattern of all nine factors in the case of each individual. For example, a 25-year-old married man states that he is tired and depressed and that he is having vague ideas about committing suicide by driving into a freeway abutment. There is no history of prior suicidal behavior. He reports difficulty in his marriage and talks of separation, but he maintains contact with his wife and he continues in a job that he has had for many years. Although many factors for suicide are present, the overall pattern of behavior suggests that this man is a low suicide risk.

In contrast, a 64-year-old man with a history of alcoholism reports he made a serious suicide attempt a year ago and was saved when someone unexpectedly found him comatose. He recounts a history of three failures in marriage along with many job changes in the past year. He further states that his physical health is failing, he has no family left, and he was thinking of killing himself with a gun kept in his house. He would be judged a very high suicide risk.

Clinical Patterns of Suicidal Behavior

On the basis of these nine factors, the most important clinical patterns of suicidal behavior can be classified as follows: adolescent turmoil, middle-age depression, and elderly hopelessness.

Adolescent turmoil

Suicide attempts by ingestion of pills and by cutting the arm or wrist occur with considerable frequency in young females and with lesser frequency in young males. These behaviors invariably indicate tension in interpersonal relationships, usually within the family or with a loved person. In young females the behavior usually reflects feelings about being rejected or unloved; in young males it often reflects doubts about masculinity and adequacy. In evaluating this particular group of patients, you should understand that the primary purpose of the suicidal act is to communicate, and that the young person is generally expressing a feeling of desperation. Is the family or others aware of this feeling? Has there been some response to his communication? Crisis management in this situation requires a strong effort to restore communication between the patient and his family. For example, a 15-year-old female ingests some of her mother's sleeping pills after being forbidden to contact her high school boyfriend. She leaves behind a note saying, "I won't be any trouble to you anymore." After gastric lavage in the emergency room, there is a tearful scene of family concern and then a reevaluation of family priorities.

Recommendations for some environmental changes are often appropriate in dealing with adolescent turmoil, especially if difficulties persist for the patient in reestablishing communication with the family. For instance, a young man of 14—president of his ninth-grade class and apparently doing well in his studies—brought snail poison to school and told friends he had ingested some of this lethal material. After medical treatment at the emergency unit, he and his family were interviewed. It became clear he could not live up to the very high standards that he felt his family expected of him. Indeed, the family was quite angry about the suicide attempt and did not seem to understand the situation. They felt disgraced. A suggestion was made to have the boy live with his grandparents in another city. Follow-up investigation several months later showed that, while not performing at quite as high a level academically, he was doing well socially.

In late adolescence a reaction of inadequacy and loss is often related to leaving the family and going away to school. College physicians and student hotline workers are familiar with the homesickness or separation anxiety experienced by a student, particularly around examination times. Such cases are worsened by feelings of shame or embarrassment which may grow strong enough to precipitate suicidal impulses. Rather than encourage the student to deny or hide his feelings, it is usually advisable to notify the student's family.

In young adults, most suicidal behaviors result from tangled or broken personal relationships. The syndrome is epitomized in their plea, "I can't live without you." The individual, feeling the sting of being rejected by someone, commonly takes pills. Often the suicidal behavior has the effect of clearing the air, leading to better communication and either a reconciliation or a decisive break in the relationship and a turning to other people. The most helpful therapeutic procedure is to encourage the patient to seek support from other relationships. Wider social contacts are beneficial—regardless of whether the relationship breaks or continues. Often friends of the patient can bring the basic emotional support to relieve his feelings of being worthless, rejected, and alone.

Middle-age depression

Depressive illnesses account for most suicidal behavior in middle age. Emergency workers should be trained to ask specifically about symptoms of depression: sleeplessness, loss of appetite, loss of interest, sadness, self-deprecation, or withdrawal from social relationships.

Clinicians distinguish two main types of depression, reactive and endogenous. Reactive depressions usually follow stressful situations, especially losses. For example, a high-ranking engineer was laid off from his job during the aerospace cutbacks and found he could not regain employment at a level anywhere near his previous position. He became morose, self-preoccupied, and irritable. His wife, unable to tolerate his behavior, went home to live with her parents. This doubled his stress, having lost both job and wife. He started to climb over the railing of a freeway overpass, but a passing patrol car spotted him and brought him into the emergency unit. He was given a sedative and placed under observation. Meanwhile, a close friend and his wife were asked to come to the unit. The engineer was released into their company on the condition that he would stay with them until further care could be obtained from a psychiatrist.

Endogenous depressions, in contrast, do not have an obvious cause-and-effect relationship. For example, a middle-aged woman was brought to the emergency care center after taking an overdose of tranquilizers. She described the gradual development of overwhelming fatigue, sadness, lack of interest in life, and inability to enjoy anything. Yet, there didn't seem to be any obvious reason for these changes. Personnel at the emergency center recognized that this was a case of endogenous depression, and they referred her for psychiatric consultation. She was eventually treated with an antidepressant medication.

Suicide among the elderly

In the older ages, suicidal behavior is often associated with a clinical pattern described as "old and sick" or "down and out." "Down and out" refers to the older person who has either outlived his personal resources or lost them gradually over the years. He experiences a steadily decreasing status in life and a deteriorating ability to function. Such a person comes to feel hopeless and suicidal. Often the feelings can be eased by an aggressive medical approach to any existing physical illness combined with an active psychological-social program administered by a social worker or senior citizens' agency. However, while these measures can lessen loneliness, isolation, and withdrawal, the risk of future suicide remains high in these lonely people.

MANAGEMENT OF THE CRISIS

Immediate Help

When a person attempts or threatens suicide, the police, a clergyman, a physician, or a rescue squad may be called to the scene of the crisis. In some cities, emergency centers operate special ambulances staffed by paramedics or other trained teams. The call may originate from the victim or from some person who is involved with him. In the case of other-than-victim calls, every effort should be made to identify the caller and to enlist his help in the rescue effort. This is particularly important since the suicidal person, often highly perturbed and agitated, may be very suspicious of potential rescuers. The third party caller can sometimes serve as an intermediary and help the worker establish rapport and trust with the patient.

Follow these guidelines in dealing with suicidal persons:

1. Gain entry to the patient's location. If the emergency team cannot enter the house because the door is locked and if there is no response to ringing or knocking, try to locate a neighbor, building manager, or someone to see if a key is available. If not, you must decide whether to break in. If possible, quickly consult by telephone with police or the emergency center staff. Report the situation to the center's team leader or medical consultant so that responsibility for any decision is distributed among several people rather than assumed entirely by the emergency crew on the scene. Follow this general rule: do not break in as long as the patient is apparently conscious and willing to talk through the closed door.

2. ***Consider armed individuals potentially homicidal as well as suicidal.*** Of particular concern to emergency teams is the person who possesses a gun or similarly dangerous weapon. Be on your guard when approaching persons who threaten to harm others as well as themselves. Do nothing to frighten them or to make them more suspicious. Above all, do not jeopardize your own life or the lives of the rescue team by futile heroic actions. For example, if a person with a gun locks himself in a room, it is foolish to try to break down the door in sudden assault so you can obtain the weapon. Instead, attempt to talk to the person in a calm, reassuring manner. At the same time, locate someone in the environment who has a special relationship of trust with the potential patient and to whom he may listen—possibly a sweetheart, spouse, clergyman, relative, or friend.

3. ***If you find the person unconscious, give emergency medical treatment, possibly establishing an airway and administering oxygen, and then transport him immediately to a hospital.*** If the individual is conscious, he might be cooperative or uncooperative, most probably some degree of both. At this point you need to evaluate the situation.

4. ***Conduct a brief crisis interview to assess the conditions and to determine further action.*** Concentrate on establishing rapport, estimating the suicidal potential, discussing alternative solutions to the problem, and seeking possible resources. In practice, the first step is to *offer help* to the victim—"How can I help you? We want to be of assistance to you in any way we can." Refrain from criticism, anger, or rejection. If you find the victim's behavior personally upsetting, remain silent or ask your partner to handle the interview.

In general, the crisis worker should appear patient, interested, self-assured, hopeful, and knowledgeable. This demeanor will convey to the patient both an ability and a willingness to help. Listen carefully to him without challenge or criticism.

Time can be a positive factor if you use it to gain the individual's confidence and to evaluate the situation. Even if the suicidal person has ingested an overdose of drugs (though not comatose), there is no need to rush. By observing the patient for a period of time, the emergency team can evaluate whether his condition is growing worse (e.g., more sedated and somnambulant) or whether it has stabilized or is improving. What you observe will help decide whether the person who is conscious actually requires further emergency room care.

5. ***Assess the suicide risk.*** Find out the answer to this basic question: what is the patient's present suicidal intent? First, direct your conversation towards obtaining information about the nine factors necessary to evaluate suicide potential which were reviewed in the preceding section. Then, turn your attention to the present situation. Ask the patient how he is feeling now. Next, go directly to the core concern by asking what happened or why he was trying to kill himself. Follow up by asking if he still feels the same way or would he attempt suicide again. If he denies further suicidal intention, the emergency team must then evaluate whether or not the patient's suicidal behavior has indeed induced some emotional change in him. Consider also whether the significant people in his environment have responded positively to the behavior. If these changes are not evident, the suicidal risk probably remains high.

6. ***Assess the patient's strengths and resources.*** This step is as important as an evaluation of the pathological aspects of his behavior. Any alarmingly negative feelings and behaviors can be mitigated by a number of positive features still present within the situation. For example, useful internal resources remain if the patient responds to the worker's first attempts to focus the interview. If the patient is able to respond by accepting suggestions and directions,

this is a hopeful sign. Improvement in mood and thinking during the course of one interview is another positive sign, indicating his ability to respond to an offer of help.

7. ***Take particular care in assessing suicidal danger in persons who smell of alcohol or appear to be drunk.*** Since the influence of alcohol can undermine ordinary prudence, self-control, and self-preservation instincts, someone who has latent self-destructive tendencies may act upon them. Consider whether the individual has ingested sleeping pills or overdosages of tranquilizers in addition to the alcohol. If a patient has taken both alcohol and medication, he is in much more serious medical danger. Check if he regularly takes pills or if he has thought about suicide. Failure to explore these questions carefully has led to loss of lives.

8. ***If your assessment suggests a high suicide risk, two steps must be taken: (1) have someone stay with the person and (2) arrange for further professional help.*** Sometimes the patient himself will agree to seek immediate help, opening the way for you to make the arrangements. But if the patient refuses or if those close to him cannot or will not help, make every effort to bring the patient directly to the psychiatric unit of the hospital. Be persuasive rather than coercive in talking with the patient. If the crisis team concludes that the person need not go to an emergency room, it becomes essential that someone—relative, friend, or neighbor—remain at the scene. Discuss provisions for subsequent treatment with the patient. As a general rule, the only time a suicidal patient should not be brought to an emergency room or a mental health center is when his threat or gesture is relatively non-lethal and when necessary family or community resources can be mobilized for effective outpatient referral.

9. ***Obtain assistance from resources within the community.*** Although resources will vary according to individual or community circumstances, certain guidelines can be followed in identifying them. In general, available resources are of two types, nonprofessional and professional.

Nonprofessional resources can be family, close friends, or a clergyman. The family, often neglected as a resource, is one of the most valuable in a time of crisis. Encourage the patient to discuss the situation and problems with his family. If it is important that someone be with the patient during the crisis, call on family members and apprise them of the situation, even though the patient may be reluctant. Inform the patient first, however, that his family will be called. Involve the family in accepting its share of responsibility for the emergency and convince its members that they must help the patient get the recommended treatment.

Close friends often can serve a similar role. In some cases the patient is better off having a friend rather than a family member stay with him during the crisis period. The friend may be more effective in talking things out and in offering a feeling of support.

If the patient is close to his church, encourage him to discuss the crisis situation with his clergyman. Many pastoral counselors are trained and experienced in dealing with these crises.

Professional resources include the family physician, an agency or clinic, individual specialists, and psychiatric facilities. A family physician is often an invaluable resource. People are accustomed to turning to him for help and, in addition, he represents a supportive authority figure often needed in crisis situations. If the patient-doctor relationship has been good, the patient will welcome this resource. Physicians can also advise on medications, consultations with a psychiatrist, or hospitalization.

In cases where you find the danger of suicide as a low risk or perhaps not even the primary problem, consider referral to a family service agency or community psychiatric clinic. This professional resource is ideal for patients whose underlying problem may be marital discord, family conflict, or chronic personal and social maladjustment. You should know the location, hours, and fees of these centers. Often a referral to an agency which works primarily with persons of the patient's own religion is desirable.

The crisis worker should be familiar with individual specialists—private therapists, psychiatrists, psychologists, or other mental health professionals—as possible professional resources. If the patient is already in treatment, ask his permission to contact the therapist.

If the community contains a psychiatric hospital or a general hospital with a psychiatric ward which offers psychiatric consultation, consider referral when the patient is disturbed to the point of doing serious harm to himself or others or disorganized to the point of no longer exercising judgment or direction in his affairs. In these instances, insist that family or friends take the patient to the hospital rather than have him go alone.

Emergency Room Care

Follow these guidelines when a suicidal person is brought to the emergency ward:

1. *Assess the patient's physical condition to determine if his life is in danger; if he is comatose, initiate immediate medical treatment.* The medical management of various life-threatening conditions is described briefly in Chapter III and in more detail in various emergency medical technician training programs.[2]

2. *If he is conscious, continue the steps begun at the scene.* Essentially, establish rapport, assess suicidal potential, discuss alternative solutions, assess helping resources, and arrange for companionship, observation, and eventual treatment.

3. *Do not react personally to the patient's frustrating, provocative behavior.* Remember the ambivalence of the suicidal act. If a suicidal patient is uncooperative, do not let this factor influence your own attitude and actions. It is even possible for an emergency room team to feel angry and resentful toward someone who has deliberately put his life in jeopardy. Emphasize helping the life-enhancing, life-strengthening side of the patient rather than dwelling on the self-destructive side. You will need to keep this positive mood. A patient can deliberately try to frustrate the wishes of a crisis worker who is dedicated to helping, healing, and caring for sick people. Be careful to refrain from provoking, punishing, or rejecting those with chronic suicidal behavior. You may sometimes be hard put to maintain self-control since this patient often seeks confirmation of his own worthless feeling.

4. *Take precautions to prevent further suicide attempts.* A person recovering from a suicide attempt requires special care within the hospital. He should be observed in a recovery room, whether this is located in the emergency ward or in a separate facility. The recovery room should contain no drugs, poisonous substances, or dangerous instruments accessible to the patient. Preferably, it should be on the ground floor. If the room has its own bathroom, no one should be able to lock it from the inside. Within hospitals, bathrooms and bedrooms are frequently sought for suicide because they are private. Belts and neckties should be removed from the patient. Electrical cords in the room should be as short as possible.

The patient in a recovery room or protective facility should be kept under close surveillance. Indeed, the most effective technique in suicide prevention is to place someone with the patient at all times. A suicide attempt is rarely made in the presence of another person. The ideal observer is a nurse in a position to assess the patient's behavior and to monitor his psychological disposition. However, the observer can also be a family member, friend, or even volunteer helper. At this point, you should find

2. See H. Grant and R. Murray, *Emergency Care*, (Bowie, Md.: Robert J. Brady Co., 1971).

out if the patient expresses relief at having been rescued or if he still conveys a sense of heavy pessimism and hopelessness. When continuous observation is impossible, place the patient in a room or area that is easily accessible to the nurse to permit frequent checks while she is conducting other activities.

5. *During the observation period, you must decide about the patient's suicidal intent and current risk status.* Has the crisis passed or is a second suicidal attempt likely? You will need to explore different ways of solving the problem with the patient. Investigate and arrange for community supports, including companionship and follow-up treatment.

6. *Consider whether psychiatric consultation is needed.* Unfortunately, most hospitals and emergency units do not have psychiatrists in attendance; therefore, a psychiatric consultation usually poses a problem and requires a special effort.

No set rules exist for requesting a psychiatric consultation, but it is wise that every patient who has attempted suicide and who is brought to a hospital should be seen by a psychiatrist. By this means, psychotic patients and those suffering from depressions can be identified and treated. Moreover, when a suicide attempt effects change in a sticky, interpersonal relationship, psychiatric consultation may help a patient make the adjustment. Also, there are special circumstances requiring absolute psychiatric evaluation, such as those in which one person survives a suicide pact.

If psychiatric consultation is required, advise the patient and his family that a psychiatrist might be of help to them. Give them the opportunity to contact a psychiatrist voluntarily. Make it easier by giving the patient the name of a mental health service or several private psychiatrists.

7. *Discharge or release from the emergency unit requires a special evaluation.* Before any decision, check the response of the patient and his environment to the suicidal act and review the plan for therapeutic referral. Telephone the patient a day or two after discharge, not only to see how he is progressing and to demonstrate your concern, but more importantly to see if he understands the therapeutic recommendations for aftercare and has acted on them.

Failure to provide the essential services of therapeutic recommendations and follow-up care is probably the greatest present deficiency in the emergency management of suicidal persons. Unfortunately, crisis teams too often resist involvement beyond the immediate emergency so that prevention of further self-destructive behavior is neglected. Yet, from among suicidal patients who required treatment in emergency medical centers, about 1 percent will commit suicide within that next year and another 1 percent, two years after treatment.

One hope for preventing suicide involves sorting out those patients who are of highest risk (based on the nine factors previously mentioned) and to encourage crisis workers in using community resources for referral and subsequent care.

SUGGESTED READINGS

Beck, Aaron T.; Resnik, Harvey L. P.; and Lettieri, Dan J., eds. *The Prediction of Suicide.* Bowie, Md.: The Charles Press Publishers, Inc., 1974.

Cain, Albert C. *Survivors of Suicide.* Springfield, Ill.: Charles C. Thomas, Publisher, 1973.

Danto, Bruce L. *Jail House Blues.* Orchard Lake, Mich.: Epic Publications, Inc., 1973.

Farberow, Norman L. *Suicide.* Morristown, N.J.: General Learning Corporation, 1974.

Farberow, Norman L., and Shneidman, Edwin S. *Cry for Help.* New York: McGraw-Hill Book Company, 1961.

Leonard, Calista V. *Understanding and Preventing Suicide.* Springfield, Ill.: Charles C. Thomas, Publisher, 1974.

Lester, David. *Why People Kill Themselves.* Springfield, Ill.: Charles C. Thomas, Publisher, 1972.

McGee, Richard K. *Crisis Intervention in the Community.* Baltimore: University Park Press, 1974.

Neuringer, Charles. *Psychological Assessment of Suicidal Risk.* Springfield, Ill.: Charles C. Thomas, Publisher, 1974.

Shneidman, Edwin S., and Farberow, Norman L., eds., *Clues to Suicide.* New York: McGraw-Hill Book Company, 1957.

Shneidman, Edwin S.; Farberow, Norman L.; and Litman, R. E. *Psychology of Suicide.* New York: Science House, Inc., 1970.

Wallenström, Jan; Larsson, Page; and Ljungstedt, Nils, eds. *Suicide and Attempted Suicide.* Stockholm: Nordiska Bokhandelns Förlag, 1972.

VII

The Management of Family Crises

Paul R. Polak, M.D.
Mary Reres, Ed.D.
Larry Fish

THE PROBLEM

While the family is potentially the most secure unit of society by virtue of its members' closeness, that same closeness may serve to have major destructive effects with any outburst in its ranks. No family is static. Family members are individuals growing physically, intellectually, spiritually, and emotionally at their own pace. Values, beliefs, needs, and desires are changing at an incredible rate within our social system. The family unit is necessarily stressed, both as its individual members begin to differ and as external events impinge upon it.

Some families grow from recognition of differences so that the members gain greater strength and self-expression. Others are threatened by differences and certain outside stimuli so that outbursts occur, resulting in both physical and emotional harm. When a family faces external forces or interpersonal conflicts so great that its members cannot adapt without undergoing major changes, a family crisis occurs. At times of stress, everyone has a breaking point when he feels trapped and compelled to strike out at others. The crisis worker must understand this essential human condition so that he may enter a crisis situation in a nonjudgmental manner and deliver care.

You must recognize that the family is, for all practical purposes, a miniature of society itself. As in any community, the members have varying dependency on one another for economics, services, support, comfort, recreation, and growth. Most crises in families and other social systems are caused by an interaction between external events, conflicts among family members, and symptomatic behavior by individual family members. When a crisis occurs within any community, its dependency is in jeopardy and great unrest occurs in all members. The smaller the community, the greater the crisis impact on the individual.

As an example, a rescue unit was called to the home of a depressed and suicidal man. Upon arriving at the scene, the emergency team found that the wife had been out of town attending her mother's funeral. Questioning revealed a man who had been extremely dependent on his wife throughout their 10-year marriage. The wife had enjoyed being overprotective, and both had strong fears of being separated. The emergency team talked to the husband about the need for psychiatric care at this time and referred him to a nearby community mental health center.

Since many physical and emotional emergencies occur in the home, more than one member of the family is usually involved when the crisis occurs and when the patient is being treated. You as a crisis worker will frequently need to deal with the family's anxiety and stress and also to administer to the patient. Pertinent family members should be involved in the crisis situation when possible. They may possibly relieve some of the anxiety and at the same time may provide an excellent opportunity for the crisis worker to understand the family situation. In cases where physical injury results from anger expressed within the family, the crisis worker may find himself in the midst of the ongoing dispute. Your primary concern is still the treatment of the victim and his family. But the presence of distraught family members further complicates the situation, requiring interpersonal skills. How you choose to approach problem-solving with the family members may speed the eventual recovery of the victim, involve others in reducing his stress, and assist the family unit in resolving its crisis situation.

Unfortunately, most family crises surface only after one of the members experiences problems. If the symptomatic member is brought for emergency treatment, the concern centers around diagnosing and treating the individual. The underlying family crisis or crises may not become apparent unless the examiner asks a few simple questions about the patient's family. A direct inquiry into recent significant family events and more specifically the answer to the question "What has been happening to you and your family recently?" are likely to lead to important information about pertinent family problems.

The kinds of family crises may be grouped according to the nature of the precipitating event: environmental stress, family conflict, or the personal crisis (individual symptomatic behavior) of a family member.

ENVIRONMENTAL EVENTS

A family asked to describe events which led up to the present crisis usually reports several critical environmental incidents. These events often produce a family crisis by triggering long-standing, unresolved family and individual conflicts. The environmental event, usually occurring within the previous two years, may be the major precipitator of the crisis. The sudden accidental death of a family member can foster a family crisis, whether or not long-standing family conflict exists. In other situations a very minor environmental event is enough to trigger a family crisis when it touches on major unresolved family tensions.

For example, police were called to a couple's home after the wife stabbed her husband with a kitchen knife. Initial questioning revealed that the cause of the violence was an argument over who should put out the cat. Probing further, the officer discovered long-standing marital discord over more serious issues. In addition to handling the legal consequences of the wife's action, the crisis worker arranged a referral to the mental health center for marriage counseling.

Described below are the most common types of environmental events which can precipitate family crises.

Death

A great deal has been written about the crisis of grief experienced by individuals as a result of the death of a loved one. (For a thorough discussion of emergency psychiatric care of the dying patient and his family, see Chapter VIII.) Less attention has been paid to the continuing crisis experienced by the whole surviving family and the processes by which the family adapts to the death.

In many ways a family crisis involving death is a prototype of all family crises. Not only does the family need to work out the processes of grief experienced by its individuals, but also it needs to undergo a complex reorganizational process as a family unit. The more sudden and violent the death, the younger the deceased, and the more meager the support from extended family and friends, the more severe the crisis.

For example, an ambulance was called for an adolescent boy who had overdosed on barbiturates–two weeks after killing his father in a hunting accident. After giving emergency care, the team learned from the mother that she had been forced to go to work immediately to support the family. Also, she had asked her son to get a part-time job. Both mother and son wanted the other to take the place of the lost father. The crisis workers helped them to understand the need to restructure their family and referred them to a local guidance clinic.

Follow these guidelines in dealing with death in a family:

1. Assist the main surviving relative in informing other family members. Children should hear that their father died in a car accident from their mother rather than from the neighbor's kids. If it is very hard for her to tell them herself, she may need help. Most families have their sources of support at the time of a death–a best friend, an understanding brother-in-law, or a respected minister. A crisis worker's immediate assistance to a family at the time of a sudden death may end when such individuals assume their role. Other families, however, may need more extended support.

2. If an individual is dying, help his family to adapt to the death before it occurs. Dying patients often have cause to feel isolated and abandoned when family members, staff members, and friends begin to avoid them as death approaches. Since most dying patients know they are going to die, it is often best for a family to discuss the approaching death openly with the dying patient.

3. For immediate management procedures, see Chapter VIII.

Separations and Moves

Over half of all psychiatric patients are members of families and social systems undergoing a separation crisis. While usually less severe than a crisis caused by a death in the family, a separation crisis nonetheless contributes to the patient's problem. Separation crises can occur after a family fight leads to a brief marital separation or after the last of three teen-agers leaves home for college. A surprising number of family blowups take place at a time when the family is moving. A move can have major disruptive influences on family members. Children may lose contact with favorite playmates, babysitters, and schools. A move to another town may deprive the mother of a three-month-old baby of daily contacts with her own mother, who lived three blocks away. Families often leave important friends and sources of social support when they move.

For example, police were called to the local high school to arrest a student who was involved in a fist fight with his teacher. Summoning the family to the police station, the officers learned that the father had lost his job due to the energy crisis. The family, with two teen-age sons, had recently moved from the city to a rural area.

The boys used to escape their parents' continual arguments by spending a good deal of time away from home with their teen-age friends. But now, they found themselves 30 miles from their old friends; nor could they rely on their usual telephone marathons. As a result of the family move and continued marital crisis at home, one son had developed severe behavioral problems at school. The police referred the entire family for further assessment and treatment at the local mental health clinic.

Follow these guidelines in dealing with crises based on separations and moves:

1. ***Clarify the forces that led to the separation for both parties.*** Perhaps you are called to help a young woman who is suicidal over breaking up with her boyfriend. Try to include the boyfriend in your meeting and focus on the factors that led to the separation. You can act as a catalyst, helping the couple to communicate and, in the process, to learn a good deal about themselves. If the meeting leads to a more final separation, help them deal with their feelings and understand the part each played in the separation. If reunion results, the relationship may now be based on a deeper understanding.

2. ***Help the parties make a decision to seek professional consultation.*** Many separation crises take place in a setting in which the family has remained chronically undecided about whether or not to separate. If you find a situation where a spouse is unable to decide, urge the couple to resolve this uncertainty. Take the role of an active intervenor by facilitating the decision-making: urge them to seek guidance, but do not urge their separation.

3. ***If helpful, arrange reunions with long-separated family members.*** A meeting to clarify what led to the separation can be very therapeutic, even a separation of many years. The parents of a 17-year-old boy who was brought to an emergency room in an acute schizophrenic state had separated when he was five. His mother constantly belittled her husband to her children, and controlled and dominated her son. The day of the emergency, the son had run into his father on the street. The feelings of tension which the meeting brought on combined with the boy's struggle to emancipate himself from his mother contributed heavily to his psychosis. At the urging of the crisis worker, the father met with the rest of the family in the emergency room. During the ensuing dramatic scene, the worker stayed with the group. Following the meeting, the boy agreed to be hospitalized to work out his problems.

4. ***Find new sources of support for a relocated family or separated family member.*** When a move or separation is a significant factor in a family crisis, you should focus on formal and informal resources available to the family in the new setting. Facilitate the development of new friends. Establish contacts with sources of help such as family doctors, ministers, and appropriate community agencies. Encourage the development of family and member relationships in the new environment.

Financial or Work Problems

Family crises can be triggered by financial problems involving actual or threatened bankruptcy, foreclosure, or repossession. Work crises commonly involve actual or threatened loss of job by the family breadwinner, although any major work change—a significant raise or an increase or a decrease in work responsibilities—can also be a cause. While financial problems and unemployment are common contributors to family crises in low-income families, many families with substantial incomes also experience problems with finances.

As an example, a paranoid young man with symptoms of psychosis was brought to an emergency room by his wife. He had complained that people were plotting against him at work. A telephone call to his supervisor revealed that he was a skilled and valued employee. However, the supervisor had decided to transfer him to another job with more responsibility, but was reluctant to discuss the change with him because of his touchiness. The nurse arranged a brief discussion between supervisor and employee the next day so that the work crisis was resolved.

Follow these guidelines in dealing with family financial or work problems:

1. *Help the family to obtain qualified financial advice through a local social service agency.* This may lead to simple adjustments such as consolidation of loans or adjustments of debts to avert financial crisis.

2. *Help the family to obtain information about available resources and benefits.* An appropriate agency can inform the family about credit rating, bankruptcy procedures, and/or available welfare benefits. The agency might also assist in job placement and training for family members.

3. *Refer the family to legal aid where appropriate.* The family may be experiencing financial difficulties stemming from unethical sales pitches, excessive interest rates on loans, or illegal contracts. A family member may be a current or potential defendant in a credit transaction or a plaintiff in a suit over unlawful dismissal or job discrimination.

4. *Contact significant members of the work setting.* With a brief phone call, you may be able to clarify and resolve a work crisis, explain a temporary problem, or effect a change.

Illness or Accident

A physical illness or accident can intensify an ongoing family conflict to the point of crisis. Family members, often not understanding the meaning and implications of the illness, have fantasies much worse than actual reality about the illness. Unfortunately, these misperceptions are often supported by doctors, nurses, and other medical staff who fail to explain fully the nature of the illness to the patient and his family.

For example, a 68-year-old man was working as a barman 12 hours a day when an unexpected eye operation for glaucoma left him with 80 percent blindness, resulting in sudden termination of employment. He became dependent on his wife, a situation unacceptable to him. His denial of his blindness was exemplified by a refusal to contact any social agencies for the blind. Shortly after his eye operation, he reached a paranoid delusional state in which he thought his wife was unfaithful and was poisoning his food. His condition led to a series of family and community crises and to his eventual admission to a psychiatric hospital.

Disasters such as floods and earthquakes often produce many different environmental stresses which take place simultaneously and overwhelm the family's abilities to cope adaptively. (For an extensive general discussion of natural disasters, see Chapter IX.) Along with the sudden death or injury of one or more family members, the family may experience the destruction of their home, loss of employment, and relocation. Families that would be able to cope effectively with one or two environmental upheavals may find it impossible to deal with the sudden overwhelming impact of many.

You can help by explaining in detail the nature, outcome and treatment of the illness to the patient and his family. Only when the family realistically understands the illness can it take practical steps to deal with the situation. Unfortunately, medical staff people are afraid that, if a patient or his family is given too much information about an illness, it will add to his anxiety and may even make him worse. However, fantasies and fears are usually worse than the actual medical problem itself. Ask family members enough questions to make sure they understand the illness or disability.

As an example, the wife of a medical student became severely depressed after two consecutive miscarriages. She began to have serious marital difficulties with her husband.

After a non-lethal suicide attempt, she was brought to the emergency room. Assessing the situation, the nurse encouraged the husband to read the latest literature on repeated miscarriages. She also informed the wife that two miscarriages did not alter the future probability for a healthy full-term infant. The wife experienced enormous relief, and the two were referred to a family planning clinic for further assistance.

Sexual Assault on a Child

This grave social concern can have lasting emotional effects on the child's psychosexual development if the crisis is not handled appropriately. Frequently the involved adult is known to the child, possibly a member of his family. Rape of a female child by an uncle or a neighbor is not uncommon. In such instances, the mother may be indirectly involved by quietly providing opportunity for such encounters or by placing the child in difficult home situations. On the other hand, the child may have been seductive or curious (neither infrequent nor psychopathological). Never assume, however, that this was the child's behavior, in any case. One last observation is in order: sexual assaults on male children, although less frequent, do occur.

Rape is a legal offense; the age of consent is established by state law. Every crisis worker should know the age of consent in his state in order to advise the parents and to know how to report the matter. Unreported cases of rape only increase the possibility of recurrence. Since this situation involves a legal matter, the interview and physical examination—especially the vaginal exam—must be done carefully by a physician, with a nurse in attendance. Make every effort not to upset the child further. Any physical examination on the scene should be limited to assessing the extent of non-pelvic injuries.

The parents may be more upset than the child, and their anxiety may heighten the child's fears. You will find yourself working with the emotional needs of both the child and the parents. At all costs, the child should be subjected to as little questioning as possible. One interview in the emergency room should be sufficient.

In most incidents of reported rape of a child, rape has occurred. However, in some cases, rape exists in the child's fantasy or is her attempt to create a difficult situation for an adult. The assessment that rape has occurred and the questioning of the child should be done in the emergency room. The following factors will be present if rape has occurred:

- The child relates in her own words that she has been sexually assaulted. In your desire to be helpful, be careful not to introduce words.
- She appears to be cautious or fearful of male personnel.
- She clings to her mother in an anxious, trembling or crying manner.
- Physical examination may reveal body bruises if force has been used, lacerations of the vagina and possibly the hymen, and the presence of sperm.

Rarely are the physical lacerations so severe that hospitalization is required. However, the incident—extremely serious for the child's mental health—requires immediate psychiatric care, most preferably by a female. If the child has been attacked by a person outside of the family, home is the best place to regain a feeling of security. If a family member living in the house was involved, relocation of the adult is preferable to placement of the child. It should be recognized, however, that the ultimate objective is to stop the behavior of sexual abuse of the child.

Follow these immediate guidelines in dealing with sexual assault on a child:

1. Direct the parents to take the child to the nearest emergency room or to their doctor for treatment. Police or crisis workers are usually notified by the parents of the child.

However, in rare instances, the child or a neighbor approaches such workers. In such cases, the child should be taken to her parents.

2. *Speak to the parents alone.* Explain that the child needs their strength and support and ask them to contain their anxiety and anger in front of the child so she will not be made to feel more anxious and guilty. Direct them not to question the child more than necessary, since questioning will also make her feel anxious. Explain that the child will be interviewed in the emergency room where the history and physical examination will be done.

3. *Do not question the child yourself.*

In emergency room care every effort should be made to have a woman physician or nurse practitioner capable of doing pelvic examinations care for the child who has been sexually assaulted. Examination by a male—no matter how skillfully done—may only trigger additional anxiety in the child.

Follow these further guidelines in treating the sexually assaulted child:

1. *Prepare for an examination in the presence of the mother.* Have the mother hold or sit physically close to the child. Explain that you have to see whether or not she was hurt, and that her mother will be close the whole time. Ask the child whether she hurts anywhere. She will probably indicate the vaginal area. Tell her that you need to check it out and that it may be a little uncomfortable, but you will try not to hurt her.

2. *Perform a vaginal examination, using a nasal speculum.* Make smears for bacterial infection and washings for sperm. Carefully record all signs of trauma.

3. *Conduct a brief humane interview with the child.* Allow the child to dress, and then carefully explain that she has a few cuts, but they'll soon be gone. In a calm manner, ask her if she can explain what happened. If she does not identify the male, ask her if she knows who he is. Tell her that she will have questions about all this, and her parents are the best ones to talk to about it.

4. *Advise the parents to seek legal counsel.*

5. *Direct them not to question the child further, but be ready to answer her questions as they arise.*

6. *Unless the child has been attacked by a member of her household, send the child home with parents.* If she was raped by a family member, suggest that person leave the household rather than dislocate the child.

7. *Report the incident to the police.*

Rape of the Adolescent or Adult

An increasingly common emergency to be handled by health workers is that of rape or forced sexual intercourse. As with so many of the psychiatric emergencies, treatment of rape is closely interwoven with establishing a basis for subsequent legal proceedings. Data taken at the time of the physical examination and police investigation are of great importance when a rape case is presented before the court. The crisis worker, aware of his grave responsibility in these matters, is faced with a difficult task of providing compassionate treatment to the victim while maintaining an objective stance in gathering necessary data. This delicate balance is frequently lost when the worker finds himself deciding whether rape or seduction has occurred. Such judgment is not only extraneous to our role as crisis workers but also tends to bias the actual delivery of care provided.

In a situation of a possible rape, the presenting victim should be given the benefit of doubt. There have been instances in which a person declaring to have experienced rape, has in reality been trying to vindicate his or her own promiscuous sexual behavior or to frame another person. Such cases are *not* the most common. Overzealousness in trying to protect potentially innocent persons from the charge of rape has frequently caused the victim to receive further abuse through dogged questioning and skepticism from all levels of crisis workers.

Aggression experienced by the physical assault of one human person on another is frightening, painful, and embarrassing to the persons involved and to others who may have observed the assault. When the aggression is expressed sexually, all of these feelings are intensified. Sex is still a difficult topic to discuss openly, and, when it occurs in a forced situation, even the more experienced crisis workers can feel less than easy in working with the victim. It is, however, an emergency situation in which the victim is both physically and emotionally traumatized and which requires great skill by the crisis worker in handling the physical and emotional situation without adding to the victim's stress.

In the majority of cases of reported rape, the victims are female, and vaginal intercourse is the prominent aggression; however, anal penetration forced on either males or females may also be regarded as rape.

Collection of data is every crisis worker's responsibility in cases where the presenting victim declares that he or she has been raped. Rape is a crime which should be reported to local authorities, and workers must be fully aware of the state laws concerning rape. Such laws vary from state to state in interpretation, evidence required, and punishment for the offense. However, in all states, the information gathered during emergency treatment of the victim is of utmost importance to subsequent legal proceedings. The crisis worker should be alert to the following observations which suggest that rape has occurred:

- The victim states that he or she has been raped or sexually attacked.
- The victim appears highly nervous but expresses great relief in being with the crisis workers.
- The victim expresses having had a greater fear than rape, e.g., "I thought he was going to kill me."
- The clothes, hair, and make-up of the victim are in disarray.
- Clothing is torn or damply spotted.
- Scratches and bruises are present.
- The victim rubs his or her upper arms, as though the muscles have been hurt.
- The victim frequently holds his or her arms about the body, as if to provide more security.
- The victim verbalizes self-accusations, e.g., "I shouldn't have been there by myself."

At this point the crisis worker should work from the assumption that rape has occurred. He should be aware that rape is usually a potentially serious situation requiring medical care but not necessarily hospitalization.

Unless the rape victim goes directly to an emergency room or a physician's office, the police are usually the first crisis workers contacted by the rape victim.

Follow these guidelines in dealing with a rape victim:

1. ***Listen to what the victim has to say.*** Then explain that he or she may have been badly cut (lacerated) or infected during the experience and that there is a possibility of pregnancy to female victims. Tell the person that you will accompany him or her to the nearest emergency room. If you cannot accompany the victim, get his or her name and address and explain that you will meet him or her later at the emergency room. At this point, do not seek additional information.

2. ***Transmit the description of the attacker to a colleague*** so that a search may begin while you accompany the victim to the emergency room. The victim will probably have given you such descriptive information.

3. ***Speak in a concerned, matter-of-fact***

way and in a low voice. Reassure the victim that the worst part of the experience is over.

4. Proceed with the victim to the emergency ward.

At the emergency room, if for any reason the patient cannot be immediately seen by the hospital staff, the police report may be taken before he or she is physically examined. The report should be taken well out of hearing of other persons in the waiting room. If possible, use an empty examining room for this purpose. Ask the questions quietly and without emphasis.

When the victim is physically examined, a nurse should be present in addition to the physician. In the physical examination the following factors should be considered.

- Written permission for the physical examination is usually required. In those settings where photographs are required as evidence, the victim should be so informed and should be given a reason for the need for such photographs.
- A complete history should be taken, detailing closely the victim's previous sexual history.
- The physician should then ask the victim to describe precisely what happened in the rape situation. If the physician is calm and concerned as well as nonaccusatory in his remarks, the victim will usually give the information without becoming upset further.
- Emphasis should be placed on the physical treatment of the victim. If the victim is overtly anxious, a minor tranquilizer may be prescribed to relax the person before the physical exam.
- The nurse should assist the victim in preparing for the examination, noting any blood or dampness on the clothing. She should instruct the victim not to wash off any secretions, hair, or discharges until after the exam. Slides must be made not only for evidence but also to detect possible infection.
- A thorough physical should be undertaken with a careful noting of all bruises and scratches. The recording of this information should be thoroughly done.
- The vaginal examination should be made. In those instances where large lacerations or tears are present, the patient is usually referred to the operating room. All lacerations and bruises to the genitalia should be carefully recorded as well as the evidence of secretions or foreign matter (e.g., hair, grass, dirt, etc.).
- Specimens of the foreign matter should be made by placing them in sterile test tubes.
- Smears should be made for the presence of sperm and gonorrhea.
- A serology for syphilis should be made. The victim should have a follow-up serology test in approximately six weeks.
- A test for pregnancy should be made.
- Prophylactic measures to abort syphilis, gonorrhea, and the possible pregnancy should be discussed with the victim. If the victim agress, then he or she is placed on a penicillin regime for gonorrhea and syphilis; 50 mg of diethylstelbesterol daily for five days is usually given to abort the possible pregnancy.
- Samples of the victim's stained clothing may be required by the local courts. Here again it is essential that the crisis workers have a working knowledge of the law in that area.
- Once the history and physical examination are complete, the nurse should take the victim aside and repeat any medical instructions. She should ask that a friend or family member be called to accompany the victim home.
- If the victim's clothing is blood stained and will be required for evidence, the nurse should instruct the victim to have the family bring in another set of clothing to be worn home.
- The victim should be told that he or she may feel anxious or depressed in the coming week. The name and phone number of the local community mental health center should be given to the victim.

FAMILY CONFLICT

In addition to external forces generating crisis, there can exist long-standing patterns of conflict or disagreement within a family that some recent change will intensify. Such patterns of conflict are common and easily identified. By interviewing the family as a group, you can discover its interactions. Certain questions asked of each family member often provide useful information. For example, what has been the individual's role in the crisis? What does he see as his own responsibility? What does he want from the family? Are these wants satisfied? What actions make him feel cared for? Do other family members know that these actions make him feel cared for?

The common types of family conflicts which create crisis situations are as follows:

Marital and Family Discord

In any close relationships, there will always be misunderstandings, arguments, and angry feelings; usually both partners contribute equally to the conflict. After such a quarrel, an adult relationship tends to become even closer or more richly rewarding. How adult a relationship really is depends on the maturity of each party. Marital discord may lead a husband and wife into activities ranging from fist fights and loud arguments to prolonged silences.

For example, a middle-aged woman was brought to the emergency room by her husband because she had suddenly lost her voice. The attending physician found no physical cause for the disorder. When the crisis worker talked with the husband alone, he learned that the wife had lost her voice several days after an argument over the husband's late working hours. After discussing the problem with the crisis worker, the couple agreed to accept a referral for marital counseling.

Follow these guidelines when dealing with marital and family discord:

1. The interviewer should be active, inquisitive, and sometimes directive. Do not be embarrassed about asking questions concerning potentially touchy areas. Talk comfortably with the whole family as a group and use informal opportunities just as much as formal interactions. Offering two members of a family a cup of coffee as they wait in the emergency room may be more productive than escorting them into a formal family meeting.

2. View the immediate crisis as an opportunity to examine and resolve long-standing problems. Families can ignore serious difficulties for years until overwhelming events force them to act. In asking the members of a family what happened *today* that pushed them to seek help, you may not only learn the "final straw" event, but also information about previous family crises. The family crisis is a unique chance to work on existing problems which otherwise might be covered up. Do not make the mistake of assuming a cautious attitude and trying to control the family members so that no open or frank discussion of the underlying problems is possible.

3. Try to interview the family together in addition to individual interviews. Too often, only the designated patient is interviewed. Every marital disagreement has at least two sides. Disruption in family communications can lead to a crisis so that messages among family members become misunderstood, distorted, or blocked. The problem intensifies: a person may make a statement one minute and contradict it the next or the family may flatly refuse to talk about certain topics. Here, nonverbal communication patterns need to be watched because a family may express one feeling through words and another through the manner in which they say them. For example, a father may verbally express warm feelings to his daughter in a cold, rejecting manner.

Encouraging family members to talk to each other about the crisis situation will often bring parts of the conflict out in the open. If arguing and fighting result, do not back off from the argument. Instead, try to mediate the argument without taking sides, giving each person a chance to express his thoughts and feelings fully. Marital conflicts can be clarified and resolved through this process. In fact, the crisis may be a family's first opportunity in years to discuss matters of mutual concern.

For example, a young girl came into a crisis unit very depressed. Involved in a homosexual relationship, she was certain that her partner was unhappy with the relationship, though neither person had discussed how she felt. The staff asked her to bring in her partner, and they were encouraged to discuss their relationship openly. The roommate said that she wished to terminate the relationship, but was afraid to talk about her feelings for fear of hurting her partner. Once the feelings were out in the open, both parties were able to go ahead with the separation.

4. *Have the couple clarify their intentions to stay together or separate without pushing them into a commitment.* If the decision is to separate, the parties may need help in dealing with the feelings of loss.

For example, a young couple appeared at an emergency room while having a loud argument. Earlier, the wife had decided to separate from her husband. When they reached the emergency room, the husband realized that he could not change his wife's mind. Consequently, he threatened to kill himself and ran out the door. After the wife and the staff had given chase and caught him, the wife confessed that she had no real intention of separating; she was just angry and trying to get back at him. They made a commitment to stay together and to seek marriage counseling.

5. *Make the family aware of the roles they are playing.* In family conflicts, members may be expected to fill roles that they do not wish to fill or prevented from taking a role that they want. Two or more family members might compete for a role like favorite child or black sheep. A wife may wish to work outside the home, but this role may conflict with the family's expectation that she should be content to be a housewife.

For example, a 28-year-old man, still the baby of the family, had difficulty holding a job. His mother was delighted with the role of taking care of him when he was unemployed. Depressed over his inability to separate from his parents and make his own life, he came with his parents to the crisis unit. The staff determined that the son's role as baby fostered his parents' continual marital difficulties. The worker succeeded in referring all three for family therapy.

6. *Identify and resolve competition for family leadership.* Power struggles are common in family conflicts. The household with a clearly defined, stable, and effective leadership will probably be able to meet most environmental difficulties with a minimum of difficulty. If, on the other hand, the leadership is unstable and contested, the family structure will be threatened even by minor day-to-day difficulties. Common leadership roles in families are breadwinner, decision-maker, performer, and family doctor. Again, it is important that the crisis worker interview the family as a group, not individually. Once it is clear who is competing for what, you might encourage open competition, acting as referree until some resolution occurs.

For example, a 19-year-old boy with acute psychotic symptoms was brought to the emergency room. The crisis worker learned that his mother and father fought frequently. When the fights became physical, the boy would rescue his mother by beating up the father. Placed in this uncomfortable position of being stronger than the head of the household, he sometimes broke down emotionally. At other times when he would attempt to assert his new power, the family would call the police. The worker interpreted the interaction to the family and they agreed to a referral for family therapy.

7. *Treat the family scapegoat as the symptom of an underlying group crisis.* Scape-

goating is a social process in which the family chooses one of its members to blame for problems that are really the responsibility of the group. Scapegoating may end when the family agrees that its problems could be solved by removing the offending member from the family. The family scapegoat usually looks bad to an outside observer. He may be psychotic, hostile, withdrawn, drunk, or unkempt. The worse he looks, the easier it is for the family to force him out. Unfortunately, the solution is only temporary because the underlying family problem remains unchanged. Usually a new scapegoat or a different expression of family conflict emerges.

For example, a depressed teen-ager was brought to an emergency room by his mother, who wanted him institutionalized. The staff learned that, six months ago, the father had died suddenly from a ruptured abdominal aneurysm. The mother refused to experience any sadness over the death, insisting instead that the rest of the family—the patient plus two daughters aged 10 and 12—make no reference to the father's death. The son's depression became the vehicle for the expression of the entire family's feelings. After one counseling session in the emergency room, the mother agreed to seek further help at the community mental health center.

It is useful to gather data in the patient's home in the presence of the family. The on-site setting can flush out family problems. When the patient is then hospitalized, you can identify the family problems involved with his symptoms for the psychiatrist or the crisis worker in the emergency room.

Wife or Husband Abuse

Commonly, verbal and physical abuse arise when the security of the emotionally dependent partner is threatened. Jealousy, arising from fear of rejection, turns into rage at the threat of what is usually an imagined loss. In some instances, both partners are immature and seek a jealous response of the mate to reassure themselves that they are wanted. Feelings of neglect or indifference by the mate frequently precipitate a partner's attempts to gain attention by aggressively striking out at the other person. Physical assault is not easily ignored and usually results in a similar response by the partner. The fighting may be severe; there is no war like a private war.

Neighbors who overhear family battles are frequently the first to notify police or emergency systems for assistance. In case of injury, the casualty arrives at the emergency room emotionally as well as physically traumatized. Be alert to these signs of possible husband or wife abuse:

- Disarray of both partners is apparent and physical injury like multiple contusions, scratches, or fractures may be present.
- Living quarters may reveal traces of a struggle or beating.
- Husband and wife, both angry and frightened, volley accusations back and forth. Both seem to be suspicious about what information the other person is giving.
- Frequent interruptions are made by one while the other is talking.
- Little or no concern is shown by the mate about a partner's injuries. Or the other will appear guilty or sheepish about them.
- Previous calls of similar circumstances have been made by this couple.

The crisis worker should be aware that, during the battle, neither party is in control of the situation. The potential is there for a life-threatening emergency. Few battling couples ever intend homicide. One or both of them are interested only in hurting the partner to the degree he or she has been emotionally hurting. But what actually happens can be serious, usually requiring medical care and occasionally hospitalization.

Entering the scene of wife and/or husband abuse can be dangerous for the crisis worker. Too frequently, the couple regard the worker as an outside threat and unite against him.

Follow these immediate guidelines in dealing with wife or husband abuse:

1. *The police should be the entering party in response to a call from the couple's neighbors.* Forced entry is indicated if the fighting continues and entry is refused.

2. *Inform the couple that a complaint has been made about the fighting, but do not identify the complainant.*

3. *Before the couple can respond with questions, identify yourself.* Tell the couple that you are there to assist them, and ask how badly they are hurt.

4. *If either person is badly beaten, call the emergency ward of the closest hospital.* Inform the ward that you are bringing in a person for evaluation.

5. *While the more severely injured person is being treated, interview the mate for the incident report.* When possible, interview the couple separately. Speak in a low voice to avoid triggering another outburst. Reassure the person by explaining that sometimes situations get out of hand; explain that you need to clarify how this situation arose since a report must be filed.

6. *Do not take sides in the dispute at any time.* Appear to be neutral and ignore accusatory or self-pitying remarks. Ask if either one wishes to file charges. Do not allow either partner to assume the role of the villain or the martyr; both persons are usually to blame.

7. *Inform the couple in a serious manner that such situations all too frequently result in death or serious injury.* Explain that family problems, which have a way of recurring, are caused by combinations of problems and needs which each one has. Do not approach the couple in a preaching or an authoritarian manner because you will have given them another target.

8. *Remain calm and in control of the situation.* If at any time either partner strikes out at the other, call that person loudly and sharply by name and tell both parties to remain seated. If either partner is crying uncontrollably or talking loudly and rapidly, tell him that you cannot understand him. Have him pause a few moments to catch his breath and collect his thoughts.

9. *If the couple still has not quieted down, suggest a physical separation for a day or two.* The separation will give each time to think.

10. *Make a referral to a helping resource.* Be specific: write down the name, address, and phone number of a local community mental health clinic. As you give it to the couple, tell them that a few marital therapy sessions can help them avoid a lot of future pain.

11. *Do not leave the couple until they have either quieted down or have been physically separated.*

Follow these guidelines in emergency room care:

1. *Give a tranquilizer to the more severely injured person to minimize anxiety or mild hysteria.* Equanil or serax, given in a dosage appropriate to the patient's weight, can help *before* treating the physical injuries.

2. *Treat the patient's wounds.*

3. *Do not discuss the cause of the patient's injuries when treating the more serious injury, i.e., broken bones, or until the tranquilizer takes effect.* While treating the minor abrasions, ask the person how he was injured. By this time, he will probably tell you the incident. If his story sounds unreasonable, press him for the real situation.

4. *Listen attentively, but without judg-*

ing. The patient will try to get you on his side against his partner by either whitewashing his role or accusing his mate. Make it clear to him that both persons had a role in the incident.

5. At this point, bring the couple together for a joint interview. Seat the couple side by side across from you. Impress them that their injuries might have been more severe than they are and that, unless they seek marital counseling, they may cause each other permanent physical and emotional harm.

6. Give them the phone number of the local community mental health center. Tell them that you expect them to make an appointment and then ask if they agree to do so.

Homicide Intent and Attempt

Most homicides that occur in this country are committed by a member of the victim's family, by someone with whom he was closely associated. These crimes are usually emotionally rather than materially motivated. Jealousy, anger, and impulsiveness form the most common triad of emotions. The murderer usually greatly regrets his action, frequently trying to take his own life as well.

Most murders in the home occur following numerous fights between the victim and the aggressor. Untreated cases of husband or wife abuse or unresolved parent-adolescent conflicts eventually reach a point where one individual, no longer able to take the stress, strikes out to destroy another. An aggressor's impulsive personality is a key factor in the realization of a homicide attempt. Intent may have been voiced angrily beforehand to the victim, who probably did not regard it seriously.

The victims of homicidal threats or attempts sometimes actively and repetitively provoke their partners to complete the act.

The crisis worker must be alert to signs of homicidal intent. Be aware that this state of mind can exist short of actual premeditation. Abuse of a husband or wife may, in fact, be a homicidal attempt. A potential homicidal situation is serious, possibly requiring hospitalization of the aggressor. Factors indicating homicidal intent or attempt are as follows:

- In cases of abuse by beating, threats to kill are made. The aggressor may remark, "if it happens again, I'll kill him" or the victim might recall that "he was so mad he tried to kill me."
- The reported focus of the fight was the bedroom or kitchen.
- Weapons, particularly guns, are present in the home.
- The aggressor in the fight is known for his impulsiveness and bad temper, though he repeatedly insists that he did not mean to do it.
- The victim, though fearful, baits the aggressor with belittling remarks.
- Previous fights have occurred between the individuals.
- With more precision, the injuries might have resulted in death.

Follow these guidelines in dealing with homicide intent or attempt:

1. Initial entry to the home should be made by police.

2. Let the police deal with the aggressor while the emergency crew treats the victim. Remove any further dangers. If a husband is threatening his wife with a loaded gun, police should separate the man from the loaded gun. If police are not there, avoid confrontation even in the case of severely injured victims.

3. Effective action by family members can often provide a practical solution in such instances.

4. Allow the aggressor to talk out his stress and try to quiet and treat the victim. Focus on his physical injury. Speak quietly to the victim and tell him that you want him to save his strength. Emotionally, both persons involved in the situation will be distraught and want to talk.

5. *If the aggressor asks to speak to the victim, allow him to do so, but only if a crisis worker is also present.* His desire to kill the victim is probably dissipated, but the victim probably still fears him.

6. *Move the individuals as quickly as possible away from the crisis scene.*

Usually just the victim comes into the emergency room after a homicide attempt. The injury—commonly a gunshot or knife wound—is probably serious, requiring hospitalization, if not surgery.

Follow these guidelines in emergency room care:

1. *Take immediate care of the patient's physical injury.* If possible, give the patient medication for pain.

2. *Reassure him that the danger is past.* If possible, while doing physical tasks, lightly put your hand on his arm. Allow him to relieve his stress if he wants to cry.

3. *If the patient says that the aggressor intended no real harm, do not contradict him.* Denial is an immediate way of coping. The patient will later accept the reality of the situation.

4. *Do not leave the patient alone.* Instruct the nurses to remain with him until sedation takes effect.

5. *Follow through with psychiatric therapy.* Pursue this at a later time when the patient's physical condition has stabilized.

6. *Remember that the risk of homicide is greater after the patient is discharged.* He will again interact with the family and encounter environmental forces which contributed to the initial homicidal threat. It is also a time when staff follow-up is minimal or absent. During the hospitalization of individuals who make homicidal threats, the risk of homicide is usually minimal. Staff members are usually acutely aware of the patient's previous homicidal behavior.

Child Abuse

One of the most difficult cases for an emergency worker is the battered child. A child is virtually defenseless in a physical fight against an adult, and the child's survival is always of concern. The crisis worker will find himself angry at parents who have beaten the child. Recognizing the defenselessness of the child, you may even find yourself unleashing a verbal onslaught against the parents. Such action is not only a waste of time, but may actually precipitate further injuries to the child or other children in the family.

Parents who abuse their children are emotionally immature persons. Unable to cope with their own stress, they lash out in disproportionate rage when upset. Frequently the crisis is triggered by situations in which the parents' needs have not been immediately gratified. Most adults can wait for satisfaction, but immature persons cannot. These persons literally throw tantrums when frustrated. Typically, the parents find themselves trapped in a situation and come to see the child as a symbol of that trap, or at least a strong factor in keeping them in the unsatisfying situation. Dissatisfaction with income, housing, food, or status can be behind the force of rage that a crying or misbehaving child may receive. Generally, the parent is the responsible aggressor; in some instances, however, a baby sitter or another adult in the household has actually committed the crime.

Child abuse, though not easily recognized, is a crime which has to be reported to appropriate local authorities or agencies. You need to be alert to the following observations that strongly suggest the child has been battered by another human being:

- Notification of the injured child to police or health personnel is made by a person other than the child's parents.
- Other than the acute injury, the child has multiple bruises, lacerations, or burns—all at different stages of healing.
- The extent of injury is out of proportion to the reason given. For example, the child has a broken arm and his parents explain that he ran into a door.
- Burns the size of the diameter of a cigarette may be spotted in varying stages of healing.
- The parents do not appear apprehensive or overly concerned about the child's injury. They may withdraw to another side of the room as the emergency worker treats the child.
- The parents make little or no direct attempt to help or comfort the child.
- In seeking comfort the child does not reach for the parent.
- The child appears physically neglected and malnourished.

If any or all of these observations are valid in a case involving an injured child, you probably are dealing with child abuse. The responsible person should be asked how the injury occurred. If he gives a story that does not seem to be supported by the injury, you should state that children frequently get on people's nerves and that sometimes the child is abused. Explain that when this situation occurs, the incident has to be reported. Usually, the parent will then relate the actual happening.

An abused child is in a life-threatening situation—not only from the physical injuries he has sustained, but also from the unpredictable and insecure environment of his home. Children have been beaten or burned to death by emotionally unstable adults. The risk of maintaining the child in such a life-threatening home environment necessitates hospitalization or temporary placement of the child. The acute physical problems of malnutrition are frequently so severe that the hospitalization is medically warranted.

Follow these immediate guidelines in dealing with child abuse:

1. *Gain entry to the home and access to the child.* If the parents placed the emergency call, gaining access is not a problem. If a neighbor placed the call, tell the parent that all such calls must be fully checked and that you will help the parent with the injured child. Speak in a low but firm voice, avoiding further upset by the parents.

2. *Focus attention on the child, administering physical first aid.* Speak softly to the child, using his name. Do not ask him to recreate the situation while he is still in an emergency state.

3. *Do not question the child about his traumatic experience.* Remember that he is still in the crisis environment and the abuser is probably present.

4. *Do not question the adults in front of the child.*

5. *After giving first aid, inform the parents that the child must be taken to the hospital for x-rays and further treatment.* Ask the parents to notify the hospital.

6. *In a room adjoining the child's, ask the parents to describe how the child was injured.* Do not glare at the parents or respond with disbelief to their explanation. Inform them that, in all cases of child injury, child abuse is a concern to be ruled out. Ask whether they have additional information they wish to share with you.

7. *Take the child to the emergency ward of the hospital.* If possible, place the child on the seat next to you. The parents should follow in their own car. In situations where this is not possible, the child should at least be placed next

to you and the parents in the rear seat out of sight. In an ambulance, be certain that the child can focus his eyes only on the attendant, not on the parents.

8. *The child probably will be very quiet or will be whimpering. Talk to the child, acknowledging that you know he is in pain, but that the pain will soon be stopped.* Lightly touch the child's arm or maintain some slight physical contact; speak in a low, deliberate, and reassuring manner.

The most mature and competent professional person in the emergency room—physician or nurse—should manage a child abuse case. The person should control the display of his emotions, obtain facts without antagonizing others, and refrain from placing himself in judgment over others. These behaviors are valuable also to every member of the emergency crisis team; once learned, they can facilitate management of any family crisis.

Many health teams direct the nurse to talk with the child and the physician to talk with the parents. How to proceed is up to the emergency team, but decisions must be made so that none of the tasks is overlooked. Try to keep an adult in the examining room with the child at all times.

Follow these guidelines in emergency room care:

1. *Physically treat the abused child.* Also, you can best meet his emotional needs. As you work, talk with the child in a soft, easy-going manner.

2. *If the child has broken bones, take x-rays for evidence of abuse.* There may be epiphyseal shearing and metaphyseal cracks from twisting or jerking the limb.

3. *Carefully examine the victim.* Note all burns, bruises, scratches, or scars. The general health status of the child should be determined.

4. *Once the child has become used to you, tell him that you need to know how he was hurt.* Do not push the child to respond. Give him time to answer as you sit with him. As the child begins to relate the event, his anxiety will increase; let him continue his story, but sit close to him, or, when possible, hold him.

5. *Let him cry if he wants, but comfort him.* Now that he is in a safe environment, he needs to release his tension. Let him know he is in a close association with an adult who will help and protect him. Tell him that now it is all over and he is safe and that you want him to stay in the hospital with the doctors and nurses. Promise him that you will talk to his parents.

6. *While the child is still in an examining room, talk with the parents in a private area.* This area should be away from the mainstream of people in the waiting room. Sit with them as you talk.

7. *Tell the parents the child's condition and the fact that he will have to remain in the hospital for a few days.* Tell them that in cases of child injury, there is a concern of child abuse. State calmly that such cases have to be reported to the appropriate authorities.

8. *If they deny abuse, quietly inform them that a report will have to be made.* Thank them for answering the questions.

9. *If the parents acknowledge their role in the child's injuries, you should recognize their difficulty in talking about it.* Tell them that adults do get angry with children, but the extent to which the anger is acted out is a grave concern to everyone.

10. *Recommend a few sessions at the local community mental health service or mental health clinic even if the parents offer assurance that the situation will not be repeated.* Tell them that in order to help them realize that goal and for the child's additional safety you want them to have an appointment at the service or clinic. Give the phone number of the service or clinic

and the name of a person to contact for an appointment. Tell them that you will contact that agency to make certain the appointment has been made and kept. Such information will be included in your report to the local police or community agency.

11. Ask them if they have other children and if a similar incident has ever occurred.

12. Ask them the details of the situation leading to the abuse. Try to determine what major frustration triggered the encounter.

13. Identify the major frustration. Begin with the following lead: "It seems that (identify conflict) was a major source of frustration that led up to your child's injury. If you experience those same frustrations tomorrow, how would you handle them differently?" If the parents' answer is appropriate, i.e., "I'd work it off," "I'd just yell," or "I'd go for a walk," tell them, "Fine, that's good. That's the sort of thinking I'd like you to start on before your appointment at the clinic."

14. Direct them to sign admission papers for the child.

15. Note whether they ask to see the child. If they want to, and the child is not extremely agitated, let them spend a few minutes with the child in your presence and in the presence of the person who has been with the child.

INDIVIDUAL SYMPTOMATIC BEHAVIOR

When an individual is brought to a police station or a hospital emergency room with such striking symptoms as homicidal, suicidal, or psychotic behavior, the fact that these symptoms are often tied to a family crisis is easily missed. Because of the dramatic nature of the symptoms, there is a natural tendency for staff members to focus their attention on the "ill" individual, missing the family upheaval that contributed heavily to the symptoms. The following types of symptomatic behavior are often associated with family crises.

Mental Illness

Symptoms of an individual's mental illness are directly related to family crises. The symptoms of an acutely schizophrenic young man, for example, may be a sort of witty, illogically accurate "state of the union" message about critical family problems.

As an example, a 35-year-old woman whose husband was preparing to divorce her was brought to the emergency room hallucinating and behaving bizarrely. Any time a man passed within 10 feet of her, she attacked him, tried to kick or grab his genitals, and said the devil was talking to her. These symptoms allowed her to express directly her present appraisal of men in general and one man in particular. Her husband, who was feeling somewhat guilty about wanting to leave his wife, decided to postpone plans for divorce, at least while his wife was seriously ill.

Follow these guidelines in dealing with individual symptomatic behavior:

1. Find out about family problems underlying the symptomatic behavior of the patient. Ask about family life at home, relationships with other family members, and the patient's feelings about family.

2. Contact the family. With the patient's permission, make one or two brief telephone calls to provide useful insight into how the mental illness fits into problems that the whole family may be having.

3. Involve the family members who brought the patient. Usually the patient is brought to a helping resource by a family member; it is a simple matter to include those members in immediate interventive procedures.

If assistance was requested over the telephone, you can arrange to involve family members during the evaluation process.

4. *Evaluate family strengths and weaknesses.* When an individual family member displays serious psychiatric symptoms, a quick appraisal of family assets and inabilities can influence decisions about immediate management. In a responsible and helpful family structure, for example, it is often possible to use rapid tranquilization procedures for acutely schizophrenic patients while they remain at home. This requires 24-hour supervision and observation for the first few days by responsible family members. In a destructive family setting or with a family exhausted by symptomatic behavior, it may be better to arrange for a separation of the patient from the family, possibly an inpatient alternative hospital setting. With less severe symptoms, individual and family treatment procedures can begin after an immediate individual and family evaluation.

5. *Intervention in family problems must take place simultaneously with individual treatment procedures in the management of mentally ill individuals.*

Antisocial Behavior

Like the symptoms of mental illness, antisocial behavior often takes place at a point in time directly related to important family crises. For example, two teen-age boys, 16 and 17, whose parents fought constantly, regularly ran away from home and got into a number of minor scrapes with the law. The father finally got fed up and kicked them out of the house, and they went to stay with their grandparents. Two weeks later, the father dropped dead of a heart attack. Within the next two months, one brother had been charged with armed robbery; the other brother was in jail after he and an accomplice robbed a small store and savagely beat the elderly store owner to death.

Follow these guidelines in dealing with an antisocial behavior situation:

1. *Determine the existence of a family crisis pursuant to the antisocial behavior.* Individuals often get into trouble with the law at a moment of family stress. Assess the type and extent of family involvement.

2. *Intervene appropriately in the family unit, using the crisis triggered by the antisocial behavior as a point of entry.*

For example, a man was arrested and charged with assault as a result of a fight in a bar which took place just after he left the house after an argument with his wife. In a visit to his home the next day, immediate intervention focused on clarifying patterns of unresolved anger between him and his wife.

In another case, a rapist had a clear pattern of committing rapes right after his unresolved arguments with a controlling, domineering mother. Intervention consisted of six family sessions with both the rapist and his mother. The sessions aimed at increasing awareness by the rapist of his anger at his mother and at helping each of them find alternatives to the angry interchanges that preceeded his antisocial behavior.

Physical and Psychosomatic Illness

Not surprisingly, when a family experiences a number of successive crises, the risk of physical illness by its members increases significantly. Studies by Reese and Lutkins show that the mortality rate of family members who have experienced a death in the family increases to six times the normal rate during the year and a half after the death. According to Holmes, illness rates also increase significantly when individuals experience more than the normal amount of significant life crises.

In dealing with physical and psychosomatic illness: assess the family difficulties contributing to the illness. Some factors will be obvious. In one case a 35-year-old Chicano male developed ulcer symptoms whenever his matriarchal, invalid mother, whom he had been taught to revere and respect, moved into his house. The symptoms went away when she moved on to stay with one of his brothers.

But the interaction between physical illness and family crisis is generally more complex. For example, a 47-year-old woman with severe emphysema was married to a binge-drinking alcoholic. They had a delicate balance between them regarding the invalid role: she took care of him after a binge and he nursed her through her chest infections. When the balance was upset—perhaps by unusually frequent recurrences of binge drinking—she increased her smoking, bringing on chest troubles. Long-term family counseling could produce only minor changes in this pattern.

Alcohol Problems

Problems around alcohol use are often directly related to family problems and crises. Men with alcohol problems often belong to families who unwittingly encourage their drinking behavior. One woman reacted to her husband's excessive drinking in bars by constantly nagging him. The husband, after usually getting drunk with friends, would return home to confront an angry and tearful wife. After she berated him, he would return to the bar and his friends. The action got him away from her nagging, provided a way of fighting back, and gave him the excuse to continue drinking. (For a complete discussion of the alcoholic himself, see Chapter IV.)

Follow these guidelines in dealing with a family alcoholism crisis:

1. ***Assess the patient's family status.*** Individuals who have been chronic alcoholics for many years often have severed family ties. But the majority of problem drinkers retain family relationships so that their crises are commonly associated with upheavals in the family.

2. ***Meet with the family and establish communication with the employer.*** One or two meetings with the whole family may clarify the roles its members play in the patient's drinking pattern. A telephone conversation with the employer—followed by a meeting which includes the patient—may help in instances where drinking has interfered with work. Encourage both the family and those in the work setting not to cover up or make excuses for drinking behavior. At work clear conditions need to be spelled out, with specific penalties for drinking behavior which interferes with work and specific inducements to decrease such behavior.

3. ***Provide resources for family members.*** Those who must live with problem drinkers might be helped by involvement in an organization like Alanon or Alateen. They may benefit from referral to a family counseling program.

Adolescent Drug Abuse

At least three-fourths of the teen-agers who come to emergency rooms or mental health resources because of problems with soft drugs also have an underlying conflict with their parents concerning the processes of growing up. Immediate management of overdoses of soft and hard drugs should involve the family. (See Chapter V for a more complete discussion of drug abuse.)

Follow these guidelines in dealing with adolescent drug abuse:

1. ***With the patient's consent, contact the parents and try to arrange a conference between the parents and the teen-ager.*** A single family meeting focusing on touchy areas like parental setting of limits, the fairness of rules, the degree of responsibility expected by parents, the degree of control and responsibility expected of the parents by the teen-ager, and open communication about areas such as drug use and sexual behavior can produce enough family change to alter significantly the symptomatic behavior of the teen-ager.

Explain to the family that drugs are taken not only as a form of pleasure, but also as a means of coping with stress. Also, adolescence is a period when major methods of handling anxiety and stress are learned. But if drugs become a solution, such coping behaviors are not learned.

2. Encourage the patient to get help at the time of the crisis. He may well change his mind when the crisis is past.

3. Refer patient and parents for family counseling.

Suicide Attempt at Home

The chosen location of home suggests that the person attempting suicide wants to shock his family with the seriousness of his problems, to make the family feel guilty, or to increase his chances of being found before the suicide is completed. The family members feel no small measure of guilt, shame, and anger concerning the attempt. (See Chapter VI for a more complete discussion.)

Follow these guidelines in dealing with a suicide attempt at home:

1. Assess the risk.

2. Avert the act.

3. Talk with the family. Tell them that a suicide attempt is essentially a cry for help and an indication that a person is overwhelmed by his problems. Ask for their ideas on identifying what his problems might be. Remind them that the person who attempted suicide will have the same problems when he returns home. Ask how they plan to help him with the problems they have identified for you.

4. Help them handle their guilt. If a family member starts assuming the full blame by such statements as, "It's all my fault; if only I had done . . . " respond by saying, "But you didn't, and at that time, you had good reasons for not doing it. Can you remember what those reasons were?" This action tends to reinstate the value of the family member. Identify the feelings of guilt, shame, and anger the family is feeling, and be careful to let them know these feelings are normal responses.

5. Refer patient and family to appropriate resources. Give them a list of resource agencies where someone who has attempted suicide can receive professional counseling.

SUGGESTED READINGS

Caplan, G. *Principles of Preventive Psychiatry.* London: Tavistock Publications, 1964.

Fish, Lawrence. "Using Social Systems Treatment Techniques on a Crisis Unit." *Hospital and Community Psychiatry* 22(1971):252-55.

Jones, M., and Polak, Paul. "Crisis and Confrontation." *British Journal of Psychiatry* 114(1968):114.

Langsley, Donald G., and Kaplan, David M. *The Treatment of Family in Crisis.* New York: Grune & Stratton, Inc., 1968.

Lindemann, E. "Symptomatology and Management of Acute Grief." *American Journal of Psychiatry* 101(1944):141-48.

Parad, Howard J., ed. *Crisis Intervention: Selected Readings.* New York: Family Service Association of America, 1965.

Polak, Paul. "The Crisis of Admission." *Social Psychiatry* 2(1968):150-58.

———. "Rapid Tranquilization." *American Journal of Psychiatry* 128(1971):640-43.

———. "Social Systems Intervention." *Archives of General Psychiatry* 25(1971):110-17.

———. "Techniques of Social Systems Intervention." In *Current Psychiatric Therapies*, edited by Jules H. Masserman, vol. 12. New York: Grune & Stratton, Inc., 1972.

VIII

Crisis Management of Dying Persons and Their Families

Elisabeth Kubler-Ross, M.D.

EMOTIONAL NEEDS OF THE DYING PATIENT

Despite much literature in recent years on the care of dying patients and their families, very little information is available on the needs of acutely ill patients who are admitted to hospital emergency rooms and have no chance for survival. Equally scarce is material on the needs of family members, who arrive ill-prepared for the shocking news of critical illness.

Ours is a youth-oriented society where fitness and health are highly valued. It is a mobile culture in which young couples rarely live with their parents or grandparents. They are thus spared the daily reminders of a father unable to adjust to retirement, or a grandparent forced to adjust to a nursing home. In avoiding the issues of old age and death, we are not attuned to such emergencies. Residences are changed so often that we have neither the advantage of a familiar neighborhood nor that of a family physician who might have known us physically, emotionally, and socially since childhood.

It is precisely within this framework—in which we are almost "strangers-on-the-go"—that illness and sudden death strike harder than in past decades, when friends, relatives, and neighbors were always close in a time of crisis.

The crisis worker should be aware of the modern day strains which accompany life and death situations. Four areas, particularly, are of concern here: meeting the needs and feelings of *the patient*, providing support and help for the *family members*, recognizing and lessening the stresses for *hospital personnel* and other helpers, and organizing *institutional services* to handle the psychiatric implications of such emergencies.

The Problem

The difficulties begin when the patient is found critically ill or injured, requiring transportation to the nearest medical facility. Typically, there is little empathy for the patient, who is carried into an ambulance and taken away—usually to a strange hospital.

When the patient reaches the emergency room, there is an air of great urgency because everyone is keenly aware that minutes may count. The emergency staff has neither time nor leisure to consider emotional needs. The victim must be quickly screened to determine the nature of the disorder and what must be done immediately to alleviate the life-threatening condition. Upon arrival the patient may already be without one or more vital signs. Evaluating the situation and acting to maintain vital functions are, in themselves, enormous tasks.

As the emergency room physicians and nurses are skillfully and frantically fighting to save a life, furthest from their minds are the patient's psychological and spiritual needs. The critically ill or injured patient, often in a state of physical and emotional shock, is usually not even aware of what is happening to him.

Sometimes, though, the patient may be conscious enough to realize the seriousness of his situation. Possibly with the ambulance's siren and flashing lights still in his mind and a twilight world of unfamiliar figures grouped around him, he may be overcome with fear for his immediate and future safety.

The patient may react to this emergency environment in one of several ways. He might ask or attempt to ask about his condition. Or he may be aware enough to be concerned about his condition, but unable to ask. He may specifically ask if he is dying. He might even inquire after family members or friends who perhaps were also injured and for whom he feels responsible.

Immediate Management of the Crisis

Follow these guidelines during the crisis:

1. ***Inform the patient who you are, what you or others are doing, and where he is to be taken.*** The patient's physical needs are the primary concern at this moment. But as soon as possible, the conscious patient deserves some explanation. Even though he is dazed or incoherent, a person is likely to feel less anxious and apprehensive if he senses that someone is keeping him informed, both on the scene and in the ambulance.

2. ***Avoid glum comments about his condition.*** The semiconscious patient can overhear expressions of fear or glib remarks about his apparently serious or hopeless condition.

3. ***Assure the patient that you will locate and notify his family.*** He may or may not be able to assist you. Make a concerted effort to reach them. Not only can the family be of great comfort to the patient, but they will want an opportunity to see or speak with him before he dies. Tell his family briefly what has happened, who you are, and where they can meet the patient. Indicate that the matter is serious and urgent.

4. ***In the emergency room, try to orient the patient to his surroundings.*** The patient may be conscious but disoriented, especially if he has suffered a head injury. Talk to him in a brief and factual manner. For example, "Mr. Jones, you have had an accident, and you are in a general hospital. I am Mrs. Smith, and I am going to help you get comfortable until the doctors get here to take a look at you."

5. ***Be honest without shocking him.*** Crisis workers must be very sensitive to each individual and decide how much the patient is able to "hear." If you can be honest without further shocking him or filling him with unnecessary information, you will be doing the patient a service. For example, a patient arriving in the emergency room with life-threatening symptoms of his basic disease—such as severe gastrointestinal bleeding as a complication of his gastric ulcer or ulcerated colitis—should be informed that his symptoms are due to internal bleeding.

6. ***Allow for hope.*** Sometimes, a patient will ask if he is dying. Since he may be, the crisis worker is frankly at a loss for words. In

situations of this nature, do not tell a patient that he is dying. The patients who have done the poorest are the ones where information is given in a cold black-or-white fashion, leaving them little hope.

Instead, simply say, "I don't know that, but we are going to fight this out together. We won't give up on you and don't you give up on yourself." The patient will then trust you and believe that everything possible will be done to save his life. If he answers, "Look, I know that I am going to die anyway," you can add, "It is possible, but we can still try the best, can't we?" The patient knows, then, you will not lie to him and he can feel secure that you will not give up on him.

7. Use discretion in relaying news to the patient about the death of a family member, passengers, victims, or others. If the patient is in critical condition, for example, wait to tell him that his wife is dead. Already subjected to emotional trauma because of his own injuries, he may go into shock or lose his will to survive if he gets additional bad news at this point. There are some exceptions to this. For example, a very badly injured man was brought to a hospital. His wife was killed, but his son was doing well. When the man asked about his family, the physician said, "I am not sure about your wife, but I saw your son and he is doing well." The man then asked, "She is dead already, isn't she?" The physician nodded.

If a man asks a straight-forward question, you have to tell him the truth—regardless of how serious his condition is. It is not acceptable to lie to him at this moment. The physician then asked if the badly injured patient could fight for his life for his son's sake; he replied, "Yes, I will."

8. Impress on the patient the seriousness of his condition. There are rare occasions when a patient is in a total state of denial. He may arrive in the hospital in critical condition, but refuse to be admitted. He might insist on returning to work or to an important meeting. You may have to contact next of kin to assist in this situation. If he still refuses, present him with the papers stating that he would have to sign out against medical advice. An alternative is to declare him temporarily incompetent and detain him while summoning relatives who may be able to reason with him.

9. If a serious operation is necessary, consult the patient if he is conscious and lucid; if he is not, ask the family. A patient may be brought into the emergency room with injuries necessitating amputations of the limbs or gross disfigurement. Usually the patient is in a state of shock and our information is directed towards relatives. There is a tendency toward great secrecy.

But if a patient is conscious and able to think clearly, hold any discussions about necessary operations with the patient alone. Follow this with brief, clear, and precise information to the family. If at all possible, a hospital chaplain might stay with the grief-striken family. The physician can then leave for the operating room while the family is free to ask further questions.

10. Lightly sedate patients who have caused a car accident first to relieve their guilt and turmoil. The sedation should not put him to sleep or make him unable to communicate. When a patient is admitted after a car accident which he caused, he is often deeply upset and guilty. He may be oblivious to his own pain or injury, often wanting to die because he feels responsible for the tragedy. A member of the health team—nurse, clergy, social worker, or specially trained volunteer—should sit with the patient in a private room and let him talk about the incident.

A patient who has been drinking and caused an accident may repeatedly recall past warnings by family members. Allow him to express his remorse and do not reassure him with false statements. By your caring and non-judgmental presence you can communicate some understanding of his turmoil.

11. Injured children are treated basically the same as adults, except for the presence of a parent or other relative. Health professionals prefer to have sobbing and hysterical relatives out of a patient's room, but this shutting out of concerned relatives only increases their anxieties and the anxiety of the injured child.

HELP FOR FAMILY MEMBERS

Their Needs

The family needs support. Crises demand quick actions and competent responses from a team. At least one team member should be available to answer relatives' questions. Someone should be able to take care of the family when they arrive, helping them face anxiety, grief, and specific decisions.

The family should be with a dying patient. When a patient is close to death, do not send the relatives out of the room "to spare them." Clinical experience shows that this action only adds to their grief and does not make it easier later on. A wife who holds her husband's hand when he takes his last breath feels better than if she had retreated to a lonely hallway or a cold waiting room until she is notified it is all over.

Notification

A relative who was with the injured or stricken person should notify the family. If no familiar person is present, a nurse or physician should. An emergency room worker should make the phone call rather than a hospital chaplain since the latter is associated with a critical or terminal condition.

Whether a patient is still alive or dead on arrival in the hospital, the family should not be informed over the telephone. When you do phone, simply state that the patient has been brought to the emergency room after a severe injury and that the family should come as soon as possible. The family members—who will arrive shocked and upset—should have been given clear information on *where* to go and *who* specifically will be waiting for them at the entrance. In these circumstances, relatives should not have to wait around until called.

When a patient dies on his way to or shortly after arrival in the emergency room, it is essential that a physician give this information to the family. He must not pass on this responsibility to a minister, social worker, or nurse. If the physician asks someone else to relay the news, the family might well conclude that no physician was in the emergency room when the patient arrived or that he may have been deprived of medical attention which could have still saved his life. Once the physician has informed the relatives, another member of the emergency team can then take over, spending more time with them.

Demands from the Family

Follow these guidelines in responding to needs of the patient's family:

1. The family may need help at the scene of the accident or at the hospital. Anyone in the family who saw the patient's accident might himself be in a state of shock. If so, he may find decisions difficult or he may act in a confused manner.

When the ambulance arrives on the scene, the first concern for a crisis worker must be the injured person. But often you are also confronted with upset and slightly injured relatives who should also be taken to the hospital for a thorough medical examination. These relatives may be needed later if the hospital staff needs further witnesses or the next of kin for the signing of consent papers.

2. They may ask to accompany the patient in the ambulance. At least one relative should accompany the victim to the hospital, comforting him and answering his questions.

The patient feels somewhat reassured if he can look up and see a familiar face; the relative, too, benefits because he is physically present and able to give reassurance. Sometimes, though, relatives are not allowed to go in the ambulance; by the time they do arrive at the hospital, the injured person has been taken to the treatment or operating room.

3. *The family may want to see the injured patient, even though a medical team may already be working to save his life.* You should arrange for a nurse, hospital chaplain, or social worker to wait for these relatives in order to inform them briefly what is happening to the patient and when they might be allowed to see the patient.

4. *If the patient died enroute or immediately after arrival, the family may wish to view the body.* The crisis worker must understand the needs of family members. Do not prevent them from viewing the body prior to its preparation in the funeral home—if that is their wish. The crisis worker may instinctively try to protect the family from the unpleasant sight of a severely mutilated body. But the option to view the body at this time belongs to the family.

5. *The family will need help after the death in expressing its grief, anger, guilt and other feelings.* This is true both immediately following the death and in the weeks to come. It is essential that the relatives not hear the bad news in a waiting area or in a public hallway. Take them into a small, private room where, after the news, they can feel free to ask questions, cry, or simply sit.

The biggest problem in a busy emergency room area is the need to get the relatives out of the hospital as soon as possible. This situation does not give the family members an opportunity to face up to reality; usually, any follow-up counseling is too brief to help in this respect. If the family members are allowed to sit in a quiet, private area within the hospital along with a chaplain, trained volunteer, nurse, or another caring person, they will be able to call other family members or just have a cup of coffee together as they try to think clearly about what steps should be taken.

6. *The family must arrange the funeral and burial and make any necessary changes in living arrangements.* Although these steps need not be done immediately, they should be dealt with during the next several hours.

7. *The family may be asked to deal with the coroner in identifying the body or granting permission for an autopsy.* If a person dies suddenly and without witnesses, the coroner very often requires an autopsy. You may need considerable tact and sensitivity to make the family understand that they have no option. The physician—in his role of requesting the autopsy—can explain to the family why the autopsy is mandatory and that it is the only way to find out the cause of death. In addition, he should reassure the family that everything humanly possible has been done to save the patient and that no other efforts could have prevented this death.

8. *The family may react with extreme anger.* It is hard to predict reactions. Some people who are not in a state of denial may berate the doctors and nurses, accusing them of not doing enough or failing to do the right thing. Others may be angry with the ambulance driver or with other relatives.

Management of Family Needs

Follow these guidelines in dealing with family members:

1. *Provide privacy for the relatives.* While conference space is not always available near the emergency room, provide what privacy you can. The family will want to stay physically close to a critically ill relative, even if family members must be limited in bedside visits.

The concept of the "screaming room" is useful in these situations. This room near the emergency room is staffed by a caring, understanding person who is familiar with the grief process and with the problems surrounding a sudden death. Some of the best trained volunteers are mothers who have lost a child and who volunteer to assist bereaved families.

2. *Do not sedate family members.* The tendency too often is to sedate crying, screaming, or hysterical relatives immediately to keep them quiet. But they are better served if allowed to cry and ask questions. They must be allowed to express an immediate reaction.

3. *Do not rush the relatives.* They should be permitted to have someone who can simply sit with them and allow them to express their feelings.

4. *Let the members of a family ventilate their feelings.* Be very concerned about relatives who remain too quiet—perhaps reacting little or not at all. The people who cry or scream after a sudden death are able to express their grief. They are much less a risk than those who keep everything inside.

5. *Stay with the family, even if the situation is prolonged.* A vigil can be long or there could be some procedural delay after death such as reaching the coroner or the attending physician to sign the death certificate. The delay may be unavoidable, but help from a volunteer in making phone calls, contacting relatives, or listening over a cup of coffee can help the family cope. Do not leave the relatives alone unless they request it, and then only if they do not appear to be in a severe state of shock or emotional turmoil.

6. *Be sensitive to suicide risks within the family.* A person who has lost an only relative or who feels responsible for a fatal accident is a potentially high suicidal risk. Never allow him to leave the hospital alone—particularly in a state of shock and denial. If necessary, admit the person to the hospital, though not to a psychiatric unit. He needs a comfortable room where he can receive warm, caring attention at this time of emotional crisis. In all probability, this will involve an overnight stay.

7. *Allow them to express anger.* A grieving relative may berate or blame the ambulance driver, the doctors, or the nurses for the death of a loved one. It is very hard to know how to help this person because he is already in an irrational state of anger. But do not judge him; try to understand that this is an expression of his pain, anguish, and grief. Let him ventilate his rage and stay nearby.

8. *Allow the members of a family to see the patient when they arrive.* If the patient is surrounded by a treatment team performing emergency surgery, starting infusions, blood transfusions, or other procedures, it is understandable that relatives cannot simply walk in. However, as soon as emergency procedures have been taken and the injured person is in the recovery room, allow one or two visitors.

Even if the injured person dies within minutes after the family arrives, it is of utmost importance that the members see their relative before death occurs. They need to express their love, guilt, or concern once more—verbally or non-verbally. They may ask for forgiveness or bring up some unfinished business before it is too late. Or they seek reassurance that everything humanly possible was done to save the patient's life.

9. *Let the family see the body if they so request.* Crisis workers often question whether a mutilated or severely injured body should be seen by the relatives, who will then have this horrible sight as a last memory. Often an encounter between the family and the deceased is avoided for reasons of the family's discomfort. However, it is very important that families be allowed to view and, if necessary, to touch the body of a suddenly deceased person in order to face the reality of his death. Preventing the family from viewing the body fosters a state of

partial denial. When a person has been severely injured, try to cover the mutilated parts—bandage the face, if necessary—but allow the family to see any identifiable part of the body.

Sometimes the deceased looks pretty grim, especially after a long attempt at resuscitation. The nurse should prepare the body by washing the face and hands with soap and water to remove emesis, blood, or foul odors. Leave the face uncovered if it is not too mutilated. If necessary, elevate the head for a few minutes to clear out some of the facial orifices. If part of the body is mutilated, cover with fresh linen. Inform the family in advance about the disfiguration. This action may be questioned; however, always give the family the option to view the body. Medical staff members are often too anxious to get the relatives out and on their way. They may rationalize that the room must be cleaned and the body should go to the morgue. This is tragic: in spite of being professionals, medical workers have their own problems with accepting death.

10. Explain the autopsy to the family. Many times, the family has begun to regain composure after an outpouring of grief and the coroner must perform an autopsy. It is mandatory in certain cases of unexplained death. Explain that the physician who will perform this operation is a specialist in diagnostic skills. Also emphasize that the disclosures from this study may turn up important information, perhaps for surviving children, or it may help other patients in the future.

11. Help them with specific decisions. Decisions are hard in these moments. Should the wedding ring be left on? Should the clothes be taken home? What funeral home should be called? Families in a state of shock, denial, or anger need help in making these decisions. If there is no church affiliation, the task of selecting the funeral home may fall to the volunteer. Leave objects like jewelry in place and await specific instructions from the family.

12. Find ways to continue the support after they leave the hospital. A grieving family will be mechanically occupied during the funeral and when all the relatives appear. It is after the funeral when the void, the silence, and the emptiness set in that help is needed. It is surprising how often marriages are threatened after the death of a child because the parents were unprepared to bear the stress of the catastrophe and medical personnel do not give them enough help after the death has occurred.

Call the relatives about four weeks after the death. By then the family is no longer in a state of shock or denial. During the interim, many questions probably have arisen which require answers. Do not visit a family at home; it is psychologically important that they return to the place where they received the tragic news.

Give the family five or ten minutes for reviewing the events of the tragedy. Their questions are predictable. Was he conscious when he arrived? Did he open his eyes once more? Did he have a lot of pain? Was someone with him when he died? Did he mention any name? Was a priest here? Did he know what was happening to him? If these questions can be answered honestly and positively, the family is able to face the reality of a sudden and unexpected death.

STRESS ON CRISIS WORKERS

Pressures and Feelings

Recently during a resuscitation attempt, a nurse in the group became very irritable and angry with a student nurse who had just asked her a routine question. In trying to find out why she had reacted this way, the emergency staff learned that her father had died a month or so ago and she had only recently returned to work. She had not yet resolved her anger at her late father who, in her opinion, had "died on her" and deserted her when they had just started to have a meaningful relationship.

The needs and feelings of staff members are important. Nurses and physicians are going to be involved in many unsuccessful resuscitation attempts. Into emergency work these people bring their own special reactions, values, and even unresolved griefs or bereavements. They must be able to share and ventilate their own feelings. It is important that a staff be trained not only in the science of medicine, but also in its art. A staff member must come to grips with his own hangups and his own fear of death. These feelings should be shared. If you feel angry, you should say so; if you feel anguish, despair or emptiness, do not bottle it up. Nurses and physicians sometimes need "screaming rooms" as much as the family does.

The Role of the Clergy

A minister, priest, or rabbi can be the most important person in the successful management of any crisis situation. When an accident victim or critically ill patient is brought to the emergency room, notify a hospital chaplain without delay. You need not know the patient's religious affiliation. It is not unusual to witness the prayer of a rabbi with a dying Christian patient or the blessing by a priest to a non-Catholic injured person.

When a patient asks for a member of the clergy, the arranged visit should be allowed to be private. Particularly, staff and relatives must step out of the room when a priest hears a patient's confession. When the priest gives communion and annoints the patient, the family may wish to return to share this moment together.

Clergy have to be prepared to face some angry patients or relatives who do not want to see them. A critically injured patient may be very upset when a priest walks into his room. The priest's presence may imply that he needs the last rites and therefore that he will not recover. In spite of the fact that the last rites are now given to all seriously ill patients, most patients still associate this ritual with imminence of death. An understanding priest simply asks for permission to pray with the patient and the family. If he is comfortable in the face of such a crisis, he will communicate his peace to the patient and family.

Management of Treatment Team in Crisis

Follow these guidelines in dealing with personal and professional grief:

1. ***Arrange a staff meeting following each crisis.*** Every emergency room team should have a brief evaluation period after a "Code Blue"—e.g., after a critical patient has been admitted to the hospital and treated. When a patient is lost, the team feels frustrated and often angry. Staff people, therefore, should be given the opportunity to ventilate their feelings.

2. ***Evaluate post-resuscitation life potential.*** The patient brought into the emergency room in cardiac arrest may not have had adequate ventilation or effective cardiac massage. The house physician must quickly evaluate this patient. If there is any sign of life, if the patient has had good cardiac massage, and if he has had adequate oxygen supply to his lungs, then he is a prime target for intensive resuscitation methods. These are tough moments when immediate decisions have to be made. Very often, an emergency team will attempt to revive a patient over too long a period of time. Sometimes, the situation presents a learning experience. But other times—especially when the patient is young—the workers just keep trying, even though they know it is futile. It is hard to stop resuscitation attempts because of the inability to accept the death of a young person. Remember, though, there is no grace in reviving someone whose brain has been oxygen-starved for too long.

A pretty 16-year-old girl with heart disease was in a hospital, bedridden and chronically depressed. Her physician did a diagnostic evaluation to see if anything else could be done to improve her condition psychologically. She was very quiet and withdrawn during this interview. While she had no fear of death, she regarded herself as a burden and without hope of ever dancing, running, or functioning normally again.

After this evaluation, the treatment team decided to allow her one hour out of bed every day to sit up, sew or do some non-strenuous activity. On one of her first days out of bed, she was permitted to attend the Hallowe'en party. She watched in sheer delight as other adolescents danced. Suddenly—at the beginning of a new modern dance—she got up from her wheelchair, grabbed her young counselor, and danced a few steps with him. Her face was beaming for the few seconds of delight. Then she collapsed in his arms and was dead within a few minutes. Residents, interns, and staff physicians attempted for hours to revive her. Counselors sat with the children and shared their grief until they were able to fall asleep.

On the following morning a staff meeting was called, enabling everyone to share his own feelings of sadness, frustration, guilt, and anger. The most predominant feeling was guilt: "I have killed her." The occupational therapist felt responsible for inviting her to the party; the recreational therapist blamed herself for asking her to get the sewing material rather than bringing it to her, and the counselor who danced with her a couple of steps reprimanded himself for not pushing her back into her wheelchair.

But the physician pointed out the girl's last three wishes shared during the recent evaluation: "I wish to really feel young and in love, to be pretty, and to dance like other girls." She had looked lovely at the party, she was very fond of the counselor, and she did get up once more and dance. Then he asked the staff whether what happened was a more acceptable death for her than to die slowly over a period of months, bedridden and inactive.

The post-emergency staff meeting not only helped the group to confront its feelings, but also raised the issue of how to better assist physicians who cannot "let go" and who continue resuscitation attempts far beyond the reasonable. The last doctor to "give up" was the only team member who could not participate in the discussion because he was "up all night and too busy." Actually, he was too upset to face the issue, requiring many individual sessions to understand his own emotional reactions.

*3. **Learn to accept the angry grief of relatives and staff.*** Three young men were brought into the emergency room after a motorcycle accident. Two were dead on arrival and the third came in with a severed leg. He was mumbling, "It can't be! It can't be!" Suddenly he started screaming; then he was dead. The family, hearing his yells, tried to get into the room. It was a horrible sight and the workers tried to prevent the family from entering. When the family members came to the door, they reacted with almost physical violence and started screaming, "What did you do to him? You killed him!"

This kind of outburst is hard on the staff members who, after all, have their own feelings of anger and frustration. Learn to differentiate between the normal reactive anger and the "stage of anger" unleased by someone who is facing a sudden loss.

If the parents of a critically ill child are sent out of her room because another electroencephalogram must be made or an infusion restarted and the child dies with the parents waiting outside, they are entitled to be very angry at the staff. They may question the necessity for the additional procedure; they will always resent the fact that they were sent away.

During a "stage of anger," the relatives are in utter anguish, bitterly resentful, and critical of anything and anybody. They may call the nursing station every few minutes or demand to see the chief of staff immediately. Instead of taking it personally and punishing these relatives with unkind, guilt-provoking remarks or avoidances, regard their outbursts as simple expressions of anguish and impotent rage in a desperate, helpless situation.

Instead of sending them away, give them simple tasks to do in the service of the patient. During a lull in activity take them aside into a private room and encourage them to verbalize their anger.

4. Learn yourself to share and express feelings about death. On-going staff meetings and seminars and workshops on death and dying facilitate the sharing of feelings and conflicts by underlining the fact that crisis workers are both medical professionals and human beings.

ORGANIZING INSTITUTIONAL SERVICES

Goals

Ideally, physical facilities, organizational structure and staff should reflect the problems and requirements of effective response to mental health crises. In practice, however, preparation is made only for the physical needs of patient and family, ignoring their emotional ones. Physicians, too, often lose interest or do not have time or training to care for patients who are beyond medical help. Nurses, who must wait for the doctor's orders, resent being put on the spot by patients or relatives who cannot communicate with a physician.

Responses

Follow these guidelines as support for a patient's family:

1. There should be a worker to help the family. A trained volunteer, social worker or hospital chaplain should be available on a 24-hour basis to comfort the relatives—especially during the night hours when needs are greatest.

2. Provide a "screaming room" for the family. Plans for new emergency room facilities should include a special room where families can ventilate their feelings. Quiet and private, this "screaming room" can be used for emotional expressions of grief. It should be close to the emergency room. There might be a writing table, a couch and some comfortable chairs, a coffee pot or coke machine, a telephone, and a clock. A bathroom facility should be in the area.

3. Provide a meeting place for staff members to share and ventilate their feelings. The staff can gather informally to share their problems and trials. If these meetings take place when the need arises, they are more useful than if artificially scheduled once a week, with the staff obligated rather than motivated to attend.

4. Provide a quiet place for family to view the body. Before admitting the family, if possible move the body out of the treatment facility into a small room which is less urgently needed. Thus, it will not be necessary to rush the family out because of another incoming patient. Then, place a chair or two nearby, and allow them to be together without being hurried or disturbed.

5. Help after the crisis is over. Most hospitals have no follow up once a body is removed to the funeral home and the family has signed the necessary papers and paid the bills. Staff members who really cared may get a thank-you note and may wonder occasionally how a family is doing. But, by then, the staff is busy with other patients.

Yet it is the human touch—this entire encounter beyond the professional role—which often teaches us more about life and its crisis, and about people's strength and inner resources. And it is this wisdom which can help us one day when we become the recipient, rather than the giver, of help.

Have the volunteer, nurse, social worker or chaplain call on the family one month later. Ask the family to come back if it wishes. Let the members sit in the same room where they received the shocking news. They will ask the same questions they did four weeks before, but now shock and anguish will not mute the answers.

Hopefully, they will associate the hospital, its staff, and the incident with a human encounter rather than remember it as a place where a loved one was taken away from them.

SUGGESTED READINGS

Becker, Ernest. *The Denial of Death.* New York: The Free Press, 1974.

Caine, Lynn. *Widow.* New York: William Morris Publishers, 1974.

Hinton, John M. *Dying.* New York: Penguin Books, 1967.

Kubler-Ross, Elisabeth. *On Death and Dying.* New York: Macmillan Company, 1969.

———. "Coping with Death and Dying." *Inservice Education Teaching Tape Series,* Flossmoor, Ill., 1973.

———. *Questions and Answers on Death and Dying.* New York: Macmillan Company, 1974.

Rheingold, Joseph C. *Mother Anxiety and Death: The Catastrophic Death Complex.* Boston: Little, Brown and Company, 1967.

IX

Mental Health Problems in Environmental Disasters

Steven R. Kafrissen, M.D.
Edward F. Heffron, M.S.
with
Jack Zusman, M.D., M.P.H.

THE CRISIS

Disasters vary in nature and severity just as individuals vary in susceptibility and reaction to stress. Nevertheless, studies of individuals who have gone through disasters provide some typical patterns of human psychological reaction as well as some methods for dealing with these reactions. The goal of disaster management is to minimize both immediate and long-range mental health problems triggered by such events.

A natural environmental disaster does not usually cause paralyzing emotional reactions. Nor is it likely that previously well-adjusted individuals will become either psychotic (unable to function) or potentially suicidal as a result of the disaster. However, disaster does cause a serious emotional crisis, and the principles of crisis intervention—although in the past seldom applied in such situations—can be very useful.

An emotional crisis in response to a disaster typically lasts a maximum of four to six weeks. It is during this time that the individual experiences his most acute disequilibrium. By the end of the typical crisis period, he has usually reestablished some degree of equilibrium. Unfortunately, without immediate and appropriate intervention, this newly established level of functioning may be of a maladaptive nature.

Periods of Disaster Response

For over two decades, authorities have recognized that there are several distinct stages of individual and community response to a common crisis. While there is not unanimous agreement upon the integrity and duration of each stage, the research literature does support the notion that at each juncture there is a range of predictable emotional responses. Such responses do not manifest themselves in the same fashion for all people. In addition to individual differences, the nature and context of the disaster will produce different levels of intensity.

Period of alarm

In some disasters, particularly those involving sudden or unexpected onset (e.g., explosion, earthquake, flash flooding), the population may receive minimal warning of the potential threat. In other circumstances, however, the slower approach and development of the potential disaster stimulus (e.g., the gradual rising of a river prior to a flood or the increasingly threatening weather and sky conditions which spawn tornadoes) cause increased public apprehension and warning of possible danger. The natural human response to this potential threat involves: heightened anxiety and gradually increasing apprehension. The psychological coping mechanisms dealing with these feelings form the basis for the individual's response to the impact. Generally, a person will not deviate radically from established behavior and coping patterns. But, when a person's anxiety is heightened and his situation becomes ambiguous, he may exhibit atypical behavior. Minor environmental changes can produce differing kinds of reactions as people struggle to maintain an equilibrium.

Those individuals who have had past experience with a similar situation may handle the warning phase better than others; those who typically become helpless in threatening situations may experience severe stress.

Period of threat

During this period the individual's problems remain the same, but there is now added an urgent warning of immediate danger. He must decide whether there is a clear threat to his life and possessions or whether the warning is premature, overcautious, or unnecessary.

An individual's choice of how to respond in face of the potential threat is influenced in varying degrees by a complicated network of personal considerations such as:

- Is the threat real? Will the potential threat materialize? How quickly?
- Should the disaster actually strike, what is the likely effect upon him?
- What possible avenues of escape or protection are available and how effective are they likely to be?
- What will be the physical, material, and emotional cost of efforts to escape?
- What is the primary mode of response by those around him?

People are not driven solely by a desire for physical safety in assessing a disaster situation. A complex set of social and personal motivations also are interacting to motivate his behavior.

Period of impact

During the impact period, the full magnitude of the disaster is brought to bear on the stricken community: that individuals are likely to be killed or injured and that substantial losses to property and personal possession will be incurred. Some of those affected exhibit extremely emotional behavior; and are completely unable to cope with the situation or even to follow the effective leadership of others.

For the majority, there is no panic reaction. They are not necessarily alert to the situation except possibly for some feelings of fear. This group instinctively turns to recognized leaders for direction or guidance.

A much smaller percentage of the disaster-affected population assumes a planning or leadership role. In the absence of recognized leaders, they emerge from the group to do what is necessary. These people seem to have particular skills or abilities which are lacking in, or needed by, the group. For this reason they receive support from the victims of the disaster.

In the period of impact, the range of responses may include: tension, disorganization, disorientation and confusion, feelings of hopelessness, or agitation.

Period of inventory

Immediately after the impact of the disaster, the survivors try to assess and come to an understanding of what has really happened. In addition to the earlier responses, individuals may evidence: multiple physical complaints, withdrawal from reality, fantasy and delusions, apathy, nightmares, chronic anxiety or fear, depression, feeling overwhelmed, anger, or social fragmentation.

During this stage, the majority will make rapid progress toward psychological recovery and will return to their previous condition. A few will stabilize at a level of moderate or serious disability. In cases of severe and prolonged stress from the disaster, symptoms may last a lifetime. Indeed, in some cases—such as survivors of wartime concentration camps—symptoms appear to have been passed on to the children through distortions in interpersonal relations within the victims' families.

During this inventory period, the social scene becomes temporarily fragmented into isolated individuals, many of whom feel overwhelmed. Almost immediately, however, many people become active in the rescue effort while others try to move through the area to better comprehend the situation. Research has indicated that the apparent mass confusion is not really what it seems to be. In fact, most individuals are engaged in highly purposeful individual activity which simply is not socially coordinated.

Period of rescue

Focus, during the rescue phase, is on helping the survivors to cope with the disaster's aftermath. While some will react with shock, only a few may be expected to manifest any continued serious emotional problems. This disaster syndrome usually takes the form of apathy, withdrawal, and regression in cognitive processes. The development of this kind of reaction seems more likely with sudden, violent disaster, but even in these cases the occurrence is not very great.

Period of remedy

The remedy phase may be the longest disaster time period. During this phase, the survivors and relief agencies begin organized activities designed to relieve the stricken community. Beginning in this period and extending into the next, disaster victims begin to feel: heightened morale, cooperative spirit (in an effort to solve problems and plan for the future), pressures of rehabilitation, and long-term emotional effects of the impact (emotional crises may occur even as late as six months after the disaster).

Period of restoration

In the final phase of a disaster—the recovery period—the community and its individuals regain former stability or achieve a new level of equilibrium. It may involve an extended period of time, contingent upon the circumstances surrounding the disaster as well as the help and resources available.

Reactions and Problems of the Victims

The emotional responses associated with an environmental crisis are quite normal, and do not represent mental illness in the usual sense. In fact, it may be a concern in itself if an individual does not exhibit some crisis symptoms when confronted with a highly traumatic event. However, because of the dynamics involved, it is possible for the troubled individual to regress, beginning habitual use of non-adaptive problem-solving techniques. Thus, the goal of psychiatric crisis management is the fostering of good coping mechanisms.

Although every disaster is in some sense unique, certain common patterns of response have been identified. Naturally, the type, magnitude, and duration of a disaster coupled with the particular characteristics of the affected community produce variations in response and recovery. Yet, throughout the seven stages of the disaster, there are common elements which affect the counter-response of various helping agents. In assessing the recovery effort, note the five factors discussed below.

Anxiety versus panic

Surprisingly, there is little evidence of panic by individuals facing a disaster situation. To the contrary, one of the major problems is the evacuation of potential victims who choose to remain where they are.

Anxiety enables individuals to mobilize necessary resources quickly. Panic, on the other hand, can lead to chaos, disorganization and failure to respond.

Finding and accepting help

Disaster typically affects a large segment of the population which has never before needed assistance from government or community resources. These individuals do not know about available services and programs or the steps they must follow in securing help.

Almost immediately, they turn to relatives or friends for shelter and support. Some, carried by an exaggerated sense of independence and self-reliance, attempt to operate without the necessary resources. Many are reluctant to ask for or accept help. These individuals will require some interested person to reach out and assist in solution of the problem. Otherwise, a frustrating spiral begins and recovery grows increasingly difficult and remote.

Disruption of natural social groupings

An environmental disaster often causes death and disruption within many families and segments of the community. The primary units of social organization, when dissolved, must be redefined. Some people are forced to relocate; some crowd in with others; others are assigned to temporary housing in unfamiliar surroundings.

As early as the period of inventory, people begin to move together into tentative groups, impelled to share experiences and to seek help and leadership. Concern at this point centers around family members; little attention is given to long-term developments within the survivor group. Thus, from the time of the impact, the individual has entered a different social situation, adding to his disequilibrium.

Reaction to "outsiders"

Shortly after the impact of a disaster, there is a convergence of individuals into the area who are eager to help. Most will stay on the scene for a short time, provide some aid, and return home reasonably self-fulfilled. In some situations, their numbers alone may interfere with their ability to help. Some arrive out of a sense of curiosity, not any real desire to help. For the most part, however, these volunteers contribute time and effort for as long as they can.

As time passes, however, communities touched by disaster develop a paradoxical situation. While demanding immediate, clearly defined direction and assistance, its members resist "outside interference." For example, the arrival of military units is helpful and often necessary for clean-up work or for supplemental law enforcement help. The community, while not ungrateful, may fear possible problems created by the outsiders, such as theft or unwanted pregnancies.

Governmental agencies suffer from the same mixed message. It is natural to expect that outsiders who are experts in their particular field will be involved. Even though large numbers of local personnel may work in the recovery programs, the key people in charge are usually outsiders. While bringing in outside expertise results in an expeditious operation, there is still that feeling among the survivors that those in charge are strangers who are ignorant of local setting. For example, in Wilkes-Barre, Pennsylvania, following the disaster triggered by tropical storm Agnes in 1972, governmental employees assigned to work in recovery programs met with this resistance. Ironically, a number of residents from Wilkes-Barre were later assigned to the Mid-West to help the victims of the Mississippi River flooding. There they themselves became the "outsiders."

Effects on the family

In a disaster situation, individuals do not experience a crisis alone. Family, friends, and other members of the community are all affected by the disaster. These people must resolve its emotional aftermath in an adaptive or maladaptive manner. While the family can be a source of strength and support for each individual member, it may itself suffer if one member experiences severe consequences from the disaster. The increased stresses triggered by family concern and worry over the affected individual, attempts to help the stricken person to deal with the problem more effectively, or an unrealistic identification with this individual's problems can all have a profound influence on the functioning of the family.

The family of every victim can expect to experience minor psychological upsets like brief anxiety and depression. There may also be shock (manifested in disbelief), loss of emotional reaction, and difficulty in concentration. Some family members function very well during the immediate crisis as long as they feel they are needed. Later, though, they may experience a serious letdown.

However, there are possible long-term, detrimental effects upon the family which can hamper the victim in his recovery. For example, a disaster might cause an injury which may disfigure or permanently disable a victim. As a result, a substantially increased financial and psychological burden on the family may be triggered. Its members may attempt to act as if the victim does not exist. The dynamics underlying this kind of behavior are similar to those sometimes observed in situations in which a member of the family is institutionalized for long-term care. In many of these situations, family members maintain increasingly irregular contacts with the victim, in effect denying the individual's continued existence as a member of the family.

An alternate course might also be followed. The family may completely and totally accept the victim but assign him a role as a permanently handicapped individual. In such cases, the family may make no provision for recovery and, indeed, may tend to discourage it. Everything is done for the individual. If he begins to show some independence, he is often cautioned not to strain himself, thereby reinforcing maladaptive behavior and promoting long-term disability.

Stresses on Helpers

In disasters, there appears to be an increased possibility that the helper himself may develop a serious emotional crisis as a result of his continued exposure to particularly difficult, emotionally draining situations. Most competent crisis workers, especially those involved in the medical aspects of emergency services, have had considerable experience with injured persons and have become relatively used to the sight and sound of serious injury and death. Despite this lack of observable reaction to stressful circumstances, most are still able to relate to disaster victims in a helpful manner.

In a disaster, however, a worker may be faced with scores of dead, dying, or injured persons and must often work for extended periods without rest or sleep. For those handling the medical problems triggered by the disaster, the results are fairly obvious. For those handling the psychiatric casualties of the disaster, the stresses can present themselves in different ways. It is possible that the helper himself may tend to increase the individual's anxiety rather than to help allay it. Concern over an individual victim's deteriorating physical or psychological condition, frustration at the crisis worker's inability to do more, personal feelings concerning the disaster itself, and other similar influences may cause the individual to lose emotional objectivity and control. The victims themselves may prove frustrating. Some disaster victims will be difficult, demanding, and unappreciative of the crisis worker's effort. In other instances, there is realistically very little that the crisis worker can contribute; as a result, he may feel helpless and ineffective.

The manifestation of the helper's malaise ranges from minor uneasiness to complete disorganization. At worst, the worker may be unable to do the tasks at hand, becoming a burden to other members of the staff. Since the nature of the disaster situation dictates that the helper will almost constantly be faced with the tragic realities of the disaster, those individuals in charge share an increased responsibility. The helper must be given adequate opportunity to share his own feelings and deal with the inherent difficulties of his role. It should also be pointed out that all those who are emotionally involved with the disaster will experience at least some minor psychological impact.

MANAGEMENT OF THE CRISIS

Follow these guidelines in dealing with a disaster-striken community:

1. Do not become overwhelmed by the immensity of the disaster. Maintain a limited perspective of feasibility: aid must be given to those who most need it. This priority should be based upon initial evaluation to determine the order of treatment among various individuals with physical or psychological problems. In this way, workers can continue to handle each individual disaster victim without being paralyzed by the enormity of the task or the scope of the disaster.

2. Obtain and disseminate information about the extent and severity of the disaster and about individual victims. The family deserves accurate information concerning the status of a patient. Such an obvious matter is often neglected in the rush to treat a victim or to meet the needs of a large group of more seriously injured individuals. As soon as possible, some of the crisis workers should be assigned to this important task. Their job will be helped considerably if accurate records have been kept. One should also consider that depending upon the nature of the disaster and the time of day in which it strikes, it is quite possible that various members of the family may be evacuated to different sections of the community and may be unaware of the whereabouts or well being of other family members. The psychological stresses placed upon individuals when they are confronted with this type of situation are obvious and should be of prime concern to crisis workers.

3. Reunite the victim and family as soon as possible. This will ease the psychological situation and help to obtain necessary medical or psychological background information which only the family may have. When the victim has been seriously injured, the family will need individual counseling to explain the extent of the injuries, the likely outcome, and the types of assistance available. Do not overlook the emotional impact of news that the victim will be seriously disabled.

4. Encourage the functioning victim to do necessary chores. Work can be therapeutic so long as the individual does not overdo it. Many disaster victims seem immobilized, unable to develop any effective plans for recovery. Emotional reactions triggered by the impact of disaster coupled with the number and variety of details to which the victim must attend can be totally overwhelming. Many people simply do not know what to do first, and as a result, do not act at all. People undergoing a crisis often disregard their normal life routine: work assignments may be overlooked and meals and housekeeping chores may go undone. The crisis worker can help the individual devise a schedule so that the necessary everyday tasks are completed and can continue to observe the victim for signs of exhaustion or overt emotional breakdowns.

5. Group displaced persons with their family and neighbors. In the face of large-scale disruption and social disorganization, the grouping will tend to decrease feelings of alienation and depersonalization. As far as possible, see that the victim is treated near his home and family.

6. Provide structure and the expectation of recovery for psychiatric casualties. The individual who is stunned and reacting ineffectively —but not severely symptomatic—should be given assistance and available material comforts. As much structure as possible should be provided for him. Tell him that he is suffering a temporary upset, that he is likely to recover rapidly, and that in the meantime minimal tasks will be expected of him. These should be carefully explained and followed up, in case he finds he is not able to do them.

The individual who has developed significant symptoms should be treated as a psychiatric casualty, with the understanding that the symptoms may subside rapidly. If they do, he will be prepared to take on a normal role. He should also be referred for examination by a mental health specialist.

7. Help the individual confront the reality of the crisis. Encourage him to talk about the crisis and to understand possible long-term effects. To adapt to a crisis situation, he must deal effectively with its reality. Help him to confront the situation in rational terms. Let him cry to ventilate his inner feelings or to begin a grief process (see Chapter VIII). Your role as crisis worker is two-fold: assist the individual in taking his mind off the crisis and act as a catalyst to encourage realism.

Urge the individual to seek out information. His speculations and fantasies are often much worse than the reality of the situation. Many times he assumes the worst; he is terrified that, by asking, his fears will be supported.

8. Use sedatives and drugs sparingly. The individual may need tranquilizers or sedatives to get him over the initial emotional shock of confronting the disaster. Few individuals are emotionally or physically strong enough to face the reality of a continued crisis situation for any extended period without some such relief. However, many experts in the field of disaster intervention warn against the indiscriminate or continued use of drugs during a crisis situation. The sustained use of drugs can postpone resolution; more dangerously, it might dampen the impact, preventing a healthy adaptation and leading to later problems.

9. Give no false assurances. Perhaps the greatest need of a person in a crisis is a desire to know that somehow things will be all right. Perhaps the greatest mistake the crisis worker can make is to provide this false reassurance without any basis in fact. What the person needs is not a promise that things will all work out, but rather a sincere offer for help in dealing with the issues. The natural human response is to empathize with the troubled person and subsequently to provide reassurance. This kind of response by a crisis worker may result in temporary relief because he was told, in effect, what he wanted to hear. Sooner or later, however, the victim must deal with the reality of the situation. If, in fact, things are really not going to be the same again, this may be much more difficult for him. The individual may become totally resistant to external intervention and suffer serious consequences.

Your best approach involves an honest appraisal of the situation, coupled with an offer of help and support, in the belief that the individual can call upon his own inner strength to handle the situation.

10. Permit limited dependency. Many people will refuse offers of assistance, claiming that they can handle the situation independently. While this is sometimes true, there are a myriad of reasons influencing the individual's decision to reject the offer of help. For some, the rejection of aid indicates a self concept which will not allow the victim to seek help. For others, cultural influences will interfere. But the refusal of help may also indicate that the individual has not accepted the seriousness of the situation.

In any event, the individual in crisis generally needs immediate, but limited help. The goal of intervention is to motivate the individual to begin meaningful activity directed toward resolution of the crisis. This frequently results in the victim's relative dependence upon the helper. In itself this temporary dependency is not bad; it may even help in resolving the crisis. Be careful, however, that the individual does not become totally dependent on you.

11. Arrange for group discussion and exchange of ideas. After the immediate physical needs of the victims have been met and the major symptoms have subsided, encourage them to discuss their feelings, plans, and reactions. They themselves may form spontaneous discussion groups. If they do not, a structure should be provided through which they can meet. For those individuals whose symptoms are prolonged, obtain a mental health specialist's consultation and consider the use of medications. When possible, place families of victims in groups to discuss the issues of recovery and to share their emotional experiences.

12. Recruit and train community gatekeepers. Within each community there are a number of people who function as gatekeepers. These are people who, because of their position, interest, personality or some other factor, are in a particularly advantageous position to help individuals in need.

These gatekeepers can be identified, recruited, and trained to provide psychological first aid during the recovery phase of a disaster. In addition, their increased sensitivity to human problems can serve a highly useful preventive mental health function long after the disaster.

13. Use existing community resources. It is better to facilitate and, if necessary, supplement the existing community expertise rather than to attempt to take over responsibility. In the short term, the take-over approach may be the most efficient. But in the longer term, the community must call upon its own resources if it is to recover.

Many groups besides gatekeepers can be mobilized to assist in the community response. Physicians, teachers, industrial and business leaders, clergymen, local public service personnel, union leaders, political and governmental leaders, news media personnel, and community volunteers are likely candidates.

14. Help the rescue workers themselves.[1] There are ways to increase the effectiveness of the crisis worker by minimizing the psychological stresses on him. Crisis workers should follow set schedules and take regular rest periods, even if brief. Organize the rescue operation so that a supervisor or administrator—someone not directly ministering to victims—can recognize early if a worker is experiencing distress. Require the worker to take a longer rest period and then return to a somewhat less stressful assignment. During rest periods, encourage workers to take nourishment, to talk with each other about their experiences and feelings, and—if time is available—to get some sleep. During conversations workers will commonly indulge in "gallows humor" in which they mimic and ridicule colleagues and patients. This is an attempt to deal with psychological stress rather than disrespect.

In general, do not administer medication to workers while they are in frontline positions and actively discourage them from using any drugs

1. This guideline has been contributed by Jack Zusman, M.D.

without consultation with the supervisor. If a worker is so upset that medication seems indicated, he should be removed if at all possible, to a less stressful assignment.

PREVENTATIVE MEASURES[2]

Many of the potentially negative psychological effects of a disaster can be eliminated, at least in part, by advance training. In this way, potential crisis workers can be sensitized to the typical emotional reactions observed in disaster victims and can be trained in the techniques of crisis intervention. Just as medical personnel are trained in first aid and emergency medical care, crisis workers also need to be trained to identify and handle psychiatric casualties. Disaster workers typically lack knowledge concerning emotional crises experienced by victims and to a great extent are ignorant of their own emotional status. Preparation in advance can help to decrease the stresses on the crisis workers while insuring increased sensitivity to the emotional status of victims.

One of the most effective ways of preparing an individual to function under stress is for him to be more aware of his own emotional reactions in general and to know what he may experience and how to deal with the negative effects. It is not necessary for the crisis worker to actually experience disaster and learn by trial and error, since appropriate intervention techniques can be learned efficiently during a brief but intensive training program prior to the disaster.

The actual training program should include at least two separate aspects. First, the workers should be made thoroughly aware of what happens to people in crisis and what methods of intervention are likely to be most effective. There is a need to help potential disaster workers respond to victims in a warm, empathic manner. The helpers need a basic framework in order to interpret, understand, and respond in a helpful fashion to victims and to each other. Without a basic understanding of typical and acceptable reactions and the dynamics of human behavior, the crisis worker will not be effective. Although some material adapts well to didactic presentation, it is best to utilize small group experiential training. Individuals can assume the roles of disaster victims while others act as helpers. Those not directly involved in the interaction can serve as observers and critics, providing input after the exercise is concluded. Specific techniques such as role playing and small-group problem solving can be extremely helpful in allowing individuals to experience and share feelings and thoughts in a controlled manner. Individuals should also be trained in interviewing techniques and recording procedures.

The other aspect of the training is more specific and related to the individual community. Individuals should know which kinds of disaster are most likely to occur and the specific effects and methods for dealing with them. For example, individuals living in tornado-prone areas should be made aware of the indications of a possible tornado, from whom and how the warning will be issued, and where the tornado is likely to come from.

The potential disaster worker should know what disaster relief operations will be operationalized and what community resources are available. A word of caution, however: while it is recommended that each community develop and publish a disaster plan, the possibility exists that the plan may not be implemented. Depending upon the magnitude of the disaster, many potential care givers find themselves victims and unable to operationalize previous plans. While there is very little the crisis worker can do to change this occurrence, he should be made aware of the possibility of encountering such a situation.

2. This section, Preventative Measures, has been contributed by Jack Zusman, M.D.

THE WILKES-BARRE FLOOD: A COMMUNITY RESPONSE

After a disaster, there is a heightened need to respond to people's emotional and physical requirements in a humanistic and sensitive manner. Utilizing local resources, individuals can be trained as effective workers in meeting the acute needs generated by the disaster. Steven Kafrissen and Edward Heffron had an opportunity to develop such a program in the immediate aftermath of the Wilkes-Barre flood.

Creating a Team

Within six weeks after the impact of the Agnes disaster, the special intervention program began operation. Project Outreach was initially proposed as a special year-long program with funds provided by the National Institute of Mental Health. The main thrust of the program was to reach out to disaster victims—through trained, indigenous workers—to promote the resolution of emotional and psychological disturbances.

The Outreach program was designed to break from more traditional mental health approaches. In the traditional model, those needing help had to seek it themselves or allow their situations to deteriorate to such a point that the community would request intervention.

A number of tactics were utilized to recruit the counselors. First, publicity appeared in the local media about the initiation of the project. In addition, referral services included public and private social agencies, churches, unions, governmental units, public and private employment agencies and—perhaps most important—the community grapevine. Later, newspaper advertisements as well as street posters described the program.

Personnel selection was guided by the consideration that the workers should be indigenous to the disaster-stricken region or be personally involved and affected by the disaster. Secondly, they needed the necessary humanistic qualities for functioning as human service counselors in a manner consistent with the philosophy and goals of the program.

From a large number of applicants, fifty were finally chosen to serve as Outreach counselors. Those hired ranged in age from 19 to 62, in education from grammar school through masters degrees and in experience from laborers to former teachers. None had had any previous mental health experience.

They also were a microcosm of the flood-affected areas and represented all the ethnic and racial groups present in the community. Individually, they brought a wide background of experience to the project. Included in the group was a recovered alcoholic, former security guard, seamstress, nutritionist, licensed practical nurse, retired Army sergeant, former union leader, Vietnam era veterans, and a number of recent college graduates.

Training the Workers

The prospective counselors were recruited and selected in about 10 days and their training program began immediately. The goal was to transform a collection of 50 individuals into a cohesive service team, equipped to deliver psychological first aid through both personal and technical counseling skills.

The initial week of training was designed to produce crisis intervention generalists who could function effectively in the community, with appropriate back-up from project supervisory staff. It was recognized quite early that a week-long training program must be limited in its scope and content, yet a longer period of training was impractical. Also, the workers should begin functioning in the community as soon as possible. In addition it was recognized that, because of the project's innovative nature, unanticipated situations would be encountered. Therefore, continued training input was recommended. A regular in-service training program was designed to meet these unanticipated changes along with specific needs developed by the workers in their own field experience. The program was continued on a regular basis throughout the year-long program.

The training itself utilized a group-experiential format, with a minimum of didactic input. Role-playing, small-group problem solving, and team-building activities were emphasized during a week-long orientation session.

The trainers operated on the assumption that the recruiting and screening methods employed would entice a kind of worker who expressed an understanding, warm, and compassionate orientation towards people with problems. These innate qualities, they believed, were necessary in crisis intervention and a training session cannot provide these traits.

Immediately after finishing the training program, the human service counselors were assigned to specific geographic areas within the two-county flood area. A member of the supervisory staff was responsible for general coordination of activities.

As their approach to the community, the Outreach workers canvassed freely in the assigned areas. They met people on the street; they knocked on the doors. Late each day, they returned to the Outreach headquarters for a team meeting to review the day's encounters. These meetings provided updated information for the counselors and a forum for group supervision and mutual learning experiences.

Early in the project the counselors began working in pairs in an effort to allay certain anxieties which had developed, to encourage continued involvement in difficult situations, and to enhance their feelings of security.

During their first year Outreach workers recorded over 16,000 client contacts.

SUMMARY AND RECOMMENDATIONS

The experience gained through the analysis of natural disasters illustrates the following important issues.

- There are fairly consistently identifiable phases of a disaster, each with its own unique features.
- There is a range of recognized emotional reactions on the part of disaster victims. Many are considered to be in the normal range, but some will lead to permanent disability or sequelae. Until quite recently, efforts directed at meeting the mental health needs of disaster victims have received a relatively low priority. This is an area too long neglected.
- The techniques of crisis intervention have been judged appropriate and successful in dealing with the emotional responses triggered by disaster.
- Experience has shown that a cadre of local residents can be recruited, selected, and trained within a very short period of time to provide crisis intervention services to disaster victims.
- In spite of disaster-triggered disruption, adequately prepared local resources can provide immediate assistance during and after the disaster.
- Groups providing assistance in disaster recovery (federal, state, and local) should be trained to provide the necessary material and human services in a manner that is not dehumanizing nor that prolongs disability.
- Local mental health personnel should be sensitized to the emotional aftermath of disaster so as to assume an active leadership role in disaster recovery.
- A national disaster team should be formed to provide immediate consultation services to disaster-affected communities.
- Emergency medical service personnel at all levels (ambulance attendants, Red Cross workers, hospital emergency room workers, military personnel, etc.) should be given ample training so as to be able to handle emotional problems during a disaster. This training should also serve to sensitize them to the psychological aspects of the activities of their jobs under ordinary circumstances.

SUGGESTED READINGS

Barker, G., and Chapman, D. *Man and Society in Disaster.* New York: Basic Books, Inc. 1962.

Barton, Allen H. *Communities in Disaster: A Sociological Analysis of Collective Stress Situations.* Garden City, N. J.: Doubleday & Co., Inc., 1969.

Blaufarb, H., and Levine, J. "Crisis Intervention in an Earthquake." *Social Work* 17(1972):16-19.

Caplan, Gerald. *Principles of Preventive Psychiatry.* New York: Basic Books, Inc., 1964.

Farberow, Norman L. "Crisis Disaster and Suicide: Theory and Therapy." In *Essays in Self-Destruction*, edited by Edwin S. Shniedman. New York: Science House, Inc., 1967.

Hirschowitz, R. "Crisis Theory: A Formulation." *Psychiatric Annals* 3(1973):36-47.

Laube, Jerri. "Psychological Reactions of Nurses in Disaster." *Nursing Research* 22(1973):343-47.

McGee, Richard K. *Crisis Intervention in the Community.* Baltimore: University Park Press, 1974.

Quarantelli, E., and Dynes, R. "When Disaster Strikes." *Psychology Today* 9(1972):67-70.

Rapoport, L. "The State of Crisis: Some Theoretical Considerations." In *Crisis Intervention: Selected Readings*, edited by Howard J. Parad. New York: Family Service Association of America, 1965.

Richard, W. C. "Crisis Intervention Services following Disaster: The Pennsylvania Recovery Project." *Journal of Community Psychology*, in press.

Tuckman, A. "Disaster and Mental Health Intervention." *Community Mental Health Journal* 9(1973):151-57.

Index